THE RISE OF
FASCISM IN EUROPE

THE RISE OF
FASCISM IN EUROPE

George P. Blum

Greenwood Press Guides to
Historic Events of the Twentieth Century
Randall M. Miller, Series Editor

Greenwood Press
Westport, Connecticut • London

Library of Congress Cataloging-in-Publication Data

Blum, George P., 1932–
     The rise of fascism in Europe / George P. Blum.
        p.   cm. — (Greenwood Press guides to historic events of the
     twentieth century, ISSN 1092–177X)
     Includes bibliographical references and index.
     ISBN 0–313–29934–X (alk. paper)
     1. Fascism—Europe.   2. Europe—Politics and
     government—1918–1945.   I. Title.   II. Series.
     D726.5.B58   1998
     335.6'094—dc21   97–43867

British Library Cataloguing in Publication Data is available.

Copyright © 1998 by George P. Blum

Library of Congress Catalog Card Number: 97–43867
ISBN: 0–313–29934–X
ISSN: 1092–177X

First published in 1998

Greenwood Press, 88 Post Road West, Westport, CT 06881
An imprint of Greenwood Publishing Group, Inc.

Printed in the United States of America

(∞)"

The paper used in this book complies with the
Permanent Paper Standard issued by the National
Information Standards Organization (Z39.48–1984).

10 9 8 7 6 5 4 3 2 1

Front cover photograph: Adolf Hitler and Benito Mussolini review a Nazi parade staged in
Mussolini's honor, Munich, Germany, October 4, 1937. Used by permission of UPI/CORBIS/
BETTMANN.

Back cover photograph: Nazi totalitarianism on the march. Used by permission of Südwest
Verlag.

Copyright Acknowledgments

The author and publisher gratefully acknowledge permission to reprint the following material:

Excerpts from *Mein Kampf* by Adolf Hitler, translated by Ralph Manheim. Copyright © 1943, renewed 1971 by Houghton Mifflin Company. Reprinted by permission of Houghton Mifflin Company. All rights reserved.

Excerpts from *International Conciliation*, No. 306, January 1935, pp. 7–10, 12–13, 15, 16–17; and No. 324, November 1936, pp. 568, 569, 572. Copyright © Carnegie Endowment for International Peace.

Excerpts from Eugen Weber, *Varieties of Fascism* (Princeton, NJ: Van Nostrand, 1964), pp. 257–258, 159–160.

Excerpts from *The Papal Encyclicals, 1903–1939*, trans. Claudia Carlen (Ann Arbor, MI: Pierian Press, 1900), pp. 525, 526–527, 534–535.

Excerpts from John Whittam, *Fascist Italy* (Manchester, England: Manchester University Press, 1995), pp. 164–165.

Every reasonable effort has been made to trace the owners of copyright materials in this book, but in some instances this has proven impossible. The author and publisher will be glad to receive information leading to more complete acknowledgments in subsequent printings of the book, and in the meantime extend their apologies for any omissions.

To Beverly

Contents

Illustrations follow page 19.

Series Foreword

As the twenty-first century approaches, it is time to take stock of the political, social, economic, intellectual, and cultural forces and factors that have made the twentieth century the most dramatic period of change in history. To that end, the Greenwood Press Guides to Historic Events of the Twentieth Century presents interpretive histories of the most significant events of the century. Each book in the series combines narrative history and analysis with primary documents and biographical sketches, with an eye to providing both a reference guide to the principal persons, ideas, and experiences defining each historic event, and a reliable, readable overview of that event. Each book further provides analyses and discussions, grounded in both primary and secondary sources, of the causes and consequences, in thought and action, that give meaning to the historic event under review. By assuming a historical perspective, drawing on the latest and best writing on each subject, and offering fresh insights, each book promises to explain how and why a particular event defined the twentieth century. No consensus about the meaning of the twentieth century emerges from the series, but, collectively, the books identify the most salient concerns of the century. In so doing, the series reminds us of the many ways those historic events continue to affect our lives.

Each book follows a similar format designed to encourage readers to consult it both as a reference and a history in its own right. Each volume opens with a chronology of the historic event, followed by a narrative overview, which also serves to introduce and examine briefly the main themes and issues related to that event. The next set of chapters is composed of topical essays, each analyzing closely an issue or problem of interpretation introduced in the opening chapter. A concluding chapter suggesting the long-term implications and meanings of the historic event brings the strands of the preceding chapters together while placing the event in the larger historical context. Each book also includes a section of short biographies of the principal persons related to the event, followed by a section introducing and reprinting key historical documents illustrative of and pertinent to the event. A glossary of selected terms adds to the utility of each book. An annotated bibliography—of significant books, films, and CD-ROMs—and an index conclude each volume.

The editors made no attempt to impose any theoretical model or historical perspective on the individual authors. Rather, in developing the series, an advisory board of noted historians and informed high school history teachers and public and school librarians identified the topics needful of exploration and the scholars eminently qualified to examine those events with intelligence and sensitivity. The common commitment throughout the series is to provide accurate, informative, and readable books, free of jargon and up to date in evidence and analysis.

Each book stands as a complete historical analysis and reference guide to a particular historic event. Each book also has many uses, from understanding contemporary perspectives on critical historical issues, to providing biographical treatments of key figures related to each event, to offering excerpts and complete texts of essential documents about the event, to suggesting and describing books and media materials for further study and presentation of the event, and more. The combination of historical narrative and individual topical chapters addressing significant issues and problems encourages students and teachers to approach each historic event from multiple perspectives and with a critical eye. The arrangement and content of each book thus invite students and teachers, through classroom discussions and position papers, to debate the character and significance of great historic events and to discover for themselves how and why history matters.

The series emphasizes the main currents that have shaped the modern world. Much of that focus necessarily looks at the West, especially Europe and the United States. The political, commercial, and cultural expansion of the West wrought largely, though not wholly, the most fundamental changes of the century. Taken together, however, books in the series reveal the interactions between Western and non-Western peoples and society, and also the tensions between modern and traditional cultures. They also point to the ways in which non-Western peoples have adapted Western ideas and technology and, in turn, influenced Western life and thought. Several books examine such increasingly powerful global forces as the rise of Islamic fundamentalism, the emergence of modern Japan, the communist revolution in China, and the collapse of communism in eastern Europe and the former Soviet Union. American interests and experiences receive special attention in the series, not only in deference to the primary readership of the books but also in recognition that the United States emerged as the dominant political, economic, social, and cultural force during the twentieth century. By looking at the century through the lens of American events and experiences, it is possible to see why the age has come to be known as "The American Century."

Assessing the history of the twentieth century is a formidable prospect. It has been a period of remarkable transformation. The world broadened and narrowed at the same time. Frontiers shifted from the interiors of Africa and Latin America to the moon and beyond; communication spread from mass-circulation newspapers and magazines to radio, television, and now the Internet; skyscrapers reached upward and suburbs stretched outward; energy switched from steam, to electric, to atomic power. Many changes did not lead to a complete abandonment of established patterns and practices so much as a synthesis of old and new, as, for example, the increased use of (even reliance on) the telephone in the age of the computer. The automobile and the truck, the airplane, and telecommunications closed distances, and people in unprecedented numbers migrated from rural to urban, industrial, and ever more ethnically diverse areas. Tractors and chemical fertilizers made it possible for fewer people to grow more, but the environmental and demographic costs of an exploding global population threatened to outstrip natural resources and human innovation. Disparities in wealth increased, with developed nations prospering and underdeveloped nations starving. Amid the crumbling of former European colonial empires, Western technology, goods, and culture increasingly enveloped the globe, seeping into, and undermining, non-Western cultures— a process that contributed to a surge of religious fundamentalism and ethno-nationalism in the Middle East, Asia, and Africa. As people became more alike, they also became more aware of their differences. Ethnic and religious rivalries grew in intensity everywhere as the century closed.

The political changes during the twentieth century have been no less profound than the social, economic, and cultural ones. Many of the books in the series focus on political events, broadly defined, but no books are confined to politics alone. Political ideas and events have social effects, just as they spring from a complex interplay of nonpolitical forces in culture, society, and economy. Thus, for example, the modern civil rights and woman's rights movements were at once social and political events in cause and consequence. Likewise, the Cold War created the geopolitical framework for dealing with competing ideologies and nations abroad and served as the touchstone for political and cultural identities at home. The books treating political events do so within their social, cultural, and economic contexts.

Several books in the series examine particular wars in depth. Wars are defining moments for people and eras. During the twentieth century war became more widespread and terrible than ever before, encouraging new efforts to end war through strategies and organizations of international cooperation and disarmament while also fueling new ideologies and instruments of mass persuasion that fostered distrust and festered old national rivalries. Two world wars during the century redrew the political map, slaughtered or uprooted two generations of people, and introduced and hastened the development of new technologies and weapons of mass destruction. World War I spelled the end of the old European order and spurred communist revolution in Russia and fascism in Italy, Germany, and elsewhere. World War II killed fascism and inspired the final push for freedom from European colonial rule in Asia and Africa. It also led to the Cold War that suffocated much of the world for almost half a century. Large wars begat small ones, and brutal totalitarian regimes cropped up across the globe. After (and in some ways because of) the fall of communism in eastern Europe and the former Soviet Union, wars of competing cultures, national interests, and political systems persisted in the struggle to make a new world order. Continuing, too, has been the belief that military technology can achieve political ends, whether in the superior American firepower that failed to "win" in Vietnam or in the American "smart bombs" and other military wizardry that "won" in the Persian Gulf.

Another theme evident in the series is that throughout the century nationalism has continued to drive events. Whether in the Balkans in 1914 triggering World War I or in the Balkans in the 1990s threatening the post–Cold War peace—or in many other places—nationalist ambitions and forces would not die. The persistence of nationalism is yet another reminder of the many ways that the past becomes prologue.

We thus offer the series as a modern guide to and interpretation of the historic events of the twentieth century and as an invitation to consider how and why those events have defined not only the past and present but also charted the political, social, intellectual, cultural, and economic routes into the next century.

Randall M. Miller
Saint Joseph's University, Philadelphia

Preface

This survey of fascism in Europe is designed to be a fresh introduction to the subject. Fascism is viewed as a singularly European phenomenon that developed into a full totalitarian political regime in Germany under Hitler and a semitotalitarian system in Italy under Mussolini. Fascist groups and some parties emerged in many of the European countries before and during World War II but failed to establish a fascist regime of any significance. There has been little continuity between historical fascism before 1945 and the neofascist groups, movements, or parties that came after the war.

The narrative opens with a historical overview of the development of Fascism in Italy and Nazism in Germany and some variations of fascism that arose in several European countries. Chapter 2 examines more specifically the political and social conditions under which Benito Mussolini and Adolf Hitler and their parties were able to attain power. Chapter 3 explores the economy and society and some of the cultural developments under Fascism in Italy and Nazism in Germany in an effort to understand what impact fascism had on these societies. Chapter 4 examines the origins of World War II, giving particular attention to Mussolini's and Hitler's role in unleashing the war. Chapter 5 describes the internal resistance to Fascism in Italy and Nazism in Germany and points out why it succeeded in toppling the ruling regime in one but failed in the other. A concluding chapter gives an assessment of traditional fascism in Europe and the prospects of neofascism after the total collapse of Fascist Italy and Nazi Germany.

The biographical sketches of major personalities related to fascism will give some insight into the life and role of these figures in their parties and countries. The selected documents illustrate the major ideas of several fascist leaders, Hitler's and Mussolini's imperialist aims, statements and manifestos from opposition groups, especially the churches, and important treaties that led to World War II. A bibliographical essay characterizes some of the more recent scholarly books, reference works, and educational films that deal with various aspects of fascism.

After experiencing Nazism and Communism at firsthand in Germany in my early youth, I began the study of fascism in Europe years later at the University of Minnesota as a graduate student under Harold C. Deutsch. I learned much from him and through the teaching of undergraduates during the past three decades in formulating my own interpretation of fascism. In preparing this summary account of fascism in Europe, I have relied for current scholarship on the works by Stanley G. Payne, Walter Laqueur, Alan Cassels, John Whittam, Philip Morgan, Karl D. Bracher, Joachim C. Fest, Jackson J. Spielvogel, Klaus P. Fischer, and the documentary compilation by Jeremy Noakes and Geoffrey Pridham. Indispensable reference aids were Philip V. Cannistraro, ed., *Historical Dictionary of Fascist Italy*, Christian Zentner and Friedemann Bedürftig, eds., *Encyclopedia of the Third Reich*, and Robert S. Wistrich, *Who's Who in Nazi Germany*.

I would like to thank the University of the Pacific for granting me a leave from my teaching obligations to enable me to complete this book in a timely fashion. Randall M. Miller, who invited me to contribute this volume to the series, has been highly supportive throughout the work on this project. He and Charles Eberline, copyeditor of Greenwood Press, read the manuscript with a critical eye, making helpful suggestions for changes in substance and style. Barbara A. Rader, executive editor of Greenwood Press, has also been supportive and encouraging in many ways. Betty C. Pessagno, production editor, was helpful in getting the book into print. Whatever shortcomings remain are my own.

Chronology of Events

1883

July 29   Benito Mussolini is born.

1889

April 20   Adolf Hitler is born.

1919

March 23   Mussolini forms the first *Fascio di Combattimento*.

September   Hitler joins the German Workers' Party in Munich. It is renamed National Socialist German Workers' Party (NSDAP) one year later.

1922

October 27–29   Mussolini threatens a march on Rome and is appointed prime minister.

1923

November 8–9   Hitler's Beer Hall Putsch in Munich fails.

1924

February–March   Hitler's trial for treason ends in a sentence of five years' imprisonment.

June 10   Giacomo Matteotti is murdered.

December 20   Hitler is released from prison.

1925

January   Mussolini defies opposition; his dictatorship begins.

February   The National Socialist German Workers' Party is re-founded.

May 25   The Nazis win 12 seats in the Reichstag election.

1929

February   Lateran Accords concluded between Mussolini and the Vatican, normalizing state-church relations.

1930

September 14   In the parliamentary elections, the Nazis increase their Reichstag seats from 12 to 107 out of a total of 577 deputies.

1932

April 10   In the presidential runoff election, Hindenburg is re-elected with 19 million votes; Hitler receives 13.5 million votes.

July 31   In the Reichstag elections, the Nazis win 230 seats (37.4 percent of the vote) in a 608-member chamber and emerge as the single largest party.

November 6   In new Reichstag elections, the Nazi vote declines to 33.1 percent, and the party's parliamentary membership drops to 196 out of 584 seats.

1933

January 30   Hitler is appointed chancellor.

March 5   In the last relatively free Reichstag elections, the Nazis gain 43.9 percent of the vote and claim 288 out of 647 seats, short of a majority.

March 23   Enabling Act on which Hitler's dictatorship will be based is passed.

July 14   NSDAP is declared the only legal party in Germany.

October   Germany withdraws from the League of Nations.

1934

June 30–August 2   Hitler carries out Röhm purge.

August 2   Upon Hindenburg's death, Hitler combines the presidency and chancellorship.

1935

March	Hitler announces German rearmament and military conscription.
September	Nuremberg Race Laws are proclaimed.
October	Mussolini's troops invade Ethiopia.

1936

March	German troops occupy the demilitarized Rhineland.
October 25	The Rome-Berlin Axis is formed by an Italian-German treaty.

1936–1939

	Fascist Italy and Nazi Germany are involved in the Spanish Civil War.

1937

March 14	Pope Pius IX issues encyclical *Mit brennender Sorge* (With burning anxiety).
November 5	Hitler outlines plans to dominate Europe in Hossbach Memorandum.

1938

March	Austria is annexed by Nazi Germany.
September 29–30	Munich Conference results in German annexation of the Sudetenland.
November 8–9	*Kristallnacht* brings the first pogrom against German Jews.

1939

March	German troops occupy the remainder of Czechoslovakia.
April	Italian troops occupy Albania.
May 22	Germany and Italy conclude Pact of Steel.
August 23	Nazi-Soviet Nonaggression Pact clears the way for Hitler's invasion of Poland.
September 1	German forces attack Poland.
September 3	Britain and France declare war on Germany.

1940

April 9	Germany occupies Denmark and Norway.

May 10	Germany invades the Netherlands, Belgium, Luxembourg, and France.
June 10	Italy declares war on France.
August–September	Battle of Britain ends in stalemate.
October to early 1941	Mussolini invades Greece and is badly defeated.
December to February 1941	Italian position in North Africa collapses.

1941

June 22	German forces attack the Soviet Union; Italy joins the war.
December 11	Germany and Italy declare war on the United States.

1942

November 5	General Erwin Rommel is defeated at El Alamein.
November 7–8	American and British troops land in northwest Africa.

1943

January 31	German troops surrender at Stalingrad.
July 25	Mussolini deposed by the Fascist Grand Council.
September 8	Italy accepts armistice with the Allies; German troops occupy the Italian peninsula.
September 12–13	Mussolini is rescued by a German commando and is soon installed as head of the Italian Social Republic in the German-occupied area of Italy.

1944

June 4	Rome is occupied by U.S. troops.
June 6	Western allies land in Normandy on D-Day.
July 20	Attempt on Hitler's life fails.
December 16 to January 1945	Battle of the Bulge ends with German defeat.

1945

April 16	Soviets make final push to Berlin.
April 28	Mussolini shot by Italian partisans.
April 30	Hitler commits suicide in his Berlin bunker.
May 7	Unconditional German surrender is signed at Reims.
May 8	V-E day is declared.

THE RISE OF FASCISM IN
EUROPE EXPLAINED

I

The Development of Fascism in Europe

FASCISM AS A NEW FORCE

The years between 1919 and 1945 have sometimes been called the age of fascism. This characterization describes a phenomenon in European history that began with Benito Mussolini's Fascist political movement and Adolf Hitler's National Socialist German Workers' Party, or Nazi Party, in the aftermath of World War I and ended ignominiously with the death of both leaders and their regimes at the end of World War II. It is important to note that Italian Fascism and German National Socialism were but one aspect of twentieth-century totalitarianism; the other was the longer-lasting political system of communism, which emerged in Russia in 1917. Fascism and communism in practice have shared certain aspects in the totalitarian state: supremacy of a leader, an exclusive ideology, a single mass party, a monopoly of communications media and education, and a secret police and terror apparatus; they both also have aimed to transform social, artistic, and literary values and to create a "new man." They differ in that European Communist regimes have adhered to the Leninist-Stalinist principle of thorough state bureaucracy, revolutionary internationalism (in theory, at least), state (economic) collectivism, and an ideology based on philosophical materialism, while fascist regimes have advanced an ultranationalist ideology with imperialist goals and have retained capitalist economic orders, albeit under very firm control.

The fascist movements and parties that arose in Italy and Germany developed into regular totalitarian dictatorial regimes in the 1920s and 1930s. But fascism also appeared in various western and eastern European countries without achieving major political power. Spain under Francisco

Franco was not a true fascist dictatorship, since the Falange, or Spanish fascist party, was firmly subordinated to the will of its authoritarian ruler, who relied on nonfascist institutions for his power. Similarly, some of the Latin American dictatorships, such as Juan Perón's regime in Argentina, though sometimes characterized as fascist, represented much more traditional military authoritarian rulerships rather than fascist, let alone totalitarian, dictatorial systems. Fascism both as ideology and as political system was a singularly European phenomenon.

Fascism everywhere was essentially a reaction against the devastating impact of World War I and its unsettling aftermath on basically liberal nineteenth-century nations that failed to achieve social harmony. Victors and vanquished alike suffered from economic and demographic devastation and moral exhaustion in a war that took close to ten million human lives, broke up empires, and undermined the political credibility of monarchs and democrats alike. Out of the ruin came extreme nationalism that called for strong state measures to restore national pride, right past wrongs, and revive the economy. Fascist leaders and supporters espoused dictatorial rule based on a distinct ideology and enforced through the actions of a mass party. In Italy, parliamentary government had found only a weak footing before Mussolini's regime was established. In Germany, parliamentary democracy during the difficult years after the war had to be established in a society that had almost no democratic political traditions. Fascist rulers in both of these societies therefore found it relatively easy to suppress democratic institutions and individual rights. Their regimes orchestrated barrages of state propaganda designed to mobilize fascist militants and the people; operated with the help of a secret police system, including prisons and/or concentration camps; regimented their populations in accordance with the aims of Fascist or Nazi policies; engaged in military aggression; and, in the case of the Nazi order, perpetrated mass murder.

The seedbed of fascist ideas can be found in the changing climate of opinion of nineteenth- and early-twentieth-century Europe. The ideals of the Enlightenment and the French Revolution—rationalism, liberalism, democracy, and egalitarianism—were increasingly challenged by new philosophical, scientific, pseudoscientific, and political precepts. These new ideas provided the intellectual source upon which some fascist ideologists and politicians would draw. Rationalism was increasingly replaced by irrationalism. Ideologically, fascism was a part of the dangerous trends inherent in the extreme nationalism, radical conservatism tinged with social Darwinism, racialism, and anti-Semitism that emerged in the late nineteenth century. It is doubtful that these extremist ideas of nationalism and racism would have produced fascism and turned it into a powerful political force without the very troubled economic and social conditions created by World War I and its aftermath. The war itself had unleashed fiery emotions of nationalism and brought total war to the citizenry of the European warring nations. Centralized authoritarian war governments assumed control of the economy, means of production, and labor relations and mobilized all segments of the society for the war effort, providing models of total dictatorship for the future.

ITALY

The first fascist totalitarian dictator was Benito Mussolini (1883–1945), self-styled Duce (leader) of Italy between the wars. From humble social origins, he became a leader in prewar Italian socialism. But in 1914, in a striking about-face, he abandoned international socialism and embraced the national cause, urging Italian entry into World War I. In March 1919 he founded fascism with the establishment of the first *Fascio* di Combattimento* (combat group) in Milan as the core of the later Italian Fascist Party. This new movement came at a time when conditions appeared to favor it. Economic and political problems engulfed Italy after the war. Close to 650,000 lives had been lost in the war, yet Italy failed to get all that had been promised for joining the Allies in the war when peace was made. The national debt had swelled as a result of the war, bringing inflated prices and depressed wages. The disorder and frustration in the postwar years raised the specter of a socialist revolution, an anathema to much of Italian society. Mussolini's movement was designed to attract converts from the many discontented, the disillusioned, and the uprooted to passionate nationalism and direct action. But above all, he was driven by a quest for power.

Ideologically, Mussolini was shallow and supremely opportunistic. Once asked to define Fascism, he bluntly responded: "I am Fascism." When the blend of nationalism and radicalism of early Fascism, mixing antiliberalism and antisocialism with attacks on big business, failed to gain recruits for Mussolini's party, he purged the party program of its proletarian pretense and sought to gain bourgeois support. He began to organize some of his veteran supporters into black-shirted paramilitary *squadristi*, or direct-action bands, to support factory owners and landowners by disrupting socialist rallies, destroying labor-union and party properties, and terrorizing leftist organizers. While Mussolini operated largely from Milan, emerging

---

*The term *fascism* is derived from *fascio*, which referred to members of this particular group. Historically, the word *fascio* stems from the Latin word *fasces*, the bundle of rods containing an axe that was carried by the lictor in ancient Rome as a symbol of authority.

local Fascist leaders, quite early called *ras* after Ethiopian tribal chiefs, were active in other northern areas: Dino Grandi in Bologna, Roberto Farinacci in Cremona, and Italo Balbo in Ferrara. As the ranks of the Fascist Blackshirts swelled, some leaders of the Liberal and Nationalist coalition government sought to tame Mussolini's hordes by co-opting the Fascist Party into a political alliance in 1921. It proved impossible to establish a stable government, since the center liberal and socialist parties refused cooperation. In 1922 the Fascist *squadristi* exacerbated the plight of the helpless government by taking over entire towns, expelling socialist or Communist mayors and councils in several regions of northern Italy.

In October 1922 Mussolini heightened the governmental crisis by threatening a "March on Rome" at a massive Fascist Party congress rally held in Naples. Confronted with this challenge, King Victor Emmanuel III avoided trouble with the Blackshirts by asking their leader to form a government. Technically, Mussolini was named prime minister of Italy according to constitutional practice. However, in a way he had forced himself into power by helping to make regular government impossible in 1921 and 1922, and relenting only when the political leaders of Italy acceded to his demand for the top ministerial post. Even though Rome alone had a military security force of 12,000 men, the king lacked the resolution to use the army to disperse the Fascist action units.

Mussolini formed a fourteen-member coalition government with representation from all major parties; only four posts were reserved for Fascists. The new prime minister, however, added the Foreign and Interior ministries to his portfolio and quickly demonstrated who was in charge. In November 1922 the Italian Chamber of Deputies granted Mussolini full powers to legislate by decree for the next twelve months. Such extraordinary power to govern by decree for a limited period of time had quite often been granted before. The Fascist leader indicated to the parliament that if he were given support for his measures, there would be no necessity for an imminent violent change of the state. Since the Fascists held less than 10 percent of the seats in the parliament, they initiated a new electoral law that would have ensured their domination. When elections were actually held in 1924, the Fascist national ticket won 66 percent of the popular vote and gave Mussolini a secure parliamentary majority even without the new law. This electoral triumph was not achieved by manipulation and violence alone; the Fascist leader, the Duce, was genuinely popular among the conservatives and even among poorer segments of the populace.

In 1925–1926 Mussolini succeeded in transforming Italy from a parliamentary monarchy into a one-party dictatorship. A series of new laws tightened control over the press and replaced all elected local officials by men appointed from Rome. Early in 1926 Mussolini was empowered to rule by decree, and later in the year all opposition parties were abolished, leaving the Fascist Party as the only political party in Italy. Even though the Duce had amassed seemingly unlimited power and authority in his hands, he had to respect the position of the monarchy, the military, and the Roman Catholic Church, for all of these long-established institutions managed to retain their relative autonomy. The king did not cede his constitutional right to appoint the prime minister. The armed forces, especially the navy, were not subjugated to the absolute control of the Duce. The Lateran Accords of 1929, concluded by the Fascist government and the Vatican, in some ways strengthened the role of the church in Italian life by normalizing the troubled state-church relations for the first time since Italy's unification. The Fascist regime dealt harshly at times with its political opponents by arresting them and confining them to wretched prisons and penal colonies; however, it never practiced abuse of justice on a scale equal to that of the Nazis or Soviets. Probably no more than 10,000 persons were imprisoned for political reasons, and only a small number of capital sentences were passed. Starting in 1938, with Mussolini's intensified alignment of Italy with Germany, policies of discrimination and harassment against Jews were enacted.

Once Mussolini had consolidated his political position, he gave concerted attention to economic affairs. Fascist economic policy in the mid-1920s and throughout much of the 1930s was designed to build economic self-sufficiency as a base for a vigorous foreign policy. Economic liberalism was denounced for promoting individual self-interest, as was socialism for creating conflicts between workers and capitalists. The Fascist solution was to join labor and capital in a self-governing corporation to decide issues of mutual interest amicably and to design economic policy for the entire society. In reality, however, Mussolini had developed a comfortable relationship with big business quite early in his regime, and his concept of corporativism did not disturb this relative harmony. In the corporations, true equality between capital and labor was not maintained, for representatives of labor generally worked with industrialists who supported the Fascist regime, allowing big business to make its own decisions with but scant attention to the corporations. Since Italy lacked the basic natural resources—oil, coal, iron ore, and strategic minerals—to ensure self-sufficiency, the Fascist regime could do little to solve Italy's long-standing dependence on imported raw materials.

In an early attempt at aggressive foreign policy, Mussolini failed to seize the Greek island of Corfu in 1923. Rebuffed, he refrained from further expansionist adventures until the mid-1930s. In 1934 he mobilized his troops on the Austrian border to thwart an Austrian Nazi coup to overthrow the archconservative government in Vienna in anticipation of unification with Germany. In October of the following year, the Duce embarked on his first colonial conquest by invading Ethiopia, a Fascist war to advance Italy's empire in Africa. Its consequence in Europe was a diplomatic realignment. Even though Britain and France, Italy's partners thus far in a common front against Germany, did not break with Italy and supported only moderate League of Nations economic sanctions against Italy as punishment for Mussolini's aggression, the Duce turned closer to Nazi Germany in order to avoid international isolation. His cool relationship with Hitler changed, and both soon teamed up to intervene in the Spanish Civil War in support of General Francisco Franco. Mussolini's motivation was to keep Spain from going Communist and, with Franco's regime in place, to contain Anglo-French influence in the western Mediterranean. In 1938 the Duce acquiesced in Hitler's annexation of Austria, and in April 1939 he occupied and annexed Albania, asserting Italy's stake in the Balkans. One month later he formally joined Germany as a somewhat dubious alliance partner, as the beginning of World War II quickly demonstrated.

GERMANY

National Socialism, or Nazism, arose in Germany under conditions that were quite similar to those in Italy. It developed in the immediate aftermath of German defeat in World War I when nationalist discontent and severe economic dislocation plagued the society. The democratic Weimar Republic that replaced the proud authoritarian empire was treated with contempt by the German elites, and the traditionally nationalistic middle class identified it with indecision, weakness, and national humiliation. During the 1920s the German government struggled with an economic slump, foreign occupation, an unprecedented hyperinflation, and harsh reparations. Yet the Weimar Republic managed to weather these crises and the persistent challenges to parliamentary democracy by opponents from the right and the left ten years longer than Italy under its constitutional monarchy. As economic conditions improved after the mid-1920s, following a currency reform and the infusion of foreign credits, the prospects of parliamentary democracy were much enhanced. It is quite likely that it would have survived in Germany and Nazism would have remained a boisterous fringe movement if the chaos of the Great Depression had not cut short economic prosperity and social stability.

The future builder of Nazi Germany was Adolf Hitler, a lower-middle-class Austrian by birth, who fancied himself an artist until his experience in the German trenches in World War I induced him to become a politician. In 1919 he joined the right-wing German Workers' Party in Munich, in which his oratorical and organizational talents quickly ensured him a leadership role. Renamed the National Socialist German Workers' Party, it extolled ultranationalism and denounced the Versailles Treaty and the Weimar Republic, as well as liberals, socialists, and Communists. Hitler added a unique racial element to German fascism, proclaiming the superiority of the Aryan, or Germanic, race and the subjugation of inferior races, especially the Jews. He was a consummate demagogue who was able to convince people that he and his party had the solution to urgent problems in Germany and could regenerate the nation.

Even though Hitler emerged quite early as the unquestioned leader of the Nazi Party, several individuals contributed significantly to its development, and some became prominent leaders in the Third Reich. Among them was Ernst Röhm, a captain in the Reichswehr (postwar German army), who helped Hitler's political career by furnishing followers, arms, and financial support for the struggling movement. He also built up the paramilitary formation of the party, the Sturmabteilung (SA), or Storm Troopers. Alfred Rosenberg, a Baltic German born in Estonia, worked as a party journalist and attempted to construct an ideology of Nazism drawn from a mixture of anti-Semitism, anti-Slavism, anti-Bolshevism, and an anti-Christian notion of world history. Though Rosenberg was later viewed as the chief ideologist of the Nazi Party, Hitler himself said that he never read Rosenberg's major work, *Myth of the 20th Century*, a ponderous if not pompous ideological treatise. Rudolf Hess, often seen with Hitler, was a student of political science at the University of Munich when he joined the Nazi Party in 1920. A rabid believer in Nazi ideology, he became a slavish devotee of Hitler and for a while served as the Führer's deputy but was overshadowed by more aggressive Nazi leaders even before his bizarre flight to England in 1941 during World War II. Hermann Göring, product of an upper-class family and a much-decorated flier of World War I fame, was a strong German nationalist and anti-Communist but cared little for Nazi ideology. He was induced to join the Nazi Party while in search of action, adventure, and comradeship. Motivated by a hunger for power, he eventually became the number two man in Nazi Germany and Hitler's designated successor. In the early years of the party, Hitler welcomed him because as an aristocrat and renowned war hero he brought respectability to the Nazi Party. At the same time, he always accepted the Führer as the dominant leader, first in the party and later in the Third Reich.

In 1923 Hitler and his associates staged a putsch (sudden political insurrection) in Munich, expecting to emulate Mussolini's coup of the year before by marching on Berlin after gaining power in the state of Bavaria.

It failed miserably, and Hitler found himself in prison instead. There he wrote *Mein Kampf*, his "autobiographical" blueprint for German political and social redemption based on territorial expansion and the suppression of "inferior" peoples. Released on parole in late 1924, he restored his party, which had fallen into disarray, and reconstituted its paramilitary arm, the SA. The Nazi Party's foray into Reichstag elections as late as 1928 gave it only 2.6 percent of the popular vote and a dozen deputies in the parliament. In 1929 the Great Depression struck Germany, bringing increasing social misery to the populace and deep political polarization to the body politic in the years that followed. As unemployment soared, more and more workers supported the Communists. Members of the middle and lower middle classes, many of whom had been devastated by the hyper-inflation of 1923, turned to the Nazis, who claimed to be the bulwark against social revolution. In the 1930 Reichstag election, the number of Nazi delegates jumped from 12 to 107, making them the second-largest party next to the Social Democrats. The advance in the Nazi and also the Communist vote deprived the government of a parliamentary majority. Without it, the country could only be governed by resort to the constitutional emergency provisions. The democratically elected, parliamentary-based cabinet was now replaced by a presidentially appointed chancellor and cabinet. Thus democracy ceased to function in Germany several years before Hitler came to power.

By 1932, due to economic collapse, unemployment peaked at 6.2 million persons, one-third of the German work force. Another round of elections confirmed the Nazis' growing popularity, and they emerged as Germany's largest political party, with 37 percent of the popular vote and 230 seats in the Reichstag out of a total of 608. Hitler refused to accept anything but the chancellorship in a coalition cabinet. Intrigue and maneuvers by conservative nationalist politicians much enhanced Hitler's chances of appointment, especially since they depended on the judgment of the aging Reich President Paul von Hindenburg, the head of the Weimar Republic. Reluctantly, he let himself be persuaded to appoint Hitler to the chancellorship in January 1933.

Like Mussolini at the outset of his prime ministership, Hitler as the new chancellor at first presided over a coalition cabinet in which his party held only a few posts. The Nazi leader skillfully outmaneuvered the nationalist and nonparty majority in the government, which sought to guarantee the preservation of conservative policies, and proceeded to make himself master of Germany. A Reichstag fire late in February 1933, which the Nazis claimed portended a Communist putsch, gave Hitler the pretext to suspend civil rights and to arrest Communists and some Social Democrats. In a new Reichstag election in March, the Nazis failed to get a popular majority, obtaining only 43.9 percent of the vote and 288 seats in the chamber. Having eliminated the Communist Party, Hitler prevailed upon the other parties (except the Social Democrats) to pass an Enabling Act that gave him dictatorial powers for four years. Within weeks after its passage, all political parties except the Nazi Party either disbanded or were dissolved. Similarly, the labor unions were eliminated and replaced by the Nazi Labor Front. By the end of the summer of 1933, the Nazi takeover of German social and political institutions was virtually completed. However, Hitler still faced three possible sources of opposition. One was Reich President von Hindenburg, who had the formal right to depose the chancellor, but the old and weary president was little inclined to act decisively on complaints about Nazi tactics. The power of the army, which in previous political crises had maintained neutrality, but could depose Hitler from office, posed a more serious challenge. The greatest immediate threat, however, came from disgruntled SA members and especially their leader Ernst Röhm, who wanted to combine the undisciplined mass SA with the much smaller orderly German military. The army leadership made it very clear that it would not tolerate Röhm's ambitious aspirations.

In June 1934 Hitler carried out a bloody purge of Röhm and many of his SA associates with the help of the elitist Schutzstaffel (SS), or Protection Squad, under Heinrich Himmler during the "Night of the Long Knives." An early member of the Nazi Party, Himmler was well on his way to becoming the ruthless bloodhound of the Nazi regime ever since he had been appointed Reichsführer SS in 1929. At that time, his order had been only an elite cadre that guarded the Führer, but it had been expanded greatly since then, and the Röhm purge resulted in the separation of the SS from the SA, to which it had been tied organizationally. Assured that the army would remain the nation's sole bearer of arms, the minister of defense, a general, thanked Hitler on behalf of the army; only weeks later, upon Hindenburg's death, the army leadership acquiesced in having the office of president and chancellor combined in Hitler's hands, making him, the Führer (he never used the title *president*), the supreme commander of all armed forces. As master of Germany, Hitler was not yet in complete control of the German army, but he enjoyed its support. In 1938 he restructured the German military high command and made it fully amenable to his will.

Even though murder became the method of treatment of many political opponents only with the onset of the war, the Nazi regime established the first concentration camp at Dachau near Munich within months after Hitler's seizure of power, first under the aegis of the SA and soon under that of the SS. Here and at other camps, imprisoned Communists, Social Democrats, and other outspoken opponents of Nazism had to endure harsh treatment and sporadic acts of murder. German Jews were generally not imprisoned in the early years of the regime, but their businesses faced a boycott as early as April 1933. The Nazis deprived Jews of citizenship rights and instituted measures that gradually displaced them from German society. Shortly after the Nazi takeover, Jews, as non-Aryans, were removed from the civil service, judgeships, the legal profession, teaching positions, cultural and entertainment enterprises, and the press. The Nuremberg Laws of 1935 forbade marriages and sexual encounters between Germans and Jews. Jews were soon barred from universities, schools, restaurants, hospitals, theaters, museums, and other public facilities. Jewish businesses were systematically "Aryanized" through confiscation by the Nazi authorities. In November 1938 a seventeen-year-old Jewish youth, driven to desperation by Nazi mistreatment of his parents, shot a German embassy secretary in Paris. The incident was used as a pretext by the Nazi authorities to organize "mobs" to loot and pillage Jewish shops all over Germany, burn synagogues, and invade Jewish homes to mistreat occupants and steal their possessions during *Kristallnacht* (Night of the Broken Glass). About 30,000 Jews were thrown into concentration camps. The Reich then exacted from the Jewish community a fine of 1 billion marks. Although some Jews managed to leave Germany, it was usually at the cost of abandoning all their possessions. Most of those who did were the lucky ones. All measures designed to drive the Jews into ghettos and starvation, which followed in the first years of the war, were but the prelude to genocidal murder of German and European Jews in World War II.

After assuming the chancellorship, Hitler recognized that he had to address Germany's economic problems, especially those caused by the Great Depression. But very important to his foreign policy goals was the ability of Germany's economy to provide the wherewithal for the development of a strong military force. Though rearmament was his foremost concern, he proceeded somewhat cautiously toward its achievement lest he alert the Western powers to German violations of the Versailles Treaty and his designs on Europe. More important at the time was the need to build the economic infrastructure in Germany. In 1933 a government plan allocated significant funds to various public works projects. A labor service begun during the Weimar Republic was expanded and made compulsory after 1935. Rearmament expenditures were systematically increased from 1934 to 1939. The German army was greatly expanded after 1935, and military service became compulsory. Not all sectors of the economy benefited from rearmament: consumer-goods industries and certain export trades suffered. One beneficial social effect of increased public spending, rearmament, compulsory labor, and military service was the rapid reduction of unemployment from over 6 million late in 1932 to less than half a million in 1937.

In foreign affairs, the Führer's plans included the destruction of the Versailles Treaty, the conquest and colonization of eastern Europe for German *Lebensraum*, (living space), and domination and exploitation of racial inferiors. Because Hitler was mindful of Germany's military weakness, his early steps were cautious and projected an air of reasonableness. The first major violation of the Treaty of Versailles came in 1935 with the official announcement of rearmament; others followed with the remilitarization of the Rhineland in 1936 and the annexation of Austria and the German-speaking Sudetenland (taken from Czechoslovakia) two years later. Great Britain and France repeatedly protested but took no military action, rationalizing that war was too horrible a means to stop Hitler's unilateral changes within his homeland or to deter him from helping German populaces to realize the principle of national self-determination accorded to other peoples by the Paris peace settlement. Ever bolder, Hitler continued to count on Western pusillanimity when he marched his army into what remained of Czechoslovakia in March 1939 and prepared an invasion of Poland several months later. When German troops smashed into Poland on September 1, 1939, France and Britain declared war on Germany, and the most devastating war in Europe was unleashed.

FASCISM IN WESTERN AND EASTERN EUROPE

Fascism was not confined to Italy and Germany. Fascist groups or parties appeared in France, Britain, the Low Countries, Scandinavia, Austria, Poland, Hungary, Rumania, and Yugoslavia. To illustrate the unique features of the varieties of fascism, however, it is informative briefly to examine the role of fascist parties in Spain, France, Poland, Hungary, Yugoslavia, and Rumania. Their experience stands in contrast to the classical forms of fascism found in Italy and Germany but mirrors aspects of the societies in which fascist parties played a limited role and short-lived fascist regimes emerged during World War II. None of the states in which fascist parties attained governmental power during the war established a totalitarian regime, since they exercised control over the political and police functions of the society but not over all economic, social, and cultural developments.

Fascism in Spain emerged in a country whose political, economic, and social development lagged behind the rest of Europe. The Spanish fascist party, the Falange Española, was formed in 1933 by José Antonio Primo de Rivera, the son of an earlier dictator. It championed authoritarian, ultranationalist, antiliberal, antiparliamentary ideas and urged social and economic revolution. When General Francisco Franco and his military associates, all of whom were staunch conservatives, rebelled against the Spanish Republican government and launched the Spanish Civil War in 1936, the ranks of the Falange swelled, and it organized its own military formations. But deprived of effective leadership after the imprisonment and execution of Primo de Rivera by the Republican government, the Falange was unable to pursue an independent course. In 1937 General Franco forced it into a new party, merging the Falange, the reactionary Catholic Carlists, and their military formations called *Requetés*. As military leader and now head of state, Franco kept the revolutionary aspirations of the Old Falangists in check and manipulated the party to his own non-fascist political ends. During his long rule as El Caudillo (the leader), he based his strongly authoritarian dictatorship on the army, the Catholic Church, the landed and industrial elite, and segments of the middle class. Fascism as a force declined and lost whatever impetus it originally had as the Franco regime unfolded.

Spain's neighbor France remained relatively stable, prosperous, and democratic during the interwar period. Even though several rightist organizations and fascist groups emerged, only one, the Parti Populaire Français (PPF), organized by the ex-Communist Jacques Doriot in 1936, gained a significant membership. With a policy based on opposition to capitalism, communism, and world Jewry, the party's political influence before World War II was limited. After the defeat of France by Nazi Germany in 1940, the country was divided into the German-occupied northern zone, whose center was Paris, and the Vichy-governed central and southern part. Several fascist splinter groups and the PPF under Doriot operated in the northern part of France and collaborated with the German authorities, who preferred to keep the French fascist factions divided and did not allow a united force to form. The Vichy government under Marshal Philippe Pétain was a regime of moderate right authoritarianism. Though moving closer to the radical right in the course of the war, it collaborated with the Nazi new order, including support of the destructive Jewish policy, but otherwise kept its distance from fascism.

The Polish government after the mid-1920s was one of several eastern European states dominated by a right authoritarian system. Marshal Józef Piłsudski and his authoritarian successors, called the Colonels, relied at times on the different rightist groups and parties for support, but the one notable fascist organization, Falanga, commanded only a small following and was of little political consequence. A more weighty role of fascist groups could be found in Hungary and Rumania.

Fascist groups in Hungary appeared in the 1930s, largely under the inspiration of German National Socialism. They flourished under the pro-fascist, anti-Semitic prime minister Gyula Gömbös. In 1937 Ferenc Szálasi, a former general staff officer, merged several of the fascist groups into his own political movement called the Arrow Cross. His program was ultra-nationalistic and imperialistic, advocating Hungarism, which combined some Christian and socialist notions to produce an enlightened national socialism. Szálasi envisaged himself as the chosen leader of a Carpatho-Danubian Great Fatherland, encompassing much of southeastern and eastern Europe, as one of the dominant forces of a new Europe along with Nazi Germany and Fascist Italy. Early in World War II, Szálasi unsuccessfully plotted to get into the government, which was headed by the regency of the conservative Admiral Miklós Horthy. With German support, Szálasi finally succeeded in 1944 in seizing power to preside over a short-lived fascist regime after Horthy was deposed under German pressure. Even though Szálasi personally considered Hitler's anti-Semitic policies excessive, his Arrow Cross regime collaborated with the Nazis in the deportation of Hungarian Jews to their destruction. An even more violent satellite quasi-fascist regime was established by Ante Pavelić with his Us-tashi in Croatia between 1941 and 1945, after the Germans invaded Yugoslavia. It unleashed a brutal wave of terrorism and murder against the Serbian and Jewish minorities. The one-party state operated with the assistance of Catholic clergy, and some scholars have characterized Pavelić's regime as, at best, protofascist, for the Ustashi appeared to have no vision of a fascist-type revolution and a "new man" other than that of an extreme, if not murderous, Catholic nationalist peasant.

Perhaps one of the most peculiar forms of fascism appeared in Rumania, which had been a "victor" state in World War I, doubling in size, but also suffered from an identity problem due to a large number of diverse minorities. In 1927 Corneliu Zelea Codreanu, son of a schoolteacher, founded the Legion of the Archangel Michael, better known by its paramilitary formation, the Rumanian Iron Guard. As a religious mystic, Codreanu and his followers developed their own idea of Rumanian Orthodoxy that aspired to achieve national salvation for the Rumanian people, or "race." The Legionaries appealed to radical nationalist youth and the peasantry, professed strident anti-Semitism, engaged in violence and sometimes murder, and maintained a rigidly hierarchical internal organization with a paramilitary external form. Since the Iron Guard came close to promoting social revolution, it was perhaps the most radical of all fascist movements. By 1938 the authoritarian regime of King Carol II felt threatened enough by the Legionaries to suppress them in the most brutal manner by arresting Codreanu and most of his associates and shooting them while they were imprisoned. But the Legion was not eliminated and remained a powerful underground movement. Within two years the Carolist dictatorial regime was overtaken by international events when Rumania was put in the German sphere of influence by the Nazi-Soviet Pact of 1939 and the German occupation of Poland. King Carol was forced to abdicate in 1940 in favor of his son Michael, and General Ion Antonescu, an ultra-nationalist right radical with a strongly authoritarian but not typically fascist bent, assumed dictatorial power. He aspired to make Rumania an important middle-sized power in eastern Europe. Antonescu formed a right-wing coalition government that included the Iron Guard, which shared his ultranationalism and authoritarian and pro-German orientation. However, when the Iron Guard proceeded to build its own power base, charged the dictator with being insufficiently "totalitarian," and finally staged a coup against Antonescu, it was ruthlessly liquidated in January 1941. During the conflict with the Legion, Antonescu retained his direct control of the army and the national police forces. He also assured Hitler of his loyalty and support of German policy in eastern Europe and received the Führer's blessing to deal with the Legion as the situation demanded. Hitler's concern was to preserve stability in Rumania to protect his oil supplies in the coming war against the Soviet Union rather than to worry about fascist orthodoxy.

FASCISM, WORLD WAR II, AND HITLER'S NEW ORDER

Wherever fascism was found, especially in the leading fascist states of Germany and Italy, it had territorial expansionism as one of its essential goals. War provided both Hitler and Mussolini with a convenient vehicle for the pursuit of their expansionist ambitions and, in fact, was a part of the raison d'être of Nazism and Fascism. The Duce was the first to resort to war, conquering Ethiopia in 1935. After turning Albania into a pliant satellite in the 1920s, he occupied it in the spring of 1939. Similarly, Hitler achieved his early expansionist aims without military violence, but on September 1, 1939, he triggered World War II in Europe by his invasion of Poland.

The German armies used *Blitzkrieg* (lightning war) strategy, a combination of airplanes, fast mobile armor, and infantry, to force Poland's surrender in less than three weeks. After a six-month interlude of Phony War with but occasional skirmishes on the French-German border, Hitler's forces occupied Denmark and Norway in April 1940 and mounted a massive successful strike against the Low Countries and France in the following month. Not to be deprived of some spoils, Mussolini advanced his own troops into France on June 10, 1940, and thereby formally entered the war on Hitler's side. His intent was to conduct a parallel war by pursuing limited conquests in Europe but larger stakes in Africa in an effort to re-create a new Roman Empire. However, as Italian performance was soon to demonstrate in Greece and then in North Africa, the Duce's appetite for foreign conquest far exceeded the inadequate economic and military resources of his country. He became utterly dependent on German sup-port and was thereby relegated to the position of the Führer's subordinate ally. After the stunning German victories in the west, Hitler expected Brit-ain to make peace but was surprised when British heroic resistance in the air Battle of Britain in the summer of 1940 resulted in a strategic deadlock. He now made the most crucial mistake of his career by launching the invasion of the Soviet Union in June 1941 before having subdued his op-ponent in the west. True, the obliteration of Bolshevism and conquest of *Lebensraum* in Russia were his cardinal goals, but by moving east before defeating Britain, he exposed Germany to a two-front war that it could not win. The *Blitzkrieg* strategy failed to bring the decisive defeat of the Soviet Union despite its enormous losses at the outset of the German invasion. In December 1941 Hitler compounded his plight by declaring war on the United States after the United States had declared war on Germany's ally Japan. A newly launched offensive in the spring of 1942 extended German lines far into the Soviet interior, but by early 1943 the tide turned inexorably against Germany.

Between 1941 and 1944 the German armies occupied most of Europe from the Atlantic to the depths of Russia. Some conquered areas were annexed outright; other lands were treated as occupied areas or satellite or client states. They were administered by German officials, ruled through local officials sympathetic to Nazism, or controlled through compliant, if not opportunistic, collaborators with the Germans. The Führer and his willing associates imposed a New Order of exploitation and terror on this expansive empire. Both material and human resources were exploited for the war effort. Whereas the Italian Fascist conquerors followed a more traditional, though harsh, military occupation policy (Ethiopia, where Ital-ians murdered many of the intelligentsia, was an exception), the Nazi treatment of occupied areas consisted largely of enacting ideological and racial policies. For vast numbers of Europeans, especially from Poland and Russia, who were viewed racially as a lower form of humanity, Nazi policy meant deportation to Germany as forced labor. Millions of Russian pris-oners of war were put in camps and systematically starved to death.

The harsh persecution of Jews in prewar Germany gave way to the extermination of millions of European Jews under Hitler's "Final Solu-tion" during the war. The Führer's New Order in Europe comprised an empire of concentration camps under Heinrich Himmler and, after 1941, death camps in Poland as well. As late as 1940, Nazi plans included the establishment of a superghetto for Jews somewhere in eastern Europe or as far away as the French island of Madagascar. But as German armies advanced into the Soviet Union in 1941, summary executions of hundreds of thousands of Jews were carried out, largely by mass machine gunning. At this point, Hitler appears to have opted for the Final Solution of physical extermination. Himmler and his associates soon searched for a more scientific method of mass killing and found it in the use of large gas chambers, which were installed at six major death camps in Poland; the largest and best known of these was Auschwitz-Birkenau. Mechanized racial genocide claimed the lives of close to 6 million European Jews. In addition, millions of Gypsies, Slavs, and others perished as victims of Nazi political and racial persecution.

Even though the Allies learned of some of the Nazi atrocities and mass killings, they found no effective way of stopping them except to expedite the defeat of Germany and its allies. Quite early after the entry of the United States into the war, President Franklin D. Roosevelt and Prime Minister Winston Churchill decided on a Europe-first strategy. After 1942 Hitler's armies had run out of military successes. Following some initial victories, the German forces and their weak Italian ally were routed from North Africa by Anglo-American armies in the spring of 1943. In July of the same year the Duce was deposed by his own Fascist Grand Council and put under military arrest. Freed by a special Nazi commando in September, he was then installed at Hitler's direction as unhappy head of the Italian Social Republic (Salò Republic) in northern Italy, which was little more than a German puppet state. In the meantime, Mussolini's successor as prime minister, Marshal Pietro Badoglio, and King Victor Emmanuel disengaged Italy from the war, switched to the Allied side, and opened Italy to Allied troops. However, the Germans had anticipated Italy's defection and quickly occupied most of the Italian peninsula. German resistance remained quite fierce in central and northern Italy until the very end of the war.

On the European continent, the Normandy invasion of June 1944 set the stage for the Allied liberation of France and the Low Countries and the conquest of Germany. Since early 1943 the Red Army had been pushing the German forces relentlessly westward. While the Allies were forging ahead in France, the Soviets were advancing into the Baltic States, Poland, and Hungary; by February 1945 they stood within one hundred miles of Berlin. By April Allied and Soviet troops were penetrating into the heart of Germany from west and east. The besieged Führer spent his last days in his underground bunker in Berlin. With Russian soldiers only blocks away, he dictated his last will and testament on April 29 in which he retracted nothing and blamed all, including the war, on the Jews. Earlier in the day, in one of the last messages to reach the bunker, he had been told of Mussolini's death at the hands of Italian partisans. Determined not to meet such a shameful end, he took his own life the following day. With the death of the fascist dictators, the most destructive war in human history ended in Europe, as did the fascist epoch.

Hitler's skillful oratory won him many followers. From Kurt Zentner, *Illustrierte Geschichte des Dritten Reiches* (Munich: Südwest Verlag, 1965). Used by permission of Südwest Verlag.

A discomfited Hitler at his first meeting with Mussolini in Venice in 1934. The Duce saw himself as the senior Fascist leader and harbored some suspicion of the new Nazi leader of Germany. From Kurt Zentner, *Illustrierte Geschichte des Dritten Reiches* (Munich: Südwest Verlag, 1965). Used by permission of Südwest Verlag.

On his visit to Germany in 1937, Mussolini appears to be impressed by Hitler's military might. As the Fascist dictator moved closer to his Nazi ally, he became more and more the junior partner. From Kurt Zentner, *Illustrierte Geschichte des Dritten Reiches* (Munich: Südwest Verlag, 1965). Used by permission of Südwest Verlag.

Nazi totalitarianism on the march: the entry of political leaders at a Nuremberg party rally. Political leaders carried the domination of the Nazi party from the regional level to the district, town, block, down to the household of the German populace. From Kurt Zentner, *Illustrierte Geschichte des Dritten Reiches* (Munich: Südwest Verlag, 1965). Used by permission of Südwest Verlag.

'PHEW! THAT'S A NASTY LEAK. THANK GOODNESS IT'S NOT AT OUR END OF THE BOAT' (1932)

Reaction of the Western powers to the Great Depression. From *Low's Autobiography* (New York: Simon & Schuster, 1957). Used by permission of Evening Standard/SOLO Syndication Limited, London.

The Girls He Left Behind Him (1935)

Mussolini was beginning to fall into the arms of Goebbels, Hitler, and Göring when he invaded Ethiopia. From *Low's Autobiography* (New York: Simon & Schuster, 1957). Used by permission of Evening Standard/SOLO Syndication Limited, London.

STEPPING STONES TO GLORY (1936)

Hitler had reoccupied the Rhineland without resistance from the Western democracies. From *Low's Autobiography* (New York: Simon & Schuster, 1957). Used by permission of Evening Standard/SOLO Syndication Limited, London.

RENDEZVOUS (1939)

Hitler and Stalin meet over the corpse of Poland. From *Low's Autobiography* (New York: Simon & Schuster, 1957). Used by permission of Evening Standard/SOLO Syndication Limited, London.

LEBENSRAUM FOR THE CONQUERED (1940)

In occupied countries the removal of Jews and inconvenient minorities to concentration camps was in progress. From *Low's Autobiography* (New York: Simon & Schuster, 1957). Used by permission of Evening Standard/Syndication Limited, London.

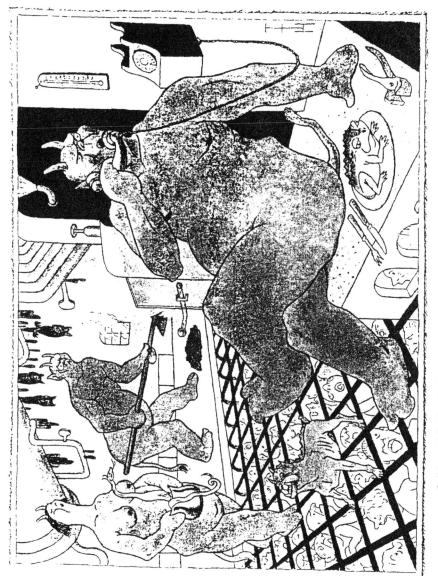

Call from Hell: 'Do stop looking for Hitler. He's here all right, but we'd be glad to get rid of him. He's always making speeches and wants to reorganize this place on the model of Belsen'

From M. Bryant, *World War II in Cartoons* (New York: W. H. Smith, 1989).

Mussolini and Clara Petacci's bodies hung up and exposed for insult in Milan, with those of other Fascists. They were caught by Italians at Donga, on Lake Como, and were tried and shot. Used by permission of Tony Stone Images / New York.

2

Fascist Seizure of Power: Italy and Germany

Fascist movements emerged in most European countries between the two world wars. However, only in Italy and Germany did fascist movements turn into parties and become major political forces that by their own efforts achieved governmental power. How did this come about? What political factors explain the success of fascism in these two societies? Both countries were states in which the old order had collapsed or no longer seemed to work. Democracy was either not deeply rooted or a system of government of short duration, and nationalist sentiment often ran high. Worst of all, Italy and Germany faced the prospect of economic breakdown and social disorder after the trauma of World War I. These conditions made it possible for the fascist movements to become established, to generate mass support, and, during times of continuing crises, to lay claim to the reins of government. The actions of conservatives and the monarchy in Italy and the Reich presidency in Germany facilitated Benito Mussolini's ascent to governmental power in 1922 and Adolf Hitler's in 1933. The willingness of the compliant King Victor Emmanuel and the reluctant Reich President Paul von Hindenburg to appoint ideological extremists to the highest political office enabled both Mussolini and Hitler to become heads of their governments according to constitutional or legal provisions. It is doubtful if either one of the fascist leaders would have dared to seize power without legal action or would have been able to maintain himself once he had done so. However, as legal appointees, Mussolini and Hitler demonstrated remarkable political skill in expanding their acquired position of power into a full dictatorship.

ITALIAN FASCISM ON THE ROAD TO POWER

Fascism gained its early prominence when Benito Mussolini organized the first *Fascio Italiano di Combattimento* (Italian combat group) in Milan on March 23, 1919. Two months earlier, Anton Drexler, a locksmith, had formed the German Workers' Party in Munich, which bore some resemblance to the new Italian Fascist association even before Adolf Hitler gave it its National Socialist stamp. The members of the Italian *Fascio* included revolutionary syndicalists turned national syndicalists, a few former Socialists who had embraced extreme nationalism, and especially members of the Italian army commandos known as *arditi*.

Mussolini and his followers attacked Catholics, Socialists, and liberals for their lack of patriotism and glorified the war, the heroism of the troops, and the camaraderie of officers and men in the front lines. However, in 1919 it was not the Mussolini Fascists who were noted for their radical nationalist initiative but Gabriele D'Annunzio, a war hero and Italy's most popular poet, who led a small expeditionary force to capture the Adriatic city of Fiume for Italy. Mussolini had private misgivings over the success of D'Annunzio's adventure, but as a radical nationalist, he lent his public support to it. When elections were held in November 1919, the patriotic Fascists suffered a major disappointment. Only one of their nineteen candidates was elected, and that in Genoa, not in their stronghold of Milan, where they received only 5,000 of 275,000 votes. In this industrial city and elsewhere, the outcome was clearly a vote against war and for the reform programs of the Socialists and Catholics. Following the election, Fascist ranks began to decline.

In 1920 the Fascists recovered by broadening their appeal among the middle classes. Starting in the fall, Fascist action increasingly shifted from the cities to the countryside as black-shirted Fascist *squadristi* attacked Socialist headquarters and broke up trade unions. These assaults brought them the support of large segments of the middle and upper classes and even some workers. Since the Italian government offered little or no protection to the frightened factory owners and landlords, they welcomed the assistance of the *squadristi*, who, organized in groups of thirty to fifty members and often led by former army officers, perpetrated more effective violence than any of the leftist groups. Their tactic was designed to protect private property against the encroachment of workers in the cities and of peasants in the countryside.

Taking the lead in a nationalist "war against Bolshevism," the Fascists saw their membership increase from 20,000 at the end of 1920 to 250,000 by the end of 1921. The Fascists had become a mass movement. They had gained a strong foothold in northern districts, where *ras* or local leaders like Italo Balbo in Ferrara, Dino Grandi in Bologna, and Roberto Farinacci in Cremona provided organizational direction. The new Fascism was more middle class and more economically moderate, but also more violent and anti-Socialist. In May 1921 the aging liberal prime minister Giovanni Giolitti decided to call for new elections to secure a more manageable Chamber of Deputies. In an attempt to tame the Fascists, he invited them to join his electoral governmental coalition. Running on a relatively moderate program, thirty-five Fascists, including Mussolini, gained seats. In his maiden parliamentary speech, Mussolini demonstrated contempt for the democratic system and for left-wing parties, but he also signalled an alternative route to power through legal and parliamentary means by indicating a willingness to forgo violence and to accept certain social and economic measures. This approach put him at odds with powerful leaders in his movement, but Mussolini worked out a compromise at the Rome congress of the Fascists in November 1921 that acknowledged *squadrismo* as an integral part of the movement. The *ras* accepted him as the indispensable Duce. The antagonistic provincial bosses, led by Dino Grandi, his most important rival, recognized that there was no real alternative to Mussolini as the leader of the party. They also went along with his more moderate and pragmatic approach to achieving power. The Fascist movement was now formally transformed into a political party, the National Fascist Party.

Early in 1922 the Duce proclaimed that "the world is turning toward the [political] right" and against democracy and socialism. He envisaged the twentieth century as an "aristocratic" century of new elites that would bring a spiritual and moral revolution to Italy.[1] To reassure the wealthy middle classes, he declared that the Fascist Party would restore Italian power and prestige, renew the economy by increasing productivity and eliminating detrimental state controls, and help restore law and order by curbing left-wing turmoil. The last assertion was egregiously cynical, for in May the Fascists launched a new offensive to take over local government in more and more districts of the north, accompanied by an escalation of violence.

The aim of the Fascist leader and his close associates became to increase their political power and to achieve a Fascist dictatorship. Their aspiration was emboldened by the political disarray of the Italian government that was brought on by disunity among the major parties, leading to what Gaetano Salvemini, a liberal critic of Fascism, called "parliamentary paralysis." Even though economic conditions were improving, the governmental crises, if anything, worsened. Socialists and Catholic Populists could not establish a common front with the Liberals to stop Fascism, since they were divided into factions that wanted to appease the Fascists and those that wanted to stop them. The more conservative Liberals were unwilling to resist the Fascists because they found them useful as a force to contain the working-class left. The election of a new pope, Pius XI who showed a benevolent attitude toward the Fascists left the democratic Catholic Populists without church support.

While political moderates were finally taking alarm at Fascist aggressiveness in the north, a Socialist protest strike in August brought new fear of the "Red menace." After the strike, Mussolini recognized that the Fascists had an unusual opportunity to push for political power, which could well be denied them if another coalition government were formed that would exclude Fascists. The *squadristi* were expanding their control of municipal and regional administrations throughout most of the north and north central regions of Italy, which confirmed their significant presence but also raised the prospect of a strong anti-Fascist backlash. In October Mussolini finalized plans for a "March on Rome." In reality, with much bluster, he only threatened a march on the Eternal City. It was not his intention to carry out an armed overthrow in Rome but to make as many people as possible believe that the control that the *squadristi* were attaining in the northern regions could also be achieved in Rome. Essentially, a military bluff enabled the Duce to attain governmental power in Italy.

The key figure who elevated the Fascist leader to the prime ministership of Italy was King Victor Emmanuel. Though not particularly forceful, he was intelligent and shrewd in sizing up the conditions of government when Mussolini threatened to march on Rome. The king realized that there was no general agreement among political leaders to head off Mussolini's move; he also feared civil war among the nonsocialist factions and wanted to discourage a revival of the left. For a short while the moderate liberal Luigi Facta, prime minister since early 1922, thought that the king would be willing to declare martial law in order to dispose of the Fascist threat and to crush any Fascist bands by military force, but Victor Emmanuel refused to grant the necessary decree, forcing the Facta government to resign on October 28. He then prevailed upon the conservative pro-Fascist liberal Antonio Salandra to organize a coalition government that included Mussolini and several Fascists. Sensing his political advantage, the Fascist leader refused to join any cabinet in which he was not granted the prime ministership. On the evening of October 29, the king invited Mussolini to come to Rome to form a new coalition government. Two days later, the Fascist leader announced his cabinet, and on the same day, after the legal transfer of power, the Blackshirts entered the city and staged a victory parade.

Mussolini presided over a fourteen-member coalition cabinet that included all major parties, from nationalists to democratic liberals, even one

Social Democrat. Of the fourteen cabinet members, only four were Fascists, but they controlled three important portfolios, prime minister, Foreign Affairs, and the Interior, all of which in fact were held by the Duce. In November, upon Mussolini's request, the Chamber of Deputies legally granted him the right to rule by decree for twelve months. To get a firmer grip over his own party, he created the Fascist Grand Council to provide a governing executive under his own direction. In the following year he sought the means to retain power by creating a more pro-Fascist parliament through the Acerbo Law, named after the Fascist deputy who introduced the bill. It provided that the party that received the highest plurality in a national election (as long as it received 25 percent of all votes cast) would have two-thirds of the seats in parliament. Liberals and democrats supported the Acerbo Law because they realized that if it was defeated, parliament would be abolished.

In the April 1924 elections, the Fascist-led coalition of Fascists, moderates, and conservatives attained 66 percent of the popular vote and secured an absolute majority in parliament even without the new law. The elections were far from free, for voters faced Fascist campaign violence, intimidation, and fraud. At the same time, Mussolini and his party appear to have enjoyed genuine support among some of the conservative segments of the established populace, especially in the south, who saw them as the means to preserve their traditional power. It is less possible to assess the sentiment of the poorer classes, especially in the countryside, where whatever Fascist "support" became evident may have been more a reflection of fraudulent campaign practice (or outright intimidation) than prevalent attitude. Overall, Mussolini was fortunate, as was Hitler in 1933, to have attained power when the economy was on the verge of a general upswing. However, Fascist dominance meant that parliamentary government as it had been known had come to an end.

Within two months after the elections, Italy was shaken by the Matteotti affair, which was brought on by the callous murder of the Socialist deputy Giacomo Matteotti, who had bitterly castigated the Fascists in parliament for their campaign violence and fraud, by Fascist thugs under the order of one of Mussolini's aides. Though there is no direct evidence that Mussolini ordered the murder, he became deeply embroiled in the political fallout of the event and was thrown into months of indecision. The leftist minority in parliament and some of the liberals walked out in protest, a move that turned out to be a serious blunder. Throughout the crisis in 1924, the king indicated no lack of confidence in his prime minister. Thus, once Mussolini recovered from what appears to have been a depression, he was able to consolidate his rule.

Early in January 1925 he addressed the Fascist-dominated Chamber of

Deputies and took personal responsibility for the events of the preceding year. He asserted that he had done nothing wrong and announced that he would assume full executive responsibility for government. He proceeded to dismiss the parliament and ordered the police to crush subversive organizations. Over a hundred people were arrested. Parties were not immediately outlawed, but opposition deputies were not allowed to return to parliamentary sessions. Parliament now rubber-stamped decrees passed by the government, censorship was introduced, and opposition newspapers were closed down. A decree at the end of the year stipulated that Mussolini was only responsible to the king and gave him virtually unlimited executive power. In 1926, with the dissolution of all non-Fascist political parties and trade unions and the replacement of elected local governments by appointed officials, a complete dictatorial state appeared in place. But, as we will see in examining the development of the Nazi model of dictatorship, Fascist Italy was far from fully totalitarian. Mussolini never controlled the monarchy and the Roman Catholic Church. Similarly, the military, the high civil servants, big business, and, to some extent, even the judiciary retained a significant degree of autonomy from Fascist interference.

NATIONAL SOCIALISM ON THE ROAD TO POWER

The rise to power of fascism in Italy and Germany followed paths that were similar, though the final outcome was different, as was the timing. The Italian Fascist leader attained the prime ministership in three years but needed three additional years to turn it into a dictatorship. The German Nazi leader struggled for over thirteen years before claiming the Reich chancellorship, but once in power, he transformed it in less than six months into a complete dictatorship.

In the immediate years after Germany's defeat, numerous radical nationalist groups were organized to battle the left and to help revive German nationalism. Few of them survived. The most notable group became the originally obscure German Workers' Party, which was founded by Anton Drexler early in 1919. Drexler was inspired by *völkisch* nationalism and aspired to inaugurate a nationalist workers' movement. *Völkisch* nationalist ideology came out of the nineteenth century and in the second half of that century combined the original idea of superiority of German culture and its universal mission with racist anti-Semitism. Adolf Hitler encountered the German Workers' Party in September 1919 when he served as an information officer in the German army, and was immediately induced to join it. His oratorical talent and the organizational skills that he developed quickly gave him a leading position. In February 1920, before an audience of 2,000, he presented the party's Twenty-Five Point Program, which he had drawn up together with Drexler. It proclaimed opposition to capitalism, democracy, and especially the Jews, who were to be excluded from German citizenship. It was emphatically nationalistic and imperialistic, demanding the union of all Germans in a Greater Germany and the acquisition of land and territory for the German people. Soon the party was given a more attractive title, National Socialist German Workers' Party (NSDAP). In July 1921, after a temporary crisis over its direction, Hitler assumed its uncontested leadership and became known as its Führer (leader).

In the early years, Hitler played the role of "drummer" to gain mass support for the nationalist cause. In his speeches, he lashed out against the Treaty of Versailles, Marxism, international capitalism, the November criminals (the democratic leaders who had stabbed the German army in the back by surrendering in World War I and acceding to the Versailles Treaty), and the Jews. When the NSDAP acquired a newspaper, the *Völkischer Beobachter* (People's observer), it notably enhanced the mass propaganda effort of the movement. From its base in Munich, the party spread to the surrounding area in Bavaria and, by 1921, began to move beyond Bavarian borders by creating units in north and central Germany. The most dramatic growth of the movement came as a result of national crises in 1923. The French occupation of the Ruhr, the German campaign of passive resistance, and unprecedented hyperinflation accompanied by economic chaos led to heightened nationalist mass agitation. By November 1923 the Nazi Party had grown to 55,000 members, and the ranks of the SA, its paramilitary formation (organized in 1921), had increased to 15,000 men. Hitler saw his first opportunity to make a bid for power by emulating Benito Mussolini's March on Rome.

Hitler hoped to seize power by exploiting the inability of the democratic Weimar government to cope with the national crises and by capitalizing on the cooperation of the rightist regime in Bavaria headed by Gustav von Kahr. He and Kahr, together with other conservative Bavarian nationalists, thought that a "march on Berlin" would receive the support of right-wing groups in northern Germany. As it turned out, the nationalist conspirators delayed their contemplated action too long.

In the fall of 1923 a strong German government was formed under Gustav Stresemann that ended the policy of passive resistance against the French and regained control of German affairs. When the Kahr government in Bavaria declared a state of emergency in September, the new Weimar government countered with its own state of emergency for all of Germany and used armed force to crush the leftist governments in Saxony and Thuringia in October. Hitler decided to strike and to force the now-reluctant Kahr and his associates into joining him in an attempt to overthrow the national government. On November 8 Hitler and his followers took over a rightist beer-hall meeting at which they pressured Kahr and the Bavarian military and police leaders to start the national revolution, but their strong-arm effort failed. The following day the Nazi leader tried a last desperate gamble to salvage his cause by staging a march with General Erich Ludendorff, a German war hero, and 2,000 supporters through the streets of Munich to generate popular support for the coup. The armed demonstrators were met by police barricades, and after a short exchange of gunfire all but Ludendorff turned and fled. The Beer Hall Putsch had failed completely. The leaders, including Hitler, were arrested and put on trial in March 1924. Unlike the March on Rome, this march had met an ignominious end, and the Nazi movement appeared to be in disarray, if not finished.

The treason trial of Hitler, Ludendorff, and several other rightist leaders made the Nazi Führer known outside of Bavaria. He used the courtroom to turn the treason charge against him against the "betrayers" of Germany who had accepted the Versailles Treaty and preserved the Weimar Republic. Sympathetic right-wing judges sentenced Hitler to the most lenient term allowed for treason: five years with the possibility of early probation. In December 1924 he was released from prison.

The failure of the Beer Hall Putsch taught Hitler an important political lesson: the Communist-style assault on the Weimar Republic to attain power did not work. He decided to obtain his objective by constitutional or legal means. That approach required the creation of a mass political party that would aggressively compete for votes with other parties in the Weimar Republic among the discontented middle and lower classes. The Nazis would also have to win the support of the army and the traditional elites. The banned Nazi Party was formally reconstituted in February 1925, and Hitler quickly regained control over party units in Munich and Bavaria and soon in other regions of Germany. Late in 1925 he faced a major challenge in the northern cities from the National Socialist Working Association, a leftist group headed by Gregor and Otto Strasser and Paul Joseph Goebbels. They hoped to obtain support for the party from the working classes and opposed participation in election campaigns. The dissidents, especially Goebbels, were soon won over by the charisma of Hitler whose messianic image and spellbinding oratory impressed and mesmerized his followers. By 1926 the *Führerprinzip* (leadership principle) was officially proclaimed, making the command of the party fully centralized and subordinated to Hitler. In the same year, the paramilitary SA was reorganized and several subsidiary organizations were formed, including the Hitler Youth and leagues for women, lawyers, doctors, teachers, and students. After a modest growth from 27,000 members (less than half of the 1923 membership) in 1925 to 35,000 in 1926, the party expanded to 75,000 in 1927, 108,000 in 1928, and 178,000 by the end of 1929.

From 1925 to 1928, the Nazi Party pursued an urban strategy designed to win blue-collar workers away from the Socialists and Communists but largely failed in its efforts. In the 1928 national elections, it received only 810,000 votes, 2.6 percent of the total vote, and captured only twelve seats in the Reichstag. The Nazis did poorly in urban areas but relatively well in rural areas, where they exploited the growing discontent among farmers caused by falling prices, high expenses, and foreclosures that accompanied a worldwide agricultural depression. This outcome prompted Hitler to make a fundamental change in the party's political strategy in the summer of 1928. It now began to become more inclusive in its propaganda and popular appeal. In cities like Berlin, the party continued to target the worker vote, but in rural regions and in small towns, it directly addressed farmers, small businessmen, artisans, white-collar workers, and civil servants. Nazi propaganda defended private property against the Marxist revolutionaries (whether socialist or Communist), charged that Jewish bankers and capitalists were the cause of the farmers' economic distress, and assailed department stores, many of them owned by Jews, as an economic threat to small businessmen. Appeals to German nationalism proved to be effective among both farmers and the middle classes. In 1929 German Nationalist Party leader Alfred Hugenberg thought that he could manipulate Hitler and the Nazis in his campaign against the Young Plan, which provided Germany with a scaled-down payment scheme on its reparations. He put at Hitler's disposal the apparatus of his enormous press empire and opened doors for him to some wealthy industrialists. The Nazis joined the rightist Nationalists in their attack on the Weimar Republic on the issue of reparations, but failed badly in a referendum that aimed to reject the Young Plan. However, as allies of Hugenberg and the Nationalists, they received increased attention throughout Germany and acquired new respectability among the middle classes in addition to gaining financial resources to wage a dynamic campaign.

The recovery from the war and the reestablishment of economic stability after the inflationary turmoil was unexpectedly disrupted by the onset of the Great Depression in the fall of 1929. The Weimar Republic also suffered an irreparable loss in October with the death of Gustav Stresemann, who was the sole able statesman who might have been able to create a moderate right governmental force to resist the Hitler movement. German society once more was subjected to a searing trauma. Business failures accelerated, and unemployment soared, reaching 3 million in 1930, 4.35 million in 1931, and exceeded 6 million by the end of 1932. The workers, under the impact of escalating unemployment, turned their backs on the Social Democrats and flocked to the radical Communists, who promised revolution and the overthrow of the Weimar Republic. The middle classes, who remembered the devastating inflation of 1923, feared for their jobs and their social status. They dreaded a Communist revolution. Small businessmen complained of big business and big labor. As the middle classes were radicalized, they became more and more receptive to the simplistic Nazi propaganda explaining the economic collapse.

The economic and social turmoil brought on by the Great Depression seriously undermined democracy in Germany by destroying the "Weimar coalition" of middle-class parties and Social Democrats that had provided the parliamentary base for government since the end of the war. As political attitudes became radicalized, parliamentary majorities supporting new coalitions became very difficult to establish when elections changed the composition of the Reichstag. Reich President Paul von Hindenburg, who was a monarchist at heart with little faith in parliament and squabbling parties, appointed Heinrich Brüning, a leader of the Catholic Center Party and a supporter of strong government, to the chancellorship in 1930. Lacking a parliamentary majority, the president granted his chancellor the power to govern by decree under Article 48 of the Weimar constitution. Such authority was to be only temporary and subject to parliamentary scrutiny. When the Reichstag rejected Brüning's measures adopted under the emergency article, he did not resign but dissolved the parliament and called for new elections, hoping to vindicate his presidential chancellorship with a supportive parliamentary majority. But he miscalculated. The worsening economic crisis and the Nazi propaganda that offered something to most threatened classes gave Hitler and his party the breakthrough they had hoped for. The Nazis' vote soared from 810,000 in 1928 to 6.4 million, or 18.3 percent of the total, giving them 107 seats in the Reichstag. Overnight the Nazis had become the second-largest party in parliament after the Social Democrats.

The reorganization of the party and shifts in strategy had definitely put the Nazis in a strong position to conduct mass campaigns. Even though the party never achieved a majority, its electoral successes bolstered Hitler's claims to the chancellorship. Nazi propaganda proved to be especially effective in reaching large segments of the German populace. The party used all available forms of media: newspaper, radio, movies, posters, billboards, leaflets, and innumerable mass meetings. In many ways, the Nazis were pioneers in electioneering techniques, covering Germany in stirring campaigns by car, train, and, as an innovation, airplane. In *Mein Kampf*, Hitler had expounded the principles of effective propaganda. It must be addressed to the masses, not the intellectuals. "The broad masses of the people can be moved only by the power of speech," he asserted. In his view, "All great movements are popular movements, volcanic eruptions of human passions and emotional sentiments," and therefore propaganda must be aimed primarily at the emotions and "only to a very limited degree at the so-called intellect." Another key aspect that he underscored was that "the receptivity of the great masses was very limited, their intelligence small, but their power of forgetting enormous." Therefore, to compensate for this shortcoming of mass audiences, "all effective propaganda must be limited to very few points and must harp on these slogans until the last of the public understands what you want to understand by your slogan." Finally, propagandists must recognize that for the great masses, "the magnitude of a lie always contains a certain factor of credibility." Given the primitive simplicity of the great masses' minds, "they more easily fall a victim to a big lie than to a little one, since they themselves lie in little things, but would be ashamed of lies that were too big."[2] Though anti-Semitic sloganeering was deemphasized during the election campaigns of the 1930s, Hitler's most egregious "big" lie was his charge that the Jews were responsible for most of Germany's and the world's problems, strove for world domination, and ultimately plunged nations into world wars.

The mastermind who put many of Hitler's propaganda principles into practice was Joseph Goebbels. He had obtained a doctorate in literature and had failed as a novelist, but began to succeed as a propagandist once he joined the Nazi Party in 1924. A cynical opportunist, but utterly loyal to Hitler after 1926, he rivaled the Führer as a dynamic orator. In 1929 he became the Reich propaganda leader of the Nazi Party and engineered many of the electoral campaigns from 1929 to 1932. His guiding principle was "That propaganda is good which leads to success, and that is bad which fails to achieve the desired result, however intelligent it is, for it is not propaganda's task to be intelligent, its task is to lead to success."[3] Under Goebbels's direction, the Reich Propaganda Office issued directives specifying themes and slogans to be used at mass rallies, printed standard posters and pamphlets, and distributed nationalist and party movies. The Nazi Party also established a Speakers' School to train propaganda speakers, especially students, to present simple speeches at public meetings. The most effective regional and national speakers appeared at the more important mass rallies. A pioneering technique was to blanket Germany in spirited campaign tours. "Hitler over Germany" was the name of one of Hitler's campaign tours, during which he appeared in fifty cities in fifteen days. The car and train were no longer adequate to carry the Nazis' prize speaker to his rallies, but the airplane made possible what no politician had achieved thus far.

In their propaganda, the Nazis claimed to be the true all-German movement, above party, class, and faction, with Hitler as the only true national leader who could save Germany from civil war and utter catastrophe. The themes of nationalism, economic salvation, and anticommunism were the mainstay of the Nazi message, and anti-Semitism was moderated and sometimes muted altogether for tactical reasons. But in practice, the Nazis were clever enough to gear campaign themes to the needs and concerns of different social groups. Thus one campaign poster was addressed to the unemployed. Under the caption "Work and Bread," it showed an arm with a Nazi armband, with the hand extending tools to the outstretched hands of unemployed workers. Another poster played on the fear of communism and the expropriation of private property. It pictured a frightful skeleton in a Communist uniform and was entitled "Only one man can save us from Bolshevism—Adolf Hitler." There were three major elections in 1932 that gave the Nazi Party an opportunity to show the full force of its mass-mobilization effort.

In the spring of 1932 Hindenburg's term as Reich president ended. Hitler decided to challenge his reelection. The eighty-four-year-old field marshal was reluctantly persuaded to stand for reelection after warnings that only he could prevent the Nazi leader's elevation to the presidency. This time the old war hero was not supported by the parties of the right but by the left and the moderates of Weimar democracy. Hitler and the Communist candidate denied Hindenburg a majority by a narrow margin, but in the runoff Hindenburg easily defeated his Nazi opponent by 53 percent of the popular vote. Hitler received 13.5 million votes, 37 percent of the total. Chancellor Brüning's austere deflationary policies had failed to solve the economic crisis and had alienated the industrial and agrarian elites. Even though Brüning had campaigned vigorously for the president's reelection, Hindenburg became angered when Brüning proposed to subdivide insolvent estates of his aristocratic friends in eastern Germany, and was persuaded by his right-wing advisors to appoint Franz von Papen chancellor. An aristocratic reactionary, Papen came from the extreme right wing of the Catholic Center Party and was determined to push the German government toward an authoritarian and rightist presidential political order. He prevailed upon Hindenburg to allow new Reichstag elections. They were held on July 31, and the Nazis, running on a law-and-order platform in an atmosphere of frequent street battles, scored their most impressive victory yet. Their popular vote rose to 13.7 million, 37.4 percent, giving them 230 seats in the Reichstag. They had become the largest single party and, together with the Communists, who also increased their support, made up 52 percent of the Reichstag. Hitler now insisted that he be appointed chancellor and that the Nazis be given the major cabinet positions. Hindenburg rejected his demand and suggested that he become vice chancellor in a coalition government. Hitler refused the offer. Papen therefore called for new elections when the Reichstag convened in September, hoping to reduce the Nazi force. In part he succeeded, for Hitler's party was psychologically and financially ill prepared for another taxing campaign when the election was held in November. For the first time, the Nazi vote fell by 2 million to 11.7 million, from 37.4 to 33.1 percent of the total, and the party's Reichstag seats were reduced to 196. It appeared to be a costly defeat, for it demonstrated that the Nazi wave could be stemmed.

However, the new Reichstag continued to be hopelessly splintered, and Papen could not expect to establish a legal majority coalition. He contemplated a kind of presidential coup by Hindenburg that would have eliminated the Weimar constitution, curtailed the Reichstag and political parties, and possibly outlawed both Nazis and Communists. Under the influence of General Kurt von Schleicher, Hindenburg's military advisor and defense minister, who argued that Papen's plan would cause a civil war, the Reich president was persuaded to dismiss Papen and to appoint Schleicher, who promised to create a new popular majority in the Reichstag in support of the government. Although the political general was no more democratic than Papen, he hoped to achieve this objective by courting Gregor Strasser and the Nazi left wing, which would have split the party. Schleicher also hoped to win over labor and the Social Democrats as well as the Catholic Center Party and to stimulate the economy through public works and government spending. The scheme misfired when Hitler vetoed the appointment of Strasser to the vice chancellorship, the Socialists remained suspicious of Schleicher, and the rightist parties became alarmed over the chancellor's overtures to the left. In the meantime, Papen schemed revenge against his successor and came forth with a plan that paved the way for Hitler's appointment as Reich chancellor.

Papen knew that to receive the Reich president's approval, he would have to promise him a government based on mass support. His solution was a parliamentary coalition government based on a working majority in the Reichstag and led by Hitler in order to tame him. Most cabinet members would not be Nazis, and Papen as vice chancellor expected to be the dominant power in government. Hindenburg, who considered Papen his favorite, was quite willing to drop Schleicher, especially when the latter proposed to revert to an authoritarian solution after the failure of his scheme. Hindenburg reluctantly appointed Hitler chancellor on January 30, 1933. The Nazi leader, not unlike his later Fascist ally in Italy, had come to power legally within the Weimar system. However, this democratic system had already been seriously undermined in the years after

1930 by the interlude of presidential dictatorship based on the emergency article of the German constitution.

In less than six months in office, Hitler consolidated his dictatorial power. Like previous chancellors, he was given power to rule by presidential decree in the first stage of his appointment. Early in February, out of concern for internal security, he first persuaded Hindenburg to issue a decree limiting freedom of the press and banning public meetings; later in the month, after a mysterious Reichstag fire, which the Nazis blamed on the Communists, another decree suspended certain civil liberties. To fulfill the promise of creating a parliamentary majority, Hitler dissolved the Reichstag and set new elections for March 5, 1933. The Nazis mounted an all-out campaign, proclaiming the "elections as the last for a hundred years." Despite deception and considerable Nazi violence in the election campaign, the outcome was disappointing for Hitler's forces. The Nazis gained 17.2 million popular votes, 43.9 percent of the total, but failed to achieve an absolute majority. Only with the 52 elected German Nationalists could the 288 Nazi deputies muster a simple majority in the parliament. But Hitler wanted permanent dictatorial power and introduced the Enabling Act when the Reichstag convened on March 23. It entailed a constitutional change and required a two-thirds majority, which Hitler achieved through cajolery, false promises, threats, and arrests of Communists and some Social Democrats. The measure passed 444 to 94 and gave Hitler the power to govern by decree for four years. Only the Social Democrats had the courage to vote against it. Parliamentary democracy had been destroyed by legal means, and Hitler had become a dictator.

He and the Nazis now proceeded to establish a single-party regime through a policy of *Gleichschaltung*, or Nazi coordination of institutions. It brought the elimination or Nazification of state governments, bureaucracies, political parties, and trade unions. Special Reich governors were appointed in states and could issue laws without the approval of state legislatures. The civil service qualifications were changed to purge Jews and supporters of democracy. May Day, traditionally observed by (leftist) organized labor, became the Day of National Labor in a move that also proved to be the prelude to the dissolution of all trade unions. The Communist Party had been officially banned in March; in June the Social Democrats were outlawed. The Nationalists, the Liberal parties, and the Catholic Center Party disbanded in the weeks that followed. A law of July 14, 1933, asserted that the NSDAP "constitutes the only political party in Germany." A widespread loss of faith in the Weimar system, the strong and dynamic Nazi image of a new Germany, and Hitler's skillful and ruthless political actions facilitated the surprisingly quick collapse of the democratic Weimar Republic.

After one year in power, Hitler eliminated the faction of Ernst Röhm in the SA through a murderous purge to appease the army leadership who violently objected to Röhm's aim of merging the SA with the German army. He thereby ensured the German army leadership's approval of combining the offices of the Reich presidency and chancellorship when Hindenburg died on August 2, 1934. Hitler was now the Führer not only of the party but of the German people as head of state and total dictator. Soldiers, civil servants, and judges now swore their oath of office not to the state or the constitution, but to Adolf Hitler. He had thereby achieved a position of state control never enjoyed by Mussolini. Although Italian Fascism invented the term *totalitarian*, its leader never succeeded in gaining complete control of all institutions. Considerable literary freedom remained under Mussolini, and he had to accept the autonomy of the monarchy, the army, and especially the church. On the other hand, in historian Stanley Payne's characterization, "The Hitlerian *Führerstaat* was a much more extensive dictatorship of one-man rule, creating agencies and institutions to regulate all sectors of economic, professional, and cultural society, with the partial exception of the churches."[4]

NOTES

1. Stanley G. Payne, *A History of Fascism, 1914–1945* (Madison: University of Wisconsin Press, 1995), 106.

2. Adolf Hitler, *Mein Kampf*, trans. Ralph Manheim (Boston: Houghton Mifflin, © 1943, renewed 1971), 107, 180–181, 231.

3. Quoted in Joachim C. Fest, *The Face of the Third Reich* (New York: Pantheon Books, 1970), 90.

4. Payne, *A History of Fascism*, 209.

3

Economy and Society under Fascism

One of the most distinctive features of fascist regimes was their effort to exercise absolute power over all important aspects of the state and society. Even though they maintained total command over political institutions, they were less successful in completely controlling economic life and social pursuits. Private property and capitalism were not abolished, as under communism, but were subjected to regulation or restrictions. There was little nationalization of private property, with the exception of Jewish property in Nazi Germany. Fascist states subordinated economic and social policies to their domestic and external objectives. However, they resorted to economic planning only haphazardly during peacetime but more rigorously during war (as did nonfascist states). Economic liberalism was frequently attacked because it advanced individual self-interest, just as socialism was castigated because it caused conflicts between labor and capital that undermined national unity. Fascist governments prohibited labor unions and strikes and promoted associations or corporations that included both workers and employers, expecting them to eliminate antagonism between the two groups. In Fascist Italy and Nazi Germany, this policy gave an upper hand to employers in their relation to the workers rather than fostering a partnership. The aim of creating a national community also was pursued through censorship and ideological propaganda and especially through the establishment of organizations that comprised youths as well as adults and exposed them to the aims of the regime.

ECONOMIC LIFE UNDER ITALIAN FASCISM

One of the most distinctive claims of Italian Fascism was to have originated a new system of economic organization based on the idea of corporativism. This system was thought to have combined the advantages of medieval guilds that had supposedly brought together workers and employers in a common productive endeavor with effective management and regulation for the good of society. Mussolini did not derive his concept of corporativism from the modern teachings of the Catholic Church but from Sorelian syndicalism, which held that the bourgeois capitalist order could be overthrown by a general strike of all laborers. His propaganda promoted corporativism as an alternative "third way" between capitalism and socialism, both of which were seen as divisive. Capitalism fostered the pursuit of self-interest, and socialism generated class war. Social cohesion was restored when economic activity in society was divided into branches and each was represented by a corporation that included both labor and capital. The base for the Fascist corporative state was created in 1925 when the *Confindustria* (Confederation of Industry) and the Confederation of Fascist Trade Unions recognized each other as spokesmen of capital and labor. A special law adopted in the following year named seven branches of economic activity: industry, agriculture, banking, commerce, domestic transport, the merchant marine, and the intellectual community. The number of corporations grew only gradually and by 1934 reached twenty-two. It was only then that mixed corporations of employers and employees came into existence. The final act came in 1939 when the Chamber of Fasces and Corporations, consisting of elected and appointed members of corporations, replaced the old Italian parliament.

Fascist corporative theory promised innovation in economic life, but in practice the corporations failed to produce very tangible results. Gaetano Salvemini wrote of them that "the mountain travailed and gave birth to a mouse."[1] The Great Depression, the involvement of Italy in the Ethiopian war, the League of Nations economic boycott of Italy triggered by this war, and at times the Duce's hesitancy made it difficult to establish a workable relationship among business, labor, and the Fascist Party when the state had to generate more taxes, control prices, and pursue an economic policy of self-sufficiency or autarky. Overall, Fascist economic policies favored the interests of commerce and industry and kept workers in cities and peasants in the countryside in a lower condition.

In practice, Fascist economic policy was variously driven by a combination of national pride, the goal of self-sufficiency, and a militarist foreign policy. One of the most controversial measures promoted by the Fascist government was the revaluation of the lira in 1926. The fairly rapid economic expansion of the 1920s had brought considerable inflation and a marked decline in the exchange value of the lira. Mussolini insisted on keeping the exchange rate artificially elevated, at 90 lira to the pound sterling, for reasons of national pride. The return to the gold standard further aggravated the economic condition of Italy. This helped to stop inflation but dampened the export trade. Thus the "battle of the lira," as it was called in accordance with Mussolini's penchant for introducing economic plans as military campaigns, turned out to be less than successful. Another policy that was conducted with much propaganda fanfare was land reclamation. It brought some successes in the Pontine Marshes near Rome and in the north, but reclamation and irrigation projects in the south were smaller in number and were frequently not completed.

The "battle of grain" announced in 1925 was supposed to enhance the self-sufficiency of Italy in wheat by significantly increasing domestic grain production and reducing the need for grain imports. Some of this was achieved, but at the expense of export-oriented diversified crops like fruits, vegetables, and olives. Livestock production also decreased because more land was being planted with wheat. All of this proved costly to the Italian consumer, who was paying higher prices for most food products. Mussolini added the "battle of births" even though many regions of Italy were over-populated and the country lacked the resources to support a large demographic expansion. It counted for little that during the Great Depression the living standard in cities and especially in the countryside declined and did not improve significantly during the late 1930s, for the campaign for grain was intended to ensure Italy's self-sufficiency in war, and the demographic campaign was intended to supply the manpower to fight wars. The Great Depression also led to a major intervention of the regime in the economic organization of Italy. In 1931 a state corporation was created to rescue the Italian banking system from collapse. Two years later a permanent Institute for Industrial Reconstruction (IRI) was set up to buy shares and infuse capital into failing industrial enterprises. On the eve of World War II, it owned controlling shares in steel, naval construction, and several other economic sectors, giving the Italian state ownership of a larger share of the national economy than in any other capitalist European country. Historians emphasize that it was the privileged economic sectors, especially cartels, that benefited from this policy.

ECONOMIC LIFE UNDER NAZISM

When Hitler became chancellor of Germany in 1933, he did not impose a systematic economic policy even though there were voices within the Nazi Party that favored conservative corporatism, on the right, and state intervention, though not full socialism, on the left. Rather, he adopted a pragmatic course that used state regulation and intervention where needed but otherwise relied on the cooperation of the traditional economic order. The appointment of Hjalmar Schacht, who was noted as a strong advocate of capitalism, first as new president of the Reichsbank and later also as economics minister, must have proved reassuring to business and industrial leaders. However, it is also clear that the direction of Hitler's economic policies was dictated by his foreign policy goals, which required the material resources for the development of a strong military force. At the same time, he understood that his goals for Germany's expansion could not be realized without a supportive unified nation, which in turn necessitated considerable improvement in the material progress of the populace and, especially, the reduction of unemployment.

In the summer of 1933, the Nazi government committed over one billion reichsmarks to various public works projects, such as the construction of bridges, canals, public buildings, and a network of four-lane superhighways, the famous *Autobahnen*. Subsidies were granted to private construction firms to renovate old buildings and to construct new housing. There were tax breaks for industrial-plant expansion. Many owners were no longer free to make individual business decisions, but they were assured of order and even prosperity. Both the economic recovery program and the rearmament that soon followed required deficit spending. Labor and wage disputes were now handled by civil servants and were not subject to union interference and strikes. The Nazi economic plan was accompanied by the continuation of the Labor Service begun during the Weimar Republic. Starting in 1935, the service became compulsory for all males between the ages of eighteen and twenty-four, requiring them to perform six months of manual labor on land reclamation and other public works projects. Military conscription usually followed the performance of labor service. A beneficial social effect of employment created by public works, expanding industry, and the soon intensified rearmament was the fairly rapid reduction of the ranks of the unemployed. Their numbers fell from 6.2 million in 1932 to 4.5 million by the end of 1933, 2.6 million in 1934, 1 million in 1936, and fewer than 500,000 in 1937. By 1939 there was a shortage of labor. Hitler's success in wiping out unemployment was his most notable economic achievement and an important source of his political appeal.

Rearmament began in earnest in 1934 when the military budget increased to 4.1 billion reichsmarks; by 1939 it escalated to 30 billion reichsmarks. Quite soon these expenditures created a very unfavorable balance of payments due to the importation of huge quantities of raw materials. Hjalmar Schacht alleviated the problem somewhat with a plan that established strict quotas on imports, accompanied by new trade agreements with other countries. This increase in state control over the economy was but the prelude to further innovations in the Nazi economy. Large-scale rearmament got under way in 1936 when Hitler declared that the German army must be "operational" in four years. Hermann Göring was put in charge of the Four-Year Plan, which was supposed to increase the production of raw materials in order to enhance Germany's self-sufficiency. It led to the building of a state-owned industry, the Reichswerke Hermann Göring, to supplement private industry, emphasizing the production of synthetics. This state enterprise was different from the Italian IRI because it constituted a new venture rather than state control of existing companies. Göring's ambition to restructure the entire private sector with the help of the Four-Year Plan and the new state-owned industries was not fulfilled. Not all sectors of the economy benefited from rearmament. Consumer-goods industries and certain export trades suffered. The real purchasing power of German workers rose to 1929 levels in 1938 but did not keep up with the enormous growth in national production after that. In the end, however, neither the economy of Fascist Italy nor that of Nazi Germany could match the growth rates of pre–World War I Germany or post–World War II West Germany.

CULTURAL DRIVE TOWARD NATIONAL UNITY

Control of economic policy by fascist regimes was essential to mobilize the material resources of the nation toward the pursuit of the goals prescribed by the ruling elite. Another major objective was the creation of a national consensus and community in which every member of the society internalized the aims of Fascist or Nazi ideology. According to Hitler, Aryan racial superiority lay at the heart of the *Volksgemeinschaft* (racial national community). This made it necessary that every aspect of cultural and social life be controlled and used to instill fascist ideological ideals at the grassroots of society and in the workplace; the aim was to influence a citizen's life in its totality. In Nazi Germany, Paul Joseph Goebbels presided over the Reich Ministry for Public Enlightenment and Propaganda and skillfully guided cultural activities along ideological lines. In Italy, an expanding propaganda ministry, in part imitating the German model, developed over several years after 1933 with the appointment of Mussolini's son-in-law Galeazzo Ciano as head of the Press Office. However, propaganda alone would not have had a more lasting impact if the regimes had not also created organizational mechanisms that encompassed the participation of many millions of the Italian and German populaces.

Both the Fascist and Nazi governments tried to silence prestigious intellectual, scientific, and artistic figures who were known to oppose fascism. In Italy, this forced the historian Gaetano Salvemini, the physicist Enrico Fermi, and the conductor Arturo Toscanini into exile once Mussolini had established a firm grip on Italian life. Only Benedetto Croce, a renowned philosopher, was permitted to continue publishing his writings in his homeland despite his opposition to Fascism. In Germany, the novelist Thomas Mann, the physicist Albert Einstein, and many other literary, scientific, and artistic luminaries became expatriates at the very start of the Nazi regime. One of the uglier incidents engineered by Nazi students was the burning of the works of Karl Marx, Sigmund Freud, Erich Maria Remarque, and many others in May 1933 as a symbolic act against the "un-German spirit" represented by their ideas. In Mussolini's Italy, where repression was less harsh and arbitrary, such incidents were rare, but intellectuals and artists either had to remain silent on political matters or compromise with the regime.

One area of creative endeavor that the Nazis in particular tried to use for political purposes was the visual arts. Since Hitler always prided himself on his artistic temperament, such blatant intervention is not surprising. Art was viewed in ideological terms, and only Aryans were deemed to produce true art. Hitler and the Nazis condemned modern art as "degenerate art" or "Jewish art." In 1937 the Nazis staged two art exhibitions, one that opened the House of German Art and a separate exhibition of "degenerate art" put on display in Munich. The latter was almost mobbed, because it contained some of Weimar Germany's greatest artistic representatives of modern art, including examples of cubism, futurism, expressionism, and dadaism. This exhibition was quickly shut down, for German art was to feature racial and heroic qualities in the figures portrayed. Stanley Payne has characterized the Nazi style as "romantic and heroic, with a strong penchant for a certain brutality of expression."[2] The themes emphasized heroes, battles, labor, and the common people (with a heavy preference for farmers), accompanied by sacrifice, readiness, and comradeship. Much of Nazi pictorial art actually was revived genre painting of the nineteenth century produced by local and provincial artists. Quite ordinary scenes were given titles that were to convey deeper messages: farms and animals could appear as *Blood and Soil*; a portrait of Hitler and his supporters in the Beer Hall Putsch had the biblical caption *In the Beginning Was the Word*; a portrayal of four female nudes by Adolf Ziegler, which Hitler considered a favorite, was entitled *Four Elements*, symbolizing elemental forces. A heroic theme was suggested by Josef Thorak's sculpture, called *The Last Flight*, of an upright female figure holding a dead youth.

The heroic (monumental) element carried over into architecture and was to express the new (racial) community spirit of Germany and national greatness. Hitler fancied himself an architectural genius and insisted that monumental buildings must reflect the ideology of the Third Reich. His personal architects, first Paul Ludwig Trost and later the young Albert

Speer, treated him to fanciful models, mostly drawn on paper or in miniature reproductions, that conceived of new and colossal structures that were to adorn the capital and other German cities. The "modernized neoclassical" House of German Art in Munich, touted as the first beautiful work of the new Germany, and the massive Reich chancellery in Berlin were actually completed. So was the gigantic and even awesome party rally grounds in Nuremberg, which had an impressive frontal colonnade behind the speaker's platform and a concrete stadium that seated 400,000. Perhaps the most ambitious project that Hitler wanted was a huge meeting hall to be constructed near the Reichstag building in Berlin. It was to consist of a structure that outdistanced St. Peter's in Rome with a dome 825 feet in diameter and was large enough to accommodate 125,000 admiring viewers.

Italian art and architecture during the Fascist period were much less ideologically charged and more fragmented in their style and genre, though they also at times emphasized themes of labor, sport, struggle, and motherhood. In practice, there was no official Fascist art style, and most forms of modern art continued in Italy. If there was occasionally a dictatorial preference for monumentality, Italian national and classical traditions could be readily used. In 1934 Mussolini even defended modernist architecture as "rational and functional" from attacks by Soviet and Nazi detractors.

Newspapers, publications, radio, and film were controlled in both fascist societies, but were used with uneven effectiveness by the leaders of the regimes. Goebbels, who was in charge of the media and the arts, showed considerable inventiveness in the effort to keep the German populace attuned to Nazi aims and psychologically receptive to the regime's message. He issued guidelines for newspaper editors and exercised direct supervision of content. All newspapers received foreign news only from the Nazi-controlled German Press Agency, and journalists were given daily directives on what could be printed. In Italy, the machinery of supervision and manipulation was considerably less well organized, although under Ciano's initiative the Fascist propaganda machine was remarkably successful in whipping up popular enthusiasm during the Ethiopian war in 1935 and 1936. The Nazis realized quite early the usefulness of radio in conveying the regime's ideology and goals. In 1933 Hitler alone made fifty broadcasts. Radio manufacturers were urged to produce an affordable set, the "People's Receiver," and by 1939, 70 percent of German households (80 percent in cities) owned a radio. The regime also encouraged communal radio listening in public places.

Mussolini failed to recognize the potential of radio. Its effectiveness was sporadic, especially since the cost of receivers remained high, allowing at best only a fraction of the Italian populace in the north and center to buy one (1 million subscribers, versus 9.5 million in Germany). The Fascist regime was only slightly more successful in the exploitation of film for propaganda purposes. After 1938 most foreign films were banned. Obvious propaganda films were seldom popular, but escapist entertainment cinema found much popular acclaim. One of the Fascist films that had a major impact was *Vecchia guardia* (1934), which exalted *squadrismo* in a small town against the "Red peril" shortly before the March on Rome. By including, for instance, sports in newsreels and producing documentaries, which were distributed to cinemas and to the network of the leisure-time Dopolavoro organization, the government reached a wider audience.

Keenly aware of popular culture's effectiveness, Goebbels, the Third Reich's propaganda master, particularly promoted films. Since he realized that continuous Nazi propaganda films would fail at the box office, he encouraged the production of entertainment films to provide plenty of escapism. These feature films offered love stories, comedies, musicals, detective stories, or even extraterrestrial color extravaganzas like *Münchhausen*. Propaganda films ranged from the grossly anti-Semitic *Der ewige Jude* (The eternal Jew) and the anti-British *Ohm Krüger*, which depicted the English mistreatment of the Boers in South Africa, to the nationalistic epic *Bismarck*. Interestingly, among the films of the Nazi era that remain best known today are the documentaries of Leni Riefenstahl, which were not produced under Goebbels's auspices. She had become known as an innovative film actress-director, especially of mountain films, and was much admired by Hitler. He invited Riefenstahl to make a film of the 1934 Nuremberg party congress, which she masterfully captured in *Triumph of the Will*. Its marching columns, the Hitler Youth camps, and the wall of swastika flags, after the prelude of Hitler descending (in an airplane) like Wotan from the clouds, were skillfully combined with the spoken words of Hitler addressing the assembled multitudes of the uniformed faithful. Her other masterpiece was *Olympia*, a Hitler-commissioned documentary of the 1936 Olympic Games in Berlin, which celebrated athletic beauty, youth, and sport. It was a mark of some courage that she included, with emphasis, the athletic successes of Jesse Owens, the African-American runner.

MOLDING SOCIETY IN THE IMAGE OF NATIONAL UNITY

Both fascist regimes made a major effort to mobilize and indoctrinate the youth. Public education from elementary to university levels was controlled by the state, and teachers, as civil servants, with but very few exceptions joined the party. However, the regimes placed their major hope for shaping the attitudes and character of the youth along ideological lines in youth organizations: the Fascist youth association, the Opera Nazionale Balilla (ONB), which included Italian males from age six to eighteen, and the Hitler Youth formations, which incorporated ten- to eighteen-year-olds. Comparable but separate leagues encompassed girls. In Italy, in contrast to Germany, there was an absence of youth groups preceding the advent of fascism. In the 1920s the ONB avoided overt political indoctrination and emphasized the submersion of youths in a mass organization that shaped character, which meant instilling obedience to authority, in line with the Fascist regime's motto "Believe, obey, fight!" Generally, youth-organization members enjoyed assembling in uniform, shouting slogans, and participating in patriotic rituals. In 1937 ONB membership became compulsory, and children who were kept from joining, apart from often feeling left out, also faced discrimination in school and later in careers, for ONB membership was the only route to Fascist Party membership. The ONB succeeded in making young Italians more sports minded. Mass gymnastic exercises of uniformly dressed youths singing Fascist songs also created the semblance of unity, order, and force that Fascism tried to generate. The enhanced sports prowess led to a strong Italian showing in the 1936 Berlin Olympic Games, boosting nationalistic pride.

The first Nazi youth organization was organized in 1922, but ended with the Beer Hall Putsch in 1923. The Hitlerjugend (Hitler Youth or HJ) was founded in 1926 and was put under the dynamic leadership of Baldur von Schirach, product of an aristocratic family, in 1931. Boys from ten to fourteen years of age were assigned to the Jungvolk, and those older, up to eighteen years of age, belonged to the regular HJ. Girls in the same age categories were grouped in the Jungmädel for younger girls and the Bund Deutscher Mädel (BDM or League of German Girls) for teenage girls, all affiliated with the HJ. Membership in the HJ became compulsory for healthy German boys and girls at age ten in 1939. The Nazis were remarkably successful in capturing the enthusiasm and sense of adventurism of the youth with various duties and activities free from parental supervision. They included arts and crafts, group singing, storytelling, camping and hiking trips, sports activities, evenings together in special youth "homes," and parades on special days like Hitler's birthday. The HJ, unlike the ONB in Italy, managed to break down quite a bit of the social and intellectual distinction between classes by offering advancement within the organization regardless of family or economic background. At the Nuremberg party rally in 1935, Hitler proclaimed that the National Socialist youth of the future must be "slim and slender, swift as the greyhound, tough as leather, and hard as Krupp steel." Nazi ideals were imparted to the youth through various programs of indoctrination, with emphasis on duty, obedience, honor, courage, service, discipline, patriotism, and utter devotion to Adolf Hitler. The motto of the HJ was "Führer command—we follow!" Boys were trained to serve Germany selflessly through exercise, competitive sports, and premilitary training; girls, in their organizations, trained for their place in the national community by preparing to become dutiful wives and mothers. They were not even supposed to use makeup, for it clashed with the Nazis' idea of natural Aryan beauty. Of the fascist youth groups in Italy and Germany, the HJ succeeded best in instilling loyalty to Germany and to Hitler that lasted to the bitter end of World War II. According to one estimate, 95 percent of the youth continued to support the Führer after the German defeat at Stalingrad (1943), when support of the general population was falling off. One of Hitler's last official acts was to decorate a group of boy soldiers in Berlin, in HJ uniforms, for their bravery in the front lines. These youths were too young to have been inducted into the German Wehrmacht, or in Italy into the Italian armed service, like their late-teenage peers of earlier years under less desperate conditions.

The stress on physical fitness and sport in the HJ very likely helped Germany to gain some of its major successes at the Olympic Games in 1936. German athletes won a total of 89 medals, compared to the second-place U.S. delegation, which garnered only 56. National enthusiasm at home and prestige outside were greatly heightened by German achievements in the Olympic competitions, as they were by German victories in soccer matches with foreign teams. The regime attributed these to the physical superiority of the Aryans. There was much special elation when the German Max Schmeling defeated the African-American Joe Louis, known as the unbeatable "Brown Bomber," in the fight for the world heavyweight boxing championship. But Nazi sentiments were soured by the athletic victories of the African-American Jesse Owens at the Olympics, and Hitler left the stadium early in order not to have to shake hands with him when he received four gold medals. The Nazis were chagrined even more when, in a return match in New York in 1938, Joe Louis knocked out Max Schmeling in two minutes and four seconds.

Adult citizens in both societies were frequently members of organizations directly affiliated with the party or under party control. According to some calculations, half of the 44 million Italian citizens in 1939 belonged to a Fascist political, economic, youth, or other organization. In Nazi Germany, the figures were most likely proportionally higher, for the German Labor Front (DAF) alone included the vast majority of working people regardless of economic or social position, workers and employers. Its budget exceeded that of the Nazi Party by 1938, which during the height of the regime had 8 million members. In Italy, the largest and most active organization for working adults was the Dopolavoro, through which the Fascist regime influenced the social and leisure-time activities of primarily urban employees and workers. Although its recreation program was not as extensive as that of the comparable Nazi Strength through Joy, an arm of the German Labor Front, it reached over 4 million people. The Nazi organization coordinated the free time of the working class by offering a variety of programs from concerts to sports events and featuring short trips and long package tours. Several professional organizations existed in Fascist Italy, but the Nazis were most notable for maintaining a great variety of party-affiliated professional organizations as control mechanisms, ranging from the National Socialist Physicians' League to the National Socialist Stenographers' League. Women in particular were urged to join the National Socialist Women's League.

In both Fascist Italy and Nazi Germany, women were generally cast in a traditional role that placed them in the home, divided between the kitchen and the bedroom. Women were not welcomed in universities and many of the professions, although the rearmament and war years forced the regimes to make some concessions. Nevertheless, official policies and differential wages very clearly discriminated against women in the professions and in the ordinary workplace. Although the Fascist program of 1919 promised political and social equality for women, this position was soon reversed by Mussolini, who looked upon women as intellectually, physically, and morally inferior to men, and the hostility of the *squadristi* and the conservative followers of the Fascist movement to female equality. In actual practice, Fascist discriminatory legislation managed to limit the opportunities of women in the so-called free professions like teaching, jurisprudence, medicine, and journalism, but forced no married or even unmarried women out of the workplace. Between 1931 and 1936 the number of married women holding jobs increased, largely because employers wanted to retain inexpensive labor. The foremost preoccupation of the regime regarding women was the "battle of births," that is, raising the birth rate. Even beyond Italy, countries with stable or declining populations were seen as old and decadent, but those with rapid population growth as young and virile, and Mussolini was intent on keeping Italy among the latter. His aim became to increase Italy's population from 40 million in 1927 to 60 million by 1950. In 1926 the Italian state instituted a tax on bachelors, criminalized abortion and the advocacy of family planning, and banned contraceptives; several years later, homosexuality was outlawed. More positive measures were the phaseout of taxes for families with six or more children, the inauguration of marriage loans and baby bonuses, and the lowering of the legal marrying age for girls from fifteen to fourteen, and for boys from eighteen to sixteen. Starting in 1937, men who were married and had children were given preference in government jobs. However, all of the regime's efforts to increase the birth rate of women essentially failed. Between 1922 and 1936 the number of births declined every year, although it rose slightly in 1937. Similarly, the attempt to bar as many women as possible from paid employment miscarried. Little was done by the state to overcome the effects of poverty. Women who had a desire for freedom realized that this could be achieved by limiting the number of children. The one beneficial result of Mussolini's policies was the various social provisions (paid maternity leaves, summer camps for children) that improved the health of mothers and children.

In Nazi Germany, women faced many of the same attitudes found in Fascist Italy: rejection of female emancipation, the desire to remove women from the workplace, and the pressure to increase the birth rate. Nazi ideology propagated the idea of racial preservation and saw women as the bearers of the children who would realize the strength of the Aryan race. By nature, women were designed to be wives and mothers, whereas men fulfilled their roles as warriors and leaders. As mentioned earlier, the Jungmädel and the BDM began the preparation of girls for their future roles as wives and mothers while they were enrolled between the ages of ten and eighteen. In 1938 a new party organization called Glaube und Schönheit (Faith and Beauty) was formed for young women between seventeen and twenty-one, before they were required to join the National Socialist Women's Association. This supposedly voluntary association, which lost its significance under the demands of the war years, offered sports, gymnastics, body care, dancing, and fashion consciousness. Once women attempted to enter the work force, they faced the Nazi regime's efforts to keep female employment restricted, especially in the civil service and teaching, but also in less skilled vocations. This policy, however, reduced overall female employment only between 1933 and 1938, when it rose again to 36 percent of the total work force, the highest percentage in the world. Rearmament and war thwarted the government's policy to get women out of the work force.

In the pursuit of combatting the falling birth rate and promoting population growth, the Nazi regime began in 1933 an extensive program of marriage loans. Newly married couples received interest-free loans of 1,000 reichsmarks (roughly $5,000 in the currency of the 1990s) to be used for household goods if the wife agreed to give up her work. For every child born to the couple, 25 percent of the loan was canceled. Four children would essentially eliminate the need to repay the entire loan. This program enjoyed a modest success, for the number of marriages increased somewhat, as did the birth rate in the first two years of the program's existence. However, the ideal average of four children per couple remained altogether elusive; surveys showed that couples receiving marriage loans (the amount was later cut in half because of a heavy demand) averaged one child. Some material benefits were provided to mothers by the National Socialist Welfare Organization. In 1938, during a campaign to exalt the role of mothers and housewives, Hitler instituted the Honor Cross of the German Mother, to be awarded annually on August 12, his mother's birthday. As in Italy and the Soviet Union, prolific German mothers were awarded honorific decorations: a bronze cross for four children, a silver cross for six children, and a gold cross for eight or more children.

In carrying out their ideologically based population policy, the Nazis did not rely only on positive inducements to increase the birth rate. The idea was to breed good Aryan stock and to reduce or eliminate inferior human stock. The usual negative measures of restricting contraceptives and outlawing abortion (which remained legal for purposes of "racial hygiene" in cases of mentally retarded, "asocial," or Jewish women) were accompanied by more questionable and, eventually, more sinister policies. Eugenics was advocated and practiced outside of Germany, including the United States, in the pre–World War II period. Many states in the United States, for instance, permitted sterilizations to "purify" the race, and early Nazi eugenics laws borrowed from American models. However, the Nazis carried such policies to extremes. Eugenics before long gave way to euthanasia. In 1933 Nazi legislation made possible sterilization of persons suffering from incurable hereditary diseases, including epilepsy, blindness, and even chronic alcoholism. Two years later, laws were enacted prohibiting marriage for those with serious infectious or hereditary illnesses and between Germans and Jews, all to preserve racial health and purity. In 1939, at the outset of the war, Hitler instituted a euthanasia program, the first part of which concentrated on the killing of mentally deficient and physically deformed children; it was soon extended to all "incurably sick," leading to the death of nearly 100,000 persons by 1941.

There were times when the Fascist and Nazi governments generated mass enthusiasm and created a feeling of community at mass rallies and during campaigns. However, it is evident that social policies and organizations failed to transform Italian and German society in the image of the fascist personality and community. The inglorious collapse of the Fascist regime during World War II quickly revealed that it had not grown deep roots despite twenty years of ideological indoctrination and streamlined dictatorial rule. In Germany, the consequences of Nazi social and cultural policies were more complex. The Nazi regime attempted to convey the idea that it had created a good order and a moral society and was on the way to enhancing the growth of a unified national or racial community. But Hitler's intent was not to create a racially superior national community in order to bring about personal happiness in an uplifted and improved society but to prepare for war and conquest for *Lebensraum*.

NOTES

1. Quoted in John Whittam, *Fascist Italy* (Manchester: Manchester University Press, 1995), 64.

2. Stanley G. Payne, *A History of Fascism, 1914–1945* (Madison: University of Wisconsin Press, 1995), 107.

4

Fascist Origins of World War II

Historians continue to debate the causes of World War I but have reached considerable agreement on the conditions that triggered the outbreak of World War II. There is no doubt that the peacemaking after the Great War, as World War I was often called, created a state configuration in Europe that fell far short of ensuring lasting harmony among nations. But the peace settlement also appeared to have established some new mechanisms, including the League of Nations, that would head off future violent conflicts. What the peacemakers of 1919 did not anticipate was the appearance of virulent nationalist ideologies like Fascism in Italy and National Socialism in Germany that, once established as ruthless dictatorships, became a threat to international peace. It is very unlikely that Mussolini's military actions alone would have resulted in a Europe-wide war. It was the unilateral action of Adolf Hitler in launching an attack on Germany's eastern neighbor Poland in September 1939 that ignited the conflagration known as World War II.[1]

The peace settlements of Paris from 1919 to 1920 broke up the German, Austrian, and Ottoman empires; the Russian Empire had collapsed even before the war ended. Germany lost some of its territory, resources, and population, but not enough to be permanently harmed. Its national pride had been hurt, and it chafed under the charge of having been guilty of causing the war, which the Allies used to justify harsh reparations. In central Europe, Poland, Czechoslovakia, Austria, Hungary, and Yugoslavia emerged as new states with disputed frontiers and diverse national minorities. The Germans left in Poland and in Czechoslovakia represented a potentially serious nationality problem, since they had previously been dominant and felt increasingly alienated under their new rule. Russia, now under the domination of the Soviet Communists, who under Stalin later assumed an increasingly aggressive stance, had lost Finland, Estonia, Latvia, and Lithuania in addition to Russian Poland. Germany and the Soviet Union became the revisionist powers in the aftermath of the war, whereas the other major powers, France and Britain, were the principal defenders of the status quo. Italy, even though on the winning side, had not received all the expected spoils from the war and considered the Paris settlement a "mutilated victory." The almost total withdrawal of the United States from European affairs after the peace conferences left the European states without a politically stabilizing force. The instability of some of the old states and the proliferation of new states heightened not only political but also economic nationalism, which was sharply exacerbated under the impact of the Great Depression. In Germany, the resulting economic and social turmoil created the conditions for Hitler's ascent to power.

THE AIMS OF FASCIST AND NAZI FOREIGN POLICY

The ideology of Fascism and Nazism glorified war and violence as a test for the achievement of the "new man" and regarded national war as a creative force in the life of nations. As social Darwinists, Mussolini and Hitler believed in the survival of the fittest, who were engaged in a perpetual struggle, and they portrayed Italy and Germany as vigorous and youthful nations that would overcome the decadent old states of Europe. Acquisition of new land, to their mind, was essential for the continued existence of their states. Through victory in war and conquest of empires, organized and conducted by their totalitarian regimes, the Duce and the Führer could expect to see their power expanded and the ultimate aims of Fascism and Nazism sanctioned. Mussolini dreamed of reviving the Roman Empire in the Mediterranean and sought territorial conquests largely outside of Europe. Hitler concentrated on the acquisition of living space to the east of Germany. He considered colonies unsuitable for large-scale European settlement and unimportant for national security. In studying the question of what made nations powerful, he had become convinced that it was the possession of a large land mass that ensured the military greatness of a nation. Germany needed more land and resources to support its growing population. A key determinant in Hitler's ideology was his belief that only the Aryans were capable of bringing forth a superior civilization. As the leaders of the Aryans, the Germans faced massive numbers of Slavic peoples who were racially inferior and must therefore be forced to cede their lands to the master race. Hitler's ideas were articulated in *Mein Kampf*, but it would be wrong to conclude that he followed a grand design. He had certain goals but took advantage of opportunities to realize them as they came along. His Fascist associate Mussolini similarly waited until he saw his chance to translate some of his expansionist aspirations into reality, even though he was the first to embark on an imperialist drive.

When Hitler became chancellor of Germany early in 1933, he had to subordinate foreign policy to more urgent political and economic concerns. He therefore publicly projected a willingness to be conciliatory and reasonable toward Germany's neighbors while he consolidated his power at home. But in a private session with Germany's military chiefs only days after his appointment, he revealed that he would restore military conscription, enlarge the German army, and pursue living space as the ultimate goal of his government's foreign policy. In May he gave a "peace speech" in the Reichstag in which he assured his audience that Germany wanted to live in "peace and friendship" with other European states, but that it also wanted equality. To make his point, in the fall Hitler ended German participation in the Geneva Disarmament Conference and withdrew Germany from the League of Nations, claiming that other states were unwilling to disarm while they kept Germany disarmed, and that the League was a front for French political domination of Europe. If this move jarred some of the European governments, Hitler startled the diplomatic community in January 1934 by concluding a ten-year nonaggression pact with Poland, supposedly Germany's most objectionable neighbor. This pact afforded Germany the opportunity to overcome its isolation among European states and to demonstrate its earnestness in the pursuit of peaceful relations, but it also chilled Germany's relations with the Soviet Union. Even though Hitler regarded Italy as a natural ally, Mussolini was not quick to establish a fascist partnership. The Duce feared German rearmament and was adamantly opposed to any violation of Austrian independence. A formal meeting of the two dictators in June 1934 ended without any significant agreement. When in the following month Austrian Nazis staged a coup in Vienna and assassinated Chancellor Engelbert Dollfuss, Italy's staunch political ally, Mussolini ordered his troops to the Austrian border to prevent an annexation of Austria by Nazi Germany. Hitler professed his innocence, and the coup collapsed.

HITLER'S AND MUSSOLINI'S EARLY EXPANSIONIST MOVES

In March 1935 Hitler felt emboldened to announce that Germany had established an air force and would reinstitute the draft and expand its army from 100,000 to 550,000 men. Both of these actions violated the Versailles Treaty, which limited German rearmament. The reaction of the Western powers was surprisingly moderate, consisting of protestations but no economic or military sanctions. The leaders of Britain, France, and Italy met in Stresa to consider a joint strategy but only affirmed their solidarity and issued a condemnation of Germany's actions. Britain's and France's domestic problems and Mussolini's contemplation of an imperialistic adventure in Africa disinclined their leaders to maintain a firm front against Germany. Hitler all along had looked upon Britain as one of Germany's natural allies—the British were racial kin of the Nordic Aryans, and he also admired the British Empire—and therefore was eager to conclude some kind of armaments agreement with Britain. Negotiations in June led to the Anglo-German Naval Pact, which tacitly recognized German naval rearmament by allowing the Germans to build a surface fleet 35 percent of the size of the British navy and by granting Germany parity in the construction of submarines. This agreement, concluded by the British without consulting France, marked a break in the Stresa Front of the Western powers.

It was only a matter of time before Nazi Germany gained the support of Mussolini's Italy. In October 1935 the Italian leader launched an invasion of Ethiopia in the pursuit of imperial conquest in Africa. France and Britain, concerned about pushing Mussolini closer to Hitler, refrained from military intervention, but acquiesced in limited economic sanctions imposed by the League of Nations. Mussolini became alienated from the Western powers, and Hitler, who was careful not to denounce the Duce's aggression, was the beneficiary. In March 1936 the Nazi leader exploited the fractured diplomatic alignment of the Western powers by marching a contingent of troops and policemen into the demilitarized Rhineland, violating the Versailles settlement and the Treaty of Locarno. Hitler knew that this was a huge gamble that could have ended in a humiliating rebuff for him if the French had resisted. But the French and the British, as he had anticipated, did not take any military countermeasures. The French, apart from grossly overestimating the strength of the German occupation force, were unwilling to move without the British, who were disinclined to give support to the French as long as remilitarization of the Rhineland was done peacefully. Hitler emerged with an enormous victory and the conviction that France and Britain were weak nations unwilling to defend the old order.

A few months after the Rhineland episode, Hitler and Mussolini drew even closer together by intervening in the Spanish Civil War in support of General Francisco Franco. The Spanish adventure gave Hitler a chance to test new weapons, win the goodwill of Franco, and gain the cooperation of Mussolini, who in turn wanted to see Spain under a friendly regime and Anglo-French influence in the western Mediterranean constrained. In secret negotiations in October, Mussolini and Hitler established their common political and economic interests. At the end of November the Duce publicly proclaimed the new Rome-Berlin Axis. During the same month a formal agreement, the Anti-Comintern Pact, was signed by Germany and Japan, in which they agreed to take a common stand against communism. Hitler could indeed be pleased with Germany's international advance, for a real "diplomatic revolution" had occurred among the European powers.

The British and French probably missed their last chance to check Hitler's aggressive violations of the Versailles settlement in the Rhineland. Why did they not act when even the Soviet Union was signalling readiness to join a collective security system to contain Nazi expansionism? Britain embarked on a policy of appeasement in the mid-1930s, expecting to avoid war if reasonable German and Italian aspirations were satisfied by negotiation. The memory of the horrors of war, the realization that Britain's resources were limited if it wanted to continue to maintain its empire, and the willingness to move beyond the international status quo in the interest of European peace were strong motivators in the pursuit of appeasement. France also had suffered enormous human losses in the war and felt the effects of a disastrously low birth rate during the war years in the decades that followed. It was plagued by economic stagnation and acute internal conflicts that brought unstable governments. Therefore, the French government seldom acted alone in the international arena to defend the status quo. The Soviet Union, once threatened by Nazi Germany, moved closer to the Western camp by concluding alliances with France and Czechoslovakia in 1935. Three years later it began negotiations with Britain and France for a three-power pact, but in the end, parallel negotiations between Germany and Soviet Russia led to the Nazi-Soviet Nonaggression Pact of 1939.

HITLER TAKES AUSTRIA AND THE SUDETENLAND WITHOUT WAR

As Hitler became ever more confident, his speeches in 1937 took on a more bellicose tone. In September a dramatic state visit by the Duce to Germany consolidated the friendship between Italy and Germany, and in November Italy joined the Anti-Comintern Pact. In early November Hitler convened a secret conference of his military and diplomatic chiefs and offered a detailed account of Germany's future plans. The Hossbach Memorandum (see Document 10) indicates that Hitler's goal was essentially that outlined in *Mein Kampf*: the conquest of living space in eastern Europe and Russia, for Germany's basic needs could not be met in any other way. The Führer was determined to solve Germany's long-range problem by 1943–1945 when German military power had reached its height, but was considering the annexation of Austria and Czechoslovakia as early as 1938 if circumstances permitted him to secure the eastern and southern flanks. Most historians agree that the ideas that Hitler outlined did not represent a systematic plan for Nazi aggression, but the conference gave him a chance to test his ideas on some of his military and diplomatic chiefs. When several of them raised reservations with respect to Germany's preparedness for a confrontation with France and the risk of a broader war against France and Britain, Hitler soon removed the doubters and replaced them with pliable subordinates.

Late in 1937 Hitler determined to turn to the Austrian problem. As an Austrian, he always believed that his homeland was German and belonged to the German Reich. He was reasonably certain that Mussolini would not raise serious objections and expected little opposition from the French and the British, especially Prime Minister Neville Chamberlain, who had become the foremost advocate of appeasement. At first, the Führer used harassment and intimidation to force the existing Austrian government to resign in order to replace it with a Nazi regime. At an invited conference at his mountain resort at Berchtesgaden in February 1938, Hitler bullied Austrian chancellor Kurt Schuschnigg into accepting Nazis into his government and speeding up Austria's economic and military coordination with Germany. Upon his return to Vienna, Schuschnigg attempted to call a plebiscite on the issue of Austrian coordination with Germany to salvage whatever he could of his homeland's independence. An enraged Hitler threatened military intervention if the plebiscite was not nullified. Even though Schuschnigg complied, Nazi troops were ordered into Austria anyway (after a sham invitation dictated to an Austrian Nazi leader), and its territory was added to the German Reich under widespread approval by the Austrian populace. France and Britain were caught in governmental crises while the *Anschluss* was under way and offered little but platitudes of objection. The original defender of Austrian independence, Mussolini, had decided to stand aside and allow developments to proceed, especially since Hitler assured him that he would not claim the German South Tyrol, which Italy had acquired in 1919. An overly grateful Hitler assured the Duce of his lasting friendship, which became a "brutal friendship," in Hitler's own words, as the proud Fascist dictator was relegated more and more to the position of a junior partner.

Germany's strategic position in central Europe was improved by the acquisition of Austria. Hitler now eyed the economic resources of industrialized Czechoslovakia. When Germany's balance-of-payments problem worsened due to large imports of raw materials as its rearmament escalated, Hitler envisaged the exploitation of conquered territories as the long-range solution to Germany's economic difficulties. At this time, the European diplomatic realities appeared to offer more opportunities for bold strategic moves. He banked heavily on the war-weariness of France and Britain and their suspicion of the Soviet Union when he proceeded to attack Czechoslovakia. His demands centered on the supposedly intolerable living conditions of the 3.5 million Sudeten Germans, who resided in the mountainous border regions next to Germany and Austria. These areas also held Czech border fortifications and many industrial centers. Hitler was prepared to attack Czechoslovakia with armed force and destroy it but proceeded in a piecemeal fashion, escalating his demands as the crisis deepened. The British government under Chamberlain felt that it could not stop the Germans from destroying the Czechoslovak state. Since the French were unwilling to honor their defense alliance without British support and Soviet assistance depended on French backing, the Czech government, under British pressure, accepted the Nazi demand for autonomy of the Sudeten Germans in late August 1938. Hitler then raised the stakes by demanding the Sudetenland itself during a meeting with Prime Minister Chamberlain in mid-September. The British leader went along and prevailed upon the French to agree, compelling the reluctant Czechoslovak government to meet Hitler's demands. When Chamberlain returned to Germany on September 22 with the Czechoslovak acceptance of German terms, he was stunned by Hitler's new demand that German troops must occupy the Sudeten region by October 1. Chamberlain angrily objected to the new proposal, saying that it was an ultimatum. Upon Chamberlain's return to London, the British cabinet rejected Hitler's new proposal as unacceptable, as did the French, and war preparations appeared to be imminent.

At the height of the Czech crisis, Mussolini, following Chamberlain's prompting, proposed that a multilateral conference be convened in Munich. It met at the end of September, with the leaders of Britain, France, Germany, and Italy in attendance. Upon Hitler's insistence, the Soviet Union was not invited, nor was Czechoslovakia. The discussion was based on a memorandum submitted by Mussolini that actually had been drafted by the Germans. The agreement that followed met practically all of Hitler's demands and delivered the Sudetenland into German hands without war. Abandoned by all European powers that they considered their friends, the Czechoslovaks had little choice but to accept their fate. Munich marked the high point of the Western appeasement policy. Chamberlain still believed that he could deal with the unpredictable Nazi dictator and returned home proclaiming that "peace in our time" had been saved by the Munich agreement. Hitler, who had been itching for an easy war with Czechoslovakia, scored his greatest diplomatic triumph by acquiring the Sudetenland, splintering the French security system, and excluding Russia from the European alliance system; he soon prepared for the final destruction of rump Czechoslovakia and the breakup of the now isolated Poland.

After Munich, Hitler was convinced that he could redraw the boundaries of eastern Europe without much restraint by France and Britain. Within weeks after the Munich Conference, he issued an order to his military to prepare for the final dismemberment of the Czechoslovak state. In March 1939 he first pressured Slovakia into declaring its independence and then forced the Czech government to accept a German protectorate over the remaining provinces of Bohemia and Moravia. German troops were placed in both areas of what once had been the Czechoslovak state. Chamberlain denounced Hitler for breaking his word, at last reaching the conclusion that the Nazi dictator could not be trusted. Only a week after his triumphant entry into Prague on March 15, Hitler sailed to Memel to reclaim it as part of the German Reich from Lithuania. Public pressure quickly changed the policy of the British and French governments and prompted them to give military guarantees to Poland, Rumania, Greece, and Turkey. In April the Western powers also opened political and military negotiations with the Soviet Union.

HITLER PUSHES GERMANY AND EUROPE INTO WAR

While the Führer was planning and then executing the destruction of Czechoslovakia, he threatened Poland. Many Germans agreed with Hitler that the Polish Corridor that separated East Prussia from the rest of Germany and the loss of Danzig were intolerable. Hitler was intent on correcting this remaining injustice of Versailles and expanding Germany's sway into the east. In October 1938 he promised the Polish government that he would respect the eastern boundaries if Germany were given Danzig and later demanded an extraterritorial passageway through the Polish Corridor. Poland refused both demands and welcomed the unexpected Anglo-French offer on March 31, 1939, to guarantee Polish territorial integrity. Hitler was enraged and on April 3 issued an order to his military chiefs to prepare plans not only for the seizure of Danzig but also the destruction of the Polish armed forces to be ready by September 1. He used the Anglo-French guarantee to Poland as a pretext to abrogate the German-Polish Nonaggression Pact of 1934. However, the Nazi leader did not take Chamberlain's guarantee to Poland very seriously, thinking that it was largely meant for British domestic consumption. To the very end of the prewar crisis, he hoped that Britain would at least remain neutral while he forged his strategy to expand into eastern Europe and eventually into Russia.

Hitler firmed up Germany's alliance with Fascist Italy and on the very eve of his invasion of Poland found a most unlikely partner, Soviet Russia. Mussolini could maintain some semblance of independence after serving as mediator at the Munich Conference, but following the Nazi annihilation of rump Czechoslovakia, he moved closer to Hitler. His foreign minister Galeazzo Ciano engineered an Italian invasion of Albania in April 1939 in response to which the British and French offered a guarantee to Greece and Rumania. This development facilitated the conclusion of the Pact of Steel in May in which Italy and Germany pledged mutual military support in case of any war. Mussolini emphasized that Italy would not be ready for war until 1943. Hitler was not deterred by such considerations and proceeded with his claims against Poland. Being unsure whether Britain and France might honor their pledges to Poland, he realized that the only way to prevent an alliance between the Western powers and the Soviet Union and the prospect of a two-front war was to conclude an agreement with Stalin.

Germany was aware that negotiations were being carried on between the Western powers and the Soviet Union. Somewhat reluctantly, both Hitler and Stalin proceeded with secret negotiations. Months later, on August 23, the world was stunned when it learned of the German-Soviet Nonaggression Pact. Since Munich, Stalin's suspicion of the Western powers had been exacerbated, and the low-level negotiations with Britain and France in the spring and summer of 1939 dragged on without the prospect of significant Western concessions. From his perspective, it was in the Soviet Union's interest to avoid war as long as possible. Stalin appears to have expected the imperialist powers—all of which he saw as hostile to Soviet Russia—to become embroiled in a mutually destructive war, the outcome of which would benefit his plans. Hitler, anxious to strike against Poland and no doubt considering the agreement with Stalin only a temporary arrangement, met many of the terms that the Soviet dictator regarded as essential to enhance his country's security. Publicly, the treaty was proclaimed as a ten-year friendship and nonaggression pact. A secret clause, not made known until after 1945, divided eastern Europe into a German and a Soviet sphere of influence. After the Polish campaign ended, the clause was amended so that the final division assigned Finland, the Baltic states, and eastern Poland to Soviet Russia and western Poland to Germany. Even though the agreement with the Soviet Union appeared to imply a stark change in Germany's hostile ideological stance toward communism, Hitler encountered no opposition in his own camp, especially since the events that followed seemed to show that a friendly relationship with Soviet Russia served Germany's interests in the east at this time.

Once Hitler had signed a pact with Stalin, he had a free hand to launch his planned invasion of Poland. Nothing would now deter him from having a war with Poland, since he was ready to embark on his ultimate goal of acquiring *Lebensraum* in the east. War started early in the morning on September 1, 1939. There is no indication that Hitler had plans to expand the German-Polish war into a Europe-wide war, let alone a world war. His expectation was that a quick crushing campaign would eliminate Poland, after which he could regroup for another strike against his next adversary, presumably Soviet Russia. But the localized conflict very quickly turned into a European war when Great Britain and France issued ultimatums to Hitler to withdraw his troops from Poland and then declared war on September 3. The Führer was left momentarily speechless when the British war declaration arrived in the Reich chancellery. The Nazi dictator faced the Western powers alone, for Mussolini, contrary to the Pact of Steel, remained a nonbelligerent until the eve of France's defeat. While Poland was being destroyed, Britain and France did not move. Immediately after the Polish campaign had ended, Hitler wanted to attack France but was persuaded by his generals to postpone action until May 1940. Before and after the swift defeat of France, Hitler hoped to disengage Britain from the war as long as it accepted Germany's domination of the Continent. Having failed to do so, he embarked on the fateful invasion of the Soviet Union in June 1941, which Nazi propaganda justified as a preventive war against a foe that was on the verge of attacking Germany. When in December the Führer unilaterally declared war on the United States after Japan's attack on Pearl Harbor, he had turned a Europe-wide war into a devastating global war. If Hitler proved successful in this war in conquering *Lebensraum* and realizing an empire ruled by the superior Aryan race, then the ultimate mission of Nazism would have been fulfilled. War became the all-or-nothing means for both Mussolini and Hitler to attain the goals of a Fascist empire in the Mediterranean and in Africa and a Nazi Aryan empire in Europe, neither of which could be achieved through peaceful means. But once they resorted to the military violence that World War II entailed, the validity and the very survival of the Fascist and Nazi regimes were staked on victory in such a war. The total defeat in the war sealed the fate of the Duce and the Führer and their dictatorial fascist states.

NOTE

1. For a more detailed overview of the causes of World War II, see Keith Eubank, *The Origins of World War II*, 2nd ed. (Arlington Heights, IL: Harlan Davidson, 1990).

5

Resistance in Fascist Italy and Nazi Germany

Resistance to fascist regimes assumed many forms. On an individual level, it might entail the refusal to use the prescribed customary German greeting "Heil Hitler" in Nazi Germany, or the refusal to participate in groups and organizations sponsored by the ruling regime; it meant also the airing of antiregime views or involvement with groups or churches that were known to be critical of policies of the government. Individual action became a group effort with committed participation in political organizations that worked actively toward the removal of the ruling regime. In this chapter, some attention will be given to individual resistance efforts, but the major emphasis will be on organized political resistance that attempted to disrupt the activities of the ruling government and to prepare for the eventual overthrow of the existing regime. In both Fascist Italy and Nazi Germany, resistance movements emerged quite early and acted independently of each other, for the challenges that they faced at various stages in the history of the regimes did not allow for any cooperation or coordination across the borders of the fascist states.

OPPOSITION IN FASCIST ITALY

From the very beginning in 1919, both the Fascists in Italy and the emerging National Socialists in Germany looked upon Socialists and Communists as their principal political foes. Other political parties were also treated as opponents by the Fascists and the Nazis, but rarely with the kind of vehemence that they reserved for the two leftist political organizations. Much of the original opposition to Fascism in Italy (and later to Nazism in Germany) came from the Socialists and Communists. When

Mussolini was appointed prime minister in 1922, his cabinet included representatives from most of the political parties, many of whom expected the Fascist Party to become part of the regular political system. It took considerably longer for an anti-Fascist force to develop outside the regular political order than in Nazi Germany since Mussolini's dictatorship did not become complete until 1926. However, views sharply opposing Fascist policies were articulated in editorials of various newspapers coming from the Catholic left and some of the Liberal Democrats as early as the spring of 1923. They often seconded the opposition that tried to resist Mussolini's policies within the Chamber of Deputies.[1] A major crisis erupted in the Mussolini government with the assassination of the reformist Socialist Giacomo Matteotti in June 1924. He had bitterly attacked the Fascists in parliament, charging them with electoral abuses. Mussolini's complicity in the murder was never fully established, but the assassins were close to the Fascist leader. A mixed group of Liberals, Catholic Populists, Socialists, and Communists boycotted the parliamentary sessions in protest and formed the Aventine Secession. However, they failed to persuade the king to remove Mussolini from the prime ministership and thus fell short of their primary objective. Even though an anti-Fascist opposition had been fashioned, it was a fractured bloc, for neither the Communists nor the conservatives were willing to join a common front.

By early 1925 Mussolini recovered from the psychological and political shock of the Matteotti affair (see chapter 2) and, capitalizing upon the indecisiveness and disarray of his political opponents, launched a counterattack with a series of repressive measures that by the end of 1926 ensured his complete dictatorship. A series of attempts on his life during 1925 and 1926 played into his hands. Only the first attempt was perpetrated by a Socialist, probably incited by an agent provocateur; the other three were carried out by individuals who could not be traced to the opposition. But all these incidents were used as justification by the government to curb the press, restrict the authority of the legislature, and suppress secret societies, parties, and trade unions. Mussolini became solely responsible to the king, and the parliament was turned into a rubber-stamp chamber. Prominent leaders of almost all parties were forced into emigration if they had not already left before the repressive actions of the government. Those who elected to remain in Italy carried on with largely passive resistance. Only some of the anarchists and Communists engaged in some violence and attempted to incite strike actions. Several attempts were made on Mussolini's life by anarchists in the early 1930s. One notable example of an intellectual oppositionist was the liberal philosopher and historian Benedetto Croce, who perhaps was too well known outside Italy to be arrested or even silenced. Though he was kept under close surveillance, he was permitted to edit and publish his review *La Critica* and to write several historical and philosophical works in which he exalted liberalism and implicitly if not explicitly cast moral aspersions at Fascism.

Two core groups of opposition were organized outside Italy among the anti-Fascist émigrés in the late 1920s. In 1927 the Anti-Fascist Concentration was formed in France under the leadership of the Socialist Pietro Nenni. This group encompassed the Socialists, the Republican Party, some of the labor groups, and anticlericals. Its program was republican, anticlerical, and reformist, thus inviting the scorn of the Communists, who wanted a more radical revolution. In 1929 a competing movement was established in Paris called Giustizia e Libertà (Justice and liberty) that tried to attract moderate socialists, democratic liberals, and libertarians, all those who did not find the Nenni group compatible. Although very antimonarchical and anticlerical, Giustizia e Libertà also refused to cooperate with the Communists. Determined to engage in action, the group attempted to maintain an organizational network in Lombardy and Turin in the early 1930s, without lasting success. For a few years, 1931 to 1933, Giustizia e Libertà joined forces with the Anti-Fascist Concentration, but that combination did not last either.

Socialists and Communists were brought together only with the advent of Hitler's dictatorship in Germany. For years, the Communists had denounced the Social Democrats as "Social Fascists" and often considered them even more reprehensible foes than the Nazis. But once the Soviet Union became concerned over its own national security, the Comintern's official stance began to soften; more and more Communist parties saw the advantage of the Popular Front strategy, combining forces with the Socialists to stem the advance of fascism. In August 1934 the Italian Socialist leaders Pietro Nenni and Giuseppe Saragat joined the Italian Communist leader Palmiro Togliatti in a "unity of action" pact. This agreement was renewed several times before August 1939, when the Nazi-Soviet Nonaggression Pact suspended the Socialist-Communist cooperation until Hitler launched his invasion of the Soviet Union in 1941. While engaged in a rapprochement with the Communists, Nenni dissolved the Anti-Fascist Concentration.

The source of some nonpolitical opposition to Fascist control of society was the Catholic Church. The Lateran Pacts of 1929 gave the church in Italy a privileged position by permitting religious education in the secondary schools, granting civil recognition to religious marriages, and assuring full autonomy to Catholic Action, an organization of Catholic laymen. After the dissolution of the Popular Party, this Catholic organization was the only one that remained in existence throughout the Fascist period. Its membership reached one million in late 1930. In 1931 the Fascist regime launched bitter attacks on the activities of Catholic Action, its efforts to organize occupational groups among Catholics, and especially its influence on youth education. Pope Pius XI responded with his scalding encyclical *Non abbiamo bisógno*, which rejected the state's claim to abrogate the rights of individual, family, and church in the education of the young. Since neither side was prepared to push the conflict to the extreme, an agreement was worked out that stipulated that the church's lay organizations would pursue only recreational and educational goals of a strictly religious nature (excluding, for instance, all athletic activity). Catholic youth groups were not abolished and thus remained an alternative to the ONB for Catholic young people. Relations between church and state improved until 1938, when the introduction of racial laws in Italy and closer relations with Nazi Germany induced the pope to express his public concern over events in Italy and central Europe.

Throughout the 1930s much of the opposition activity was carried on outside of Italy. Its achievements, both inside and outside of Italy, were limited. Mussolini's Ethiopian adventure successfully resisted the sanctions of the League of Nations and greatly enhanced his and the Fascist regime's popularity. However, the Duce's hasty intervention in the Spanish Civil War on Franco's side in 1936 bogged him down in encounters in which his armed forces were facing not only the Spanish defenders of the Republic and their foreign supporters but also anti-Fascist Italian volunteers. They included contingents of Giustizia e Libertà, who were among the first anti-Fascist Italians to fight on the side of the Spanish Republicans. Italian Socialists and Communists soon rallied their supporters in international brigades. Among these, the Garibaldi Battalion achieved a certain notoriety when it scored a major psychological victory at the Battle of Guadalajara in March 1937 by decisively defeating attacking forces of Mussolini's corps of Italian volunteers. Newspaper headlines of Guadalajara throughout the world kept reminding an infuriated Mussolini of the humiliation and instilled hopes in many of the Italian anti-Fascists that a similar civil war would eventually erupt in Italy. Some 3,000 anti-Fascists participated in the Spanish Civil War, many less than the 60,000 Mussolini "volunteers."

Mussolini's regime was never seriously threatened by the anti-Fascist opposition until 1942–1943, when deteriorating living conditions due to food and consumer-goods shortages caused economic unrest and military setbacks put Italy's Fascist future into question. It also was clear that as long as Mussolini stayed in power, Italy would remain Germany's partner in war. These developments energized several of the political parties— Socialists, Communists, Christian Democrats, Labor Democrats, and Liberals—secretly to reconstitute their organizations in anticipation of the eventual overthrow of Mussolini. Similarly, within the army leadership, resistance began to stir when Italian forces suffered one setback after another. Mussolini had dragged his generals into war in June 1940 at the collapse of France, but after assuming supreme command he failed to correlate his ambitious political goals with military means in disastrous campaigns in Greece and North Africa. After the Battle of El Alamein in November 1942 forced the Italian and German forces into retreat in North Africa, the Italian High Command advocated a separate peace.

However, the actual impetus for the Duce's fall from power came from within the Fascist Party leadership and the conservatives around King Victor Emmanuel. Discontent in the highest quarters of the Fascist Party spread when in February 1943 several of the top leaders, including Dino Grandi and Galeazzo Ciano, were removed from their ministerial positions. They banded together with several others who had lost their posts and formed the heart of the opposition to Mussolini. Their strategy was to convene the Fascist Grand Council, which had not met since December 1939, to bring about a change in Italian policy. The king had generally admired his prime minister in the early years but had become increasingly disenchanted with Mussolini as he altered constitutional arrangements in his favor and, after 1940, arrogated to himself decision making regarding the war. By 1943 the king was ready to consider the removal of Mussolini and made soundings to other members of the royal circle and politicians who had been Fascist fellow travelers or even belonged to the pre-Fascist era. The action of the Fascist conspirators forced the issue and enabled the king to act.

Shortly after the landing of the Allies on Sicily, a deputation of the dissident Fascist leaders prevailed upon Mussolini to set a meeting of the Fascist Grand Council. He reluctantly agreed, and it was convened on July 24, 1943. Mussolini had very recently met with Hitler and again succumbed to his promises of aid and ultimate victory rather than stand up to the Führer and inform him that Italy could not continue the war, as some of the Duce's military advisors had urged. Dino Grandi prepared a motion that expressed a vote of no confidence in the Duce's leadership and called for the reactivation of the legal organs of the state and the restoration of political initiative to the king. Mussolini, who had been apprised of the motion prior to the meeting, offered an elaborate defense of his foreign and military policy at the sometimes heated and lengthy session of the Grand Council. When the Grandi motion was finally passed by a vote of nineteen to seven, Mussolini did not seem unduly perturbed since he assumed that he still had the king's support. In the afternoon of July 25, hours after the fateful Grand Council session, he made his report to the king in what otherwise would have been a routine conference. The royal palace, upon hearing of the decision of the Fascist Grand Council, had mobilized the army and the police. During the course of Mussolini's report, the king interrupted him and asked for his resignation. Upon leaving the king, the dumbfounded Duce was arrested.

The sequel to the Duce's removal from office moved beyond the confines of the anti-Fascist resistance. Under Marshal Pietro Badoglio, Mussolini's successor, Italy extricated itself from its alliance with Germany and soon declared war against Germany. In September 1943 the Duce was freed by a special German commando, brought to Germany, and installed upon Hitler's order as head of the Italian Social Republic. He eked out the rest of his life as a puppet of his Nazi fellow dictator. German military forces occupied northern and central Italy and only slowly yielded to the Allied advance. Worst of all, Italy exploded into a full-blown civil war in which Mussolini loyalists fought anti-Fascist armed resisters, who consisted of bands of escaping officers and soldiers reacting to the German invasion and disbanding of Italy's army, as well as large numbers of men wanting to escape military and labor conscription by the new enemy. The ranks of the anti-Fascist partisans also came to include members of the anti-Fascist parties, Communists, Socialists, and a new liberal-socialist group, the Action Party. In January 1944 a broad alliance of anti-Fascist parties, the Committee of National Liberation for Upper Italy (CLNAI), was formed in Milan to serve as a five-party clandestine government and to coordinate the struggle in German-occupied Italy. Representatives of these parties were also found in the Ivanoe Bonomi–led government, which succeeded the Badoglio government in June 1944 after the Allied liberation of Rome. Early in April 1945 the Allies fought their way into the Po Valley. Anti-Fascist partisans were prominent in the liberation of the Apennine-Liguria region, Genoa, Bologna, Milan, and Venice. Mussolini was caught between anti-Fascist partisans and the German military's attempts to arrange a surrender to the advancing Allies. Fleeing north with a small German military contingent, he was caught and met his inglorious end at the hands of a band of Italian Communist partisans in late April 1945.

RESISTANCE IN HITLER GERMANY

Both Mussolini and Hitler achieved power under legal conditions, and thus the initial opposition to their respective governments operated quite openly. However, whereas in Italy traditional political debate, newspapers, literary periodicals, and political parties managed to carry on for several years, in Germany this transitional phase of relative political openness lasted only a few months. By the summer of 1933 anti-Nazi groups were pushed into the underground and compelled to operate illegally. As in Fascist Italy, in Nazi Germany the resistance groups were centered in the remnants of the political parties. This was especially true in Germany during much of the 1930s. By 1938 a group of army officers formed a somewhat loosely organized resistance movement that lasted until the fateful assassination attempt of July 1944.[2] It was this core of military officers that drew civilians and political leaders into its network and maintained a resistance organization that neither illegal political parties, labor unions, nor existing but weak church organizations could provide. Although Hitler made every effort to beat the army leadership into submission, he was not able to gain total control over all segments of the officer corps. Senior officers, largely in the army, were conservative. Many were aristocratic in origin and mindful of the Prussian military tradition in their attitude toward the state and their conception of the role of the army. Even though they felt bound by their oath to Hitler, some of them were imbued enough with patriotism to set the well-being of Germany above the policies of the Nazi regime. They resented Hitler's intrusion into military affairs and considered his adventurous foreign policy dangerous to Germany's interests. It was from such ranks that military resisters emerged.

Communists and Socialists felt the brunt of Nazi hostility from the very beginning of Hitler's takeover. After the enactment of the Enabling Law in March 1933, in part facilitated by a widespread arrest of Communist deputies, Hitler needed only two months to disband the leftist parties. Operating under the illusion that the Nazi regime would not last but only prepare the ground for a proletarian successorship, the Communist leadership used illegal organizations to distribute literature and to engage in public agitation. Such activity could easily be detected by the Gestapo and led to massive arrests of Communist activists. Starting in 1935, the Communist Party adopted a more realistic approach by organizing illegal cells in factories and even in some Nazi organizations to spread its message. During the war, the exiled party leadership in Moscow decided to intensify its anti-Nazi activity by establishing a centralized party system in Germany and by infiltrating party officials into Germany. Some small Communist groups operated independently, and several individual Communists or sympathizers engaged in espionage activities from within non-Communist resistance circles. Socialists and Communists very rarely united, since they distrusted each other. Because the Social Democrats learned from the very start that resistance groups could easily be destroyed by the secret police, they maintained small forces in a number of German towns that helped to distribute socialist publications that were smuggled into Germany. A unified socialist resistance organization never developed inside Germany. However, several Social Democratic leaders had close links to the conspiratorial groups within the German armed forces after the war began. In 1944 these socialist resistance leaders attempted to bring Communist resistance leaders into the plot against Hitler but were arrested after they made contact, only confirming thereby that Communist groups had all too often been penetrated by Gestapo agents. The remnant groups of the once-sturdy labor-union movement also did not rise in power or effectiveness above the level of resistance of the leftist parties and thus demonstrated that the Nazi regime did not have much to fear from the working-class opposition.

Resistance from within the churches was basically not politically motivated wherever it appeared. The Catholic Church concluded a concordat with the Nazi government in 1933, hoping to improve its standing in Germany, but the Catholic leadership was soon dismayed by Nazi attacks on Catholic organizations, the dismissal of Catholic teachers, and interference with Catholic youth groups. Many priests and even nuns soon were harassed; numerous clergy were arrested and sent to concentration camps once the church began to defend itself and attacked Nazi practices. Pope Pius XI's 1937 encyclical entitled *Mit brennender Sorge* (With burning anxiety) constituted a high point in the church's response to the Nazification efforts of the Hitler government. A prevailing group of the Catholic hierarchy favored negotiation rather than protest. However, the vehement public protest of Bishop Clemens August Count von Galen against the ongoing Nazi practice of euthanasia of mentally impaired and physically disabled persons in 1941, which was also sharply condemned by the Protestant leader Theophil Wurm and others, prompted Hitler to suspend the program. Opposition within the Protestant fold centered in the Confessing Church of the Lutheran and Reformed faiths. It was formed in April 1934 to resist the attempt to Nazify the Protestant churches and to protect their religious activities. The Confessing Church became a rival authority to the increasingly Nazified Reich Church and comprised many clergy of the Pastors' Emergency League, which had been organized in September 1933 under the leadership of Martin Niemöller, pastor of a notable Berlin-Dahlem congregation. Niemöller was arrested and sent to a concentration camp in 1937 as Hitler's "personal prisoner." He survived and was liberated in 1945. His shining example and that of other Protestant and Catholic clergy, a good number of whom died, cannot conceal the rather limited achievement of the churches' resistance.

Youthful idealism was especially shown in the small student resistance organization called the White Rose in Munich. The most celebrated members of this student group were the young brother and sister Hans and Sophie Scholl. Together with several of their friends and a philosophy professor, Kurt Huber, they wrote, printed, and distributed leaflets in which they denounced the Nazi government and Hitler for their criminal policies and actions. The student resisters knew that they could not overthrow the Nazi regime, and so they called for acts of sabotage and passive resistance, hoping to raise the consciousness of fellow students in Munich and also in Hamburg, Freiburg, Berlin, and Vienna. Less than a year after becoming active, the Munich circle was denounced to the Gestapo in February 1943; its leaders were arrested, sentenced to death by a People's Court, and guillotined.

The efforts of the various political, labor, church, and student groups could produce actions of protest and minor disruption directed against the Nazi regime, but they lacked an effective organizational network and also, quite often, individuals in powerful positions to constitute a significant threat to the Hitler government. It is important to note that any resistance group would not have been able to receive broad support as long as most Germans accepted Hitler's government as legitimate and this government appeared to be successful in its economic achievement in peace and its military expansion in war. Even under the impact of major military reversals toward the end of the war, popular loyalty was not seriously affected. Also, the Nazi police state, relying on twentieth-century techniques and instruments, was able to maintain and certainly create the appearance of an ever-present surveillance system that was ready to strike against any opposition. The Gestapo and security intelligence services could also count on agents and informers of the party in the state, from provincial and district down to block levels, to provide them with reports on suspicious activities. The one institution that was relatively immune to secret police surveillance and penetration was the army and the officer corps. However, at first, the German military was receiving significant benefits from the Hitler government and therefore was disinclined to oppose its policies.

Active opposition developed originally among some officers who resented Hitler's high-handed way of removing military leaders who disagreed with him and became concerned over the Nazi leader's daring expansionist plans. The original military opposition group emerged in 1935 in the Abwehr, the intelligence section of the armed forces, whose chief, Admiral Wilhelm Canaris, and his chief of staff, Major General Hans Oster, showed early disaffection toward Hitler. When the Führer outlined his plans of aggression at the Hossbach conference in 1937, Ludwig Beck, chief of the general staff of the army, became the driving force to resist Hitler. Beck had contact with the Abwehr group and also reached out to the civilian opposition, headed by Carl Goerdeler, the former mayor of Leipzig, who had become vociferous in his anti-Nazi stand. Although Beck had no objection to enlarging the German armed forces, he was deeply concerned that Hitler was preparing for reckless war instead of negotiating revisions of the postwar settlement. Beck also favored the union between Austria and Germany. But when Hitler threatened war to bring it about and, having annexed Austria, months later ordered preparation of military action against Czechoslovakia, Beck intensified his effort to rally senior military commanders for protest action against Hitler's plans. In August 1938, one month before the Munich Conference that gave Hitler the Sudetenland, Beck resigned and, together with several leaders of the opposition, concentrated on preparing a coup d'état against Hitler. The conspirators assumed that the Führer would go to war against Czechoslovakia and thereby compel the Western powers to declare war on Germany. Their plan was to arrest Hitler and to establish a temporary military dictatorship to be succeeded by a new political government. However, when British prime minister Neville Chamberlain announced that he was ready to come to Germany to negotiate and Hitler scored a diplomatic triumph at Munich, the resisters' scheme collapsed. The military and civilian opponents revived various plans for action against the dictator after the war started but did not mount another coup attempt until July 1944.

Once the war broke out, the resisters faced increasing difficulties. As long as Hitler was successful in the war, any action against him would be viewed by the German people as treason not only against the Nazi rulership but also against Germany. Under such conditions, few military leaders were willing to act. The Allies were being kept apprised of some of the resistance activity by German opponents through various diplomatic channels in 1939 and 1940. France and Britain informally indicated willingness to consider peace with a non-Nazi Germany. But the longer the resisters delayed action, the more they lost credibility in the eyes of the Allies. By 1942 the Churchill government refused to grant any further recognition to the resistance movement, and the Allies soon declared unconditional surrender as their war aim.

Starting in 1940 and continuing into 1943, an important diverse resistance group known as the Kreisau Circle met at the estate of Count Helmuth James von Moltke in Silesia and at times in Berlin. Most of the members were in their thirties and included civil servants, aristocrats, Socialists, trade-union leaders, and Protestant and Catholic theologians. In addition to Moltke, one of the most active members was Adam von Trott zu Solz, who used his position as a lawyer in the Foreign Office to maintain contact with Allied officials outside Germany. The Kreisau Circle drafted several proposals for the postwar Hitler era that, in contrast to the conservative and nationalist ideas of the civilian Goerdeler group, favored a new European international order without the hegemony of Germany. The circle maintained ties to the other resistance groups until Moltke's arrest in January 1944 and Trott's after the failed July plot broke up the conspiracy.

After 1941 a younger generation of officers joined the military opposition who turned against Hitler when they witnessed Nazi occupation and Jewish policies. Prominent among them were Colonel Count Claus von Stauffenberg and General Henning von Tresckow, both products of the aristocracy but willing to move beyond the conservative and nationalist frame of mind of the older generation of conspirators. Stauffenberg in particular made contact with the socialist resistance group. In 1943 he energized those resisters who were convinced that Hitler had to be removed by assassination and were willing to overthrow the Nazi regime without any Allied assurances of a post-Hitler government. Several attempts on Hitler's life were planned by this group, but all of them either miscarried or had to be aborted. By the end of 1943 and the beginning of 1944, urgency to carry out a major coup intensified as members of several opposition circles linked to the military group of resisters were arrested by the Gestapo, and Canaris and Oster were removed from their Abwehr positions. With the worsening condition of the German fronts in the early summer of 1944, the resisters found support among several of the army commanders in France, including Field Marshal Erwin Rommel. Lists of possible leaders who could carry on the new government after Hitler had been overthrown were established and included the names of Goerdeler and Beck of the older group as well as those of the younger generation. All of this was of no avail when the bomb that Stauffenberg placed at Hitler's headquarters on July 20, 1944, failed to kill the dictator and the coup collapsed. With it ended all organized German resistance against Hitler, who took frightful vengeance on its participants and others who were suspected of having links to the opposition. Beck and Tresckow managed to commit suicide. Stauffenberg was shot. Goerdeler and many others were charged with treason before a People's Court and hanged. Some 200 people were executed as a result of the failed coup after a trial by a People's Court. Many hundreds were arrested, including family members of the major participants in the conspiracy, and thrown into prison or concentration camps.

The history of the anti-Fascist resistance in Italy and the German opposition to Hitler demonstrated the enormous difficulty of mobilizing an effective force against a dictatorial regime that was headed by a popular leader and commanded the instruments of complete control. The Mussolini regime collapsed only under the most severe strain of war, and the dictator was toppled by his own associates who enlisted the support of the king and the army leadership. The leaders of the anti-Hitler resistance faced a much more formidable problem of establishing and maintaining a conspiracy within a segment of the armed forces and the loose political circles; they could count on the support of only a very few of the top leaders of the armed forces who were on active duty and none of the civilians in the highest governmental offices. Many of these military and civilian resisters showed great courage by being ready to give their lives to combat an evil regime when the prospects of overthrowing it appeared to be doomed. The only country in which fascism was devastated well before it was destroyed by the Allies was Rumania. Here the fascist Iron Guard was eliminated by the ultranationalist General Ion Antonescu on the eve of Rumania's entry into the war and at a time when Nazism and Fascism were in their heyday. It was ironic that Hitler raised no objections when Antonescu proposed to take action against his fascist partner.

NOTES

1. The standard work on the resistance against Fascism is still Charles F. Delzell, *Mussolini's Enemies: The Italian Anti-Fascist Resistance* (Princeton, NJ: Princeton University Press, 1961).

2. For a very readable account of the German resistance, based on current scholarship, turn to Joachim C. Fest, *Plotting Hitler's Death: The Story of the German Resistance* (New York: Henry Holt and Co., 1996).

6

Fascism: Assessment and Legacy

Fascism as an ideology and political system thrived solely in Europe during the first half of the twentieth century, a time in modern history during which two global wars and unprecedented totalitarian dictatorships brought enormous turmoil to Europe and the world. In many ways, totalitarian fascist and Communist states became a singular hallmark of this century. Whereas traditional modern dictatorships exercise primarily political domination over citizens, twentieth-century totalitarian regimes like fascism and communism have sought to secure complete political, social, and cultural control over individuals and societies. Under totalitarian dictatorships, there is no distinction between public and private spheres of life. Historians regard fascism as a form of right-wing totalitarianism (in contrast to communism, which represents a brand of left-wing totalitarianism) that derived from the movement that Benito Mussolini organized in 1919 and turned into Italy's ruling regime in just a few years. In the actual development of fascist states, only National Socialist Germany under Hitler achieved a full form of fascist totalitarianism. Mussolini's Italy became at best only a quasi-totalitarian fascist state.

Since the 1930s the term *fascism* has also been applied to extreme nationalist movements and regimes like the Falange in Francisco Franco's Spain, the Arrow Cross in Hungary, the Iron Guard in Rumania, and, by some scholars, even to non-European states like the pre–World War II imperial-army regime of Japan, certain dictatorships like Juan Perón's in Argentina, and, more recently, Saddam Hussein's rule of Iraq. However, even though these regimes have shown some fascist features (and the fascist Arrow Cross Party even briefly ruled Hungary in 1944–1945), they cannot be called fascist states, let alone be considered totalitarian in tendency, when compared to the regimes of Mussolini's Italy and Hitler's Germany.

Without the devastating experience of World War I and the postwar political, social, economic, and cultural crises, fascism as an ideology and political system would have remained a fringe phenomenon or perhaps not have appeared at all. Interestingly enough, it made its first entry into politics on a national scale in Italy, which was among the victors of the war, and spread in Germany, a loser, only later. Britain, France, the United States, and some other smaller states remained largely immune to the fascist virus during the aftermath of the war and even during the Great Depression, which brought almost as much economic and social hardship to Britain and the United States as Germany had endured. Western countries lacked certain preconditions favoring the vigorous germination of fascism. They had been consolidated national states for a long time; democracy had established quite deep roots, and their representative political institutions functioned adequately; they were economically developed, relatively prosperous, and socially reasonably well balanced, with a large segment of well-educated citizens. In contrast, Italy and Germany had achieved their nationhood only in the 1860s and early 1870s and, in searching for a balanced idea of national identity, were given to waves of national resentment and extremism. Italy lived under a liberal constitutional monarchy in which parliamentary government performed inadequately at times and democracy had been barely planted. For Germany, World War I brought the collapse of its authoritarian empire, and democracy was established in the wake of military defeat.

The most striking features of fascist movements and regimes were their intense nationalism and their drive for territorial expansion beyond the borders of their homelands. They vehemently opposed socialism and Marxism and sought to destroy working-class parties and organizations. They repudiated liberalism and democracy and, once in power, abolished nonfascist political parties and crippled or eliminated traditional parliamentary institutions. The success of fascist movements and fascist states depended ultimately on the charisma, the ability, and the ruthlessness of outstanding leaders; neither Italy nor Germany would have gone fascist without Mussolini and Hitler. These two future dictators came to power not following an armed struggle or a sudden coup d'état but as a result of political machinations. The Fascist "March on Rome" never took place, for Mussolini arrived in the Italian capital in a railroad sleeping car after the king invited him to join the government. The idea of Nazi "national revolution" became a legend, even though Hitler took over the government only after Hindenburg, prompted by his archconservative advisors, appointed him, as the leader of the largest political party, to the chancellorship.

Even though the Fascist Party in Italy and the Nazi Party in Germany were very important organizations, Mussolini and Hitler, their subordinates, and government officials were the rulers. The party served much more as an instrument of indoctrination than as a mechanism of government. In Italy, the Fascist Party membership gradually grew from 500,000 men in 1926 (only males could belong) to 2.6 million in 1939 and reached 4.7 million in 1942. Around 25 million Italians were affiliated with some kind of Fascist association, including the multimillion-member Dopolavoro leisure organization. The duties of party members were not very exacting; at times, they did not go much beyond annual membership registry and participation in occasional party activities and planned mass rallies. Mussolini himself did not regard the party as the most suitable instrument for control after the early years of the regime, and starting in the late 1920s, power was formally shifted from the party to the state organs like prefects (provincial governors) and the police. Civil servants were required to be party members starting in the 1930s, but in practice often gave more allegiance to the state than to the party. There was a clear perception that the party was subordinated to the state, and Mussolini wielded his power as head or chief of the government rather than as Duce of the party (though the title Duce applied to both).

In Germany, the role of the Nazi Party was more far-reaching and critical than in Italy. This was due in part to Hitler's scorn for bureaucrats and officialdom, but especially because party leaders were regarded as important decision makers on the central and regional levels. Party membership stood around 1 million at Hitler's takeover in 1933, escalated to 2.5 million in 1935 and 5 million in 1938, and peaked at 8 million Germans during the war. About 15 percent of the members were women. The party endeavored to encompass most members of German society and keep them attuned to Nazi ideas and, wherever possible, under control of the regime through numerous affiliated organizations from the German Labor Front to the Hitler Youth, the Women's League, the Motor and Flying Corps, and leagues for teachers, lawyers, judges, physicians, students, stenographers, and others. As for the Nazi Party's governing role, the Hitler regime was vague on the relationship between party and state. There was no suggestion that the party was subordinated to the state, as was true of the Fascist Party and the Italian state. At the regional level, party officials like *Gauleiter* (regional leaders) were generally also appointed to the state post of Reich governor, combining party and state positions. As party officials, regional leaders theoretically had direct access to the Führer via his deputy Rudolf Hess and later Martin Bormann, director of Hitler's chancellery; but as Reich governors, they were subordinated to the Reich minister of the interior. Below the regional level, party and state offices were generally kept distinct and separately manned by appointees from the party and the state. Party officials at the county level, however, shared in the state appointment of those below. The overlap of lines of authority and the inclination of some of the top party leaders and Reich ministers to engage in rivalries led to conflicting relationships within the party, within the state, and between party and state. Hitler, who was loath to become involved in the petty squabbles of his underlings, stood in the position of ultimate decision maker and absolute ruler. The Führer's orders had the power of law and bypassed normal governmental channels. As the war dragged on, the power of top party officials like Bormann, the *Gauleiter* corps, and party functionaries at the county level increased in control over the state apparatus.

The elitist SS, commanded by Heinrich Himmler, increasingly assumed a very powerful and unique role in the Third Reich after the Röhm purge in 1934 and the formal separation of the SS from the paramilitary SA. Himmler championed a worldview that linked notions of a Germanic racial utopia with extreme nationalism and anti-Semitism. He became the architect of the Nazi system of control and terror, which he built with the help of the SS. The SS assumed police, state security, intelligence, and, in World War II, military functions. It was solely responsible for the murder of millions of Jews and other "enemies" of Nazi rule. The SS eventually became a state within a state with loyalty and ultimate responsibility only to the Führer. Its official motto was "Unsere Ehre heisst Treue" (Our honor is loyalty). Even though Himmler wielded enormous power, he remained one of Hitler's most faithful servants almost to the very end of the war. Mussolini's Italy with its party militia never developed an organization comparable to Hitler's praetorian guard SS.

The question inevitably arises: How totalitarian were the Fascist and Nazi dictatorships? The term *totalitarian* must be understood as an ideal type rather than a historical reality. No one regime, fascist or Communist, has been visualized as more than an approximation of a full model of totalitarianism. Mussolini's and Hitler's regimes had in common an ideology, a mass party, a one-man dictator, and the aim of achieving total control over a citizen's life. Whereas Hitler became unchallenged head of state and complete dictator in a little over a year, Mussolini never achieved such a position. He exercised personal rule over a party-state regime as head of the government. In his position as Duce of Italy and of the Fascist Party, he subordinated the party to the state. In his principal state role as prime minister or chief of government, he remained constitutionally responsible to the king, the head of state, who retained the right to appoint and dismiss him. The king was also the titular commander in chief of the armed forces until June 1940. When Mussolini became commander of the armed forces during the war, he lacked the staff to plan and carry out actions effectively and thus found that the army and especially the navy retained much of their autonomy. The military, the civil service, and the police swore their oath of loyalty to the king. The judiciary remained autonomous, and the police acted with more restraint than in Germany. There was no concentration-camp system in Fascist Italy, and the use of terror was relatively moderate. Artists and writers were left quite free to pursue their interests as long as they did not challenge the regime politically. Mussolini's personal rule was even overshadowed by the Fascist Grand Council, which acquired legal authority over party and state organizations. Although the Duce was able to control and ignore it during the heyday of his rule, it was the council's action in July 1943 that led to Mussolini's ouster. Overall, the Duce's dictatorship had to recognize the monarchy, the armed forces, the state apparatus, and the Catholic Church as significant centers of power and to incorporate them into the Fascist state rather than to confront them or attempt to control them completely. In sum, the Fascist regime originated the term *totalitarian*, but in its makeup and achievement, it can only be characterized as semitotalitarian at best.

The National Socialist system under Hitler was very definitely totalitarian in its aim and also in its achievement. Here the party assumed a much more important role than in Fascist Italy, and the Führer's party leadership position was further bolstered by his close relationship to the very powerful SS. In contrast to Mussolini, the Nazi dictator established a much more dominant state foundation for his one-man rule by combining the Reich presidency (head of state) with the chancellorship (head of government) after Hindenburg's death in 1934. From this combined office of Führer and Reich chancellor Hitler could not be legally removed and thus wielded virtually absolute power. The Nazi government established agencies and institutions to regulate the economic, professional, and cultural aspects of society. Hitler rejected economic corporatism, one of the hallmarks of Mussolini's system, because it appeared to foster autonomy for some of its elements, in favor of a structure of state controls and regulations. He exercised complete authority over the military, requiring a personal oath of loyalty and obedience of all soldiers (as was true of civil servants, judges, and others), and during the war he actually assumed operational command of the army. In contrast to Mussolini, Hitler had acquired extensive knowledge of military affairs and thus fancied himself superior to his generals in planning and implementing military actions.

Moreover, he could rely on the compliant staff of the supreme command of armed forces to carry out his orders. In short, Hitler and the Nazi state gained much more effective control over the state bureaucracy, the armed forces, the economy, and the society than Mussolini's regime. Perhaps the one institution over which the Nazis had only limited control was the church, both Protestant and Catholic, but not many of the intimidated clergy and church members were willing to risk imprisonment or death to stand up against the actions of the regime. The adulation and personal cult of Mussolini was paralleled by an elaborate Hitler cult orchestrated by Goebbels's propaganda machinery. Since Hitler could not be removed from power legally, as his Fascist partner was in 1943, when the war appeared to be lost, assassination of the Führer appeared to be the only option left to his sworn opponents.

The rise of fascism in Italy and Germany inspired fascist movements and parties in various European countries, but none of them produced a fascist regime of any duration. The absence of able charismatic fascist leaders and the presence of authoritarian and nationalist parties that dominated states in which fascist movements emerged inhibited, if not prevented, the establishment of fascist regimes. Spain under Francisco Franco appeared to have the prospect of becoming a fascist state when its military dictator made Falangism the basis of a united right-wing party in 1937. Had the Nazis and Fascists triumphed in World War II, Franco, who based his dictatorship on the army, most likely would have embraced fascism more overtly. But as authoritarian Caudillo, he kept the radical aspirations of the Falangists as much in check as he restrained Spanish expansionist designs. In Austria, a right-wing nationalist government thwarted a domestic Nazi coup d'état in 1934. In Hungary and Rumania, fascism and reactionary politics were intertwined, but not to the advantage of fascism. Under the moderate right-wing regime of Admiral Miklós Horthy, between 1922 and 1944, the fascist Arrow Cross Party was at times tolerated and much of the time combatted; it achieved power only briefly in 1944 when Horthy was ousted by the Germans. In Rumania, the Iron Guard, or Legion of the Archangel Michael, represented a notable fascist movement and party with a checkered history throughout the 1930s. The ultra-nationalist authoritarian General Ion Antonescu accepted fascist participation in his government in 1940 but violently suppressed it in the following year when fascist Legionaries threatened his authority. It is significant to note that the most effective opponents of fascist parties and their attempts to gain power were authoritarian right-wing or archconservative governments or regimes, not socialist, Communist, or democratic parties and governments. In Italy and Germany, a concerted effort of the authoritarian-minded political parties and the military under bolder leadership of the Italian monarchy and the German presidential government might well have thwarted Mussolini's and Hitler's ascent to power. Once the Fascist and Nazi dictators were firmly established, they were not easily dislodged. In Hitler's case, it took a world war to bring him down.

Fascist efforts to consolidate the nation through political, economic, and sociopsychological means were not ends in themselves but were designed to ready the people for the achievement of national greatness through imperial expansion. Italian Fascism and German Nazism shared the idea that nations (and races, according to Nazism) were engaged in a perpetual struggle for self-assertion and survival. Hitler's foreign policy went beyond traditional German expansionist efforts, striving to attain German living space and to restructure racial Europe under a Germanic territorial hegemony from the Atlantic to the depths of Russia. Mussolini's ambitions remained largely within the sphere of traditional Italian imperialist policy, pursuing colonial expansion and the exploitation of limited war in the Mediterranean area with the aim of achieving some kind of new Roman Empire. Even though Mussolini was the first to resort to war, he was pulled into a Europe-wide and soon world war (which he avoided when acting alone) through Hitler's reckless aggression. The fascist era in Europe came to an abrupt end in the spring of 1945 with the total military defeat of Nazi Germany and Hitler's suicide. Only two days before the Nazi dictator's violent end on April 30, Mussolini had been shot by Italian Communist partisans.

Fascism as an ultranationalist, imperialist, and even racial ideology and political system was entirely a European phenomenon closely tied to the personalities of Hitler and Mussolini. It was principally a German and Italian phenomenon, for it had only a limited impact upon states like Spain, Hungary, and Rumania, where internal fascist aspirations and movements became submerged in the political ambitions of traditional, albeit nationalist, military dictators. The legacy of Italian Fascism was moderate in destruction but significant in postwar institutional change. It prepared the end of monarchy in Italy and led to a more decentralized government once democracy was restored. But vehement Nazism inflicted a vast sea of material destruction, caused the loss of tens of millions of lives, and left memories of the horrors of genocide and of unprecedented dehumanization. Until quite recently, Germany and Europe were ideologically divided and dominated by two world powers as a reminder of fascism's defeat. Only the internal collapse of the Soviet Communist empire has finally restored Europe to its prewar state. On a similarly positive note, the utter defeat of the Third Reich also discredited racism, anti-Semitism, and extreme nationalism beyond the borders of Germany, if not Europe. Within Germany, the liquidation of a great many members of the German aristocracy by Hitler after the July 1944 assassination attempt weakened the rigidity of the traditional social structure and facilitated the opening of German society to liberal democratic values after the war. Given the massive defeat of fascism and the national, social, economic, and international changes that followed, it is not likely that a totalitarian fascist regime of the magnitude of Nazi Germany or Fascist Italy will arise in Europe. This would require certain cultural preconditions—a unique combination of a seductive nationalist ideology, a mass party led by a charismatic leader, and a developed society under severe socioeconomic stress—to respond to the all-or-nothing solutions of a future ruthless dictator.

But what about fascist groups and parties that seem to have sprung up in various European countries, sometimes within just a year or two after the total failure of the Italian and German fascist regimes, and have become quite notorious even in former Communist states in the wake of the collapse of the Soviet empire? Do such fascist movements represent a continuity of historic fascism? Most likely not. Just as there were varieties of fascism among the classic forms, so the postwar fascist groups are different enough to be seen as something less than a direct continuity of the Italian Fascist or the German Nazi parties. The several different kinds of fascist organizations and parties that emerged after World War II are best characterized as a form of neofascism.[1] They profess a number of ideas that carry over from the fascist age—zealous nationalism, belief in the dominance of the state and the pureness of the people, an antipathy toward liberal-democratic values and institutions, and rejection of American hegemony and earlier Soviet domination—but they frequently favor international contacts and have a concern for the future of Europe, which they envision as a collaborative new Europe based on "Eurofascism." It is also very important to distinguish neofascist groups from moderate to radical rightist parties, many of which accept their role within the liberal-democratic order. On the other hand, some of the most extremist neofascist factions have embraced terrorism as a means of political action. A brief survey of some of the representative neofascist parties in Italy, Germany, France, and eastern Europe will exemplify some of the particulars.

In Italy, the motherland of Fascism, the first major neofascist party, the Movimento Sociale Italiano (Italian Social Movement, MSI), was organized in December 1946 with a hefty influx of supporters of Mussolini's Republic of Salò. It espoused strong nationalism, centralized state power, a bold foreign policy, and the establishment of a corporate state in which workers and employers were full partners. It also accepted Catholicism as the prevailing state religion. Due to a constitutional prohibition of fascism, the MSI could not openly embrace Mussolini's ideas, but its leanings were more toward fascism than toward the radical right. Factors that favored the early development of Italian neofascism, even though executions (or plain murder) by political groups toward the end of the war had claimed the lives of close to 15,000 Fascists, were the short defascistization efforts that followed and the weakness of the postwar Italian democracy in coping with the arduous internal and social problems. By 1953 the MSI was receiving 5.9 percent electoral support, which put it among the most successful neofascist or extreme right-wing parties of Europe.

In its strategy the MSI pursued a double course: it propagated ideas and tactics reminiscent of the "good" government of Mussolini, but also asserted that not everything about fascism was suitable for today. It purported to represent a party that was "postfascist." Far from being monolithic, the MSI was divided into right, left, and center factions. At times it promoted violence in the streets, and some of the dissident groups that broke off resorted to terroristic bombings that emulated the violence of the leftist Red Brigades. But already in the 1950s and 1960s there were intermittent party efforts to collaborate with moderate centrist forces, emphasizing electoral and parliamentary tactics. Starting in 1969, under the leadership of the former Fascist Giorgio Almirante, the MSI pursued a more isolationist course that mixed conservative moderation with radical action while keeping its official distance from the neofascist terrorist groups. By the early 1980s the moderates increasingly won out in the divided party, and more pragmatic policies were adopted, even though the party continued to affirm the Fascist past as a historic legacy.

A crisis in the postwar Italian party system opened the opportunity for the MSI, now under the pragmatic leadership of Gian Franco Fini, to escape from its political wilderness and to score remarkable electoral successes in 1993 and 1994. This came about only when the MSI joined a broader National Alliance with former right-wing Christian Democrats and conservatives. The National Alliance positioned itself as a parliamentary and nationalist right-wing party, and the MSI was a major beneficiary. Under this alignment, Mussolini is still respected as a "great statesman," but, according to Fini, Fascism is "not repeatable." The local elections of 1993, in which Fini almost reached the mayor's seat of Rome and Alessandra Mussolini, the granddaughter of the Duce, barely missed being elected mayor of Naples, presaged the achievement in the national elections of 1994: in March the National Alliance gained 13.5 percent of the vote and sent 107 deputies to parliament, the overwhelming majority of whom came from the MSI. The National Alliance was now the third-largest party in Italy. With five seats in the new ministry, fascists now held government posts for the first time since the end of World War II. In June eleven National Alliance members were elected to the European Parliament, where they had four seats before. Even though some feared that behind the parliamentary facade of the MSI lurked a totalitarian fascist core, Fini and his party alliance had attracted unexpected support from a broader electorate and had also gained growing respect even from opponents.

Neo-Nazism in Germany never matched the burgeoning of neofascism in Italy. After four years of Allied military government, the Federal Republic of (West) Germany was established in 1949. Numerous trials of war criminals in the aftermath of the war were supposed to help the German public comprehend the evil side of Nazi policies and of their perpetrators. In West Germany, denazification was prolonged and quite thorough, albeit not always successful. But the economic miracle that gave West Germany prosperity less than ten years after the war especially contributed to the containment of the growth of Nazism in postwar Germany. The utter defeat of the German armies could not help but also discredit Nazism. Finally, once West Germany regained its own government, it operated under a constitution that outlawed Nazi activities.

Nevertheless, various groups emerged by 1948 that advocated ultranationalist and even neo-Nazi policies. Only one of them, the Socialist Reich Party, achieved some prominence before it was outlawed by the West German Supreme Court in 1952 as a neo-Nazi organization. In practice, it operated legally as a right-wing radical group but without being able to conceal its neo-Nazi leanings, especially since its supporters were mainly Nazis and discontented war veterans. The adherents of the outlawed Socialist Reich Party splintered into numerous grouplets of no political significance after the party's dissolution. Archconservatives, reactionaries, and right-wing radicals could find a home in the two more moderate radical right parties, the National Democratic Party (NPD) and the German Reich Party (DRP). The NPD was the more important of the two, with 56,000 members in the late 1950s. It carefully differentiated itself from neo-Nazi taint by stressing adherence to conservative values and the "national idea." However, all its efforts to gain representation in the federal parliament failed because it never mustered the required 5 percent minimum electoral support in national elections.

As the popularity of the NPD waned, the place of a radical right party was taken by the Republican Party in 1983. On the eve of German reunification, it was scoring regional electoral successes in West Berlin and several West German states and also sent a few members to the European Parliament. Its political concerns, apart from denying any neo-Nazi connections, concentrated on immigration restrictions, the presence of foreign minorities, and the growing prevalence of crime. This moderate right authoritarian party fared poorly during the reunification events and has declined in importance. Neo-Nazi activities were somewhat on the increase in the 1980s and 1990s when neo-Nazi youth groups, "skinheads," and a few individuals perpetrated acts of violence and terrorism, bringing them wide publicity. Such groups, though boisterous and violent, are generally sects made up of youthful admirers of some of Hitler's ideas, but they do not muster any electoral following or political significance. Overall, efforts to generate neo-Nazism in Germany have failed.

Elsewhere in Europe, the phenomenon of neofascism must be examined in its varied impact and threat. Spain experienced considerable extreme rightist and neofascist terrorism in the 1970s and 1980s, but the beginning of democracy after Franco's death in 1975 did not bring a significant emergence of an ultraright or neofascist force. The inefficient Franco regime left a residue of hate among many, and the Socialists proved to be popular and prestigious. When they began to falter, many Spanish turned to the conservatives, leaving the party that identified with the old Franco regime on the sidelines.

France largely escaped neofascist and ultraright terrorism in the decades after the war. Memories of the German occupation and the Vichy regime discredited any neofascist group that might have tried to establish itself. However, France produced two major movements that were rooted in the politics of the right. In the 1950s Pierre Poujade generated a following that used antiliberal, nationalist, anti-Semitic, and antiforeign slogans to promote the interests of farmers and small traders. This movement failed to create a lasting political organization. More significant has been the National Front that Jean-Marie Le Pen formed by uniting various right-wing splinter groups in the 1980s. This rightist-nationalist movement or party opposes immigration, foreign minorities, and crime; it rejects modern egalitarianism and supports law and order. In the parliamentary and presidential elections in the 1980s, the party gained between 9.9 and 15 percent of the popular vote and at its high point sent thirty-two deputies to the French parliament. This representation has been greatly reduced. In the 1993 election, the party failed to gain an assembly seat, even though it received 12.5 percent of the popular vote. The success of the National Front has been mainly due to Le Pen's image and effectiveness as a leader, but its role has been more that of a protest movement than a party that expects to gain power or that can offer effective alternatives to the problems of France.

Even though neofascism and the extreme right have found a niche in most western European countries since the end of World War II and, from time to time, show flashy electoral advances, they have not secured a permanent base in the political culture of these societies that could be expanded into an authoritarian regime. It is too early to assume that neofascist movements in western Europe have been tamed and have come to embrace parliamentary democracy, given their authoritarian approach and outlook. However, it is difficult to imagine that these parties could break out of the parliamentary mold of Western politics and sustain an authoritarian approach even in times of economic crises.

Since the fall of communism, ultranationalist movements and some neofascist and a few neo-Nazi groups have cropped up in all eastern European states, with the possible exception of Bulgaria. In Hungary, the land of the Arrow Cross, several neofascist groups have been organized but have played no role in the political arena. Even Hungarian right-wing followers have not achieved much political significance due to limited popular support. The situation is not much different in Rumania, where the ruling party is following a nationalist course and thus discourages the expansion of right-wing movements. Marshal Ion Antonescu, executed as a war criminal after World War II, was rehabilitated as a national hero in 1991 with quite wide support from the populace, and not just from the right. He was remembered by much of the Rumanian media as "Rumania's greatest anti-Communist." Neofascist groups have had little chance to compete successfully with the Rumanian radical right, since it was Antonescu who had eliminated the Iron Guard in 1941, and there is very little of the checkered pre–World War II heritage of Rumanian fascism that can be revived. In Russia, several neofascist-leaning groups like Pamyat emerged on the eve of the collapse of communism but had a short life. Much more notorious has been the maverick extreme right-wing Liberal Democratic Party led by Vladimir Zhirinovsky, which gained 25 percent of the vote in the first free parliamentary election in 1993. Zhirinovsky's use of shocking ideas and provocative schemes, some of which are contradictory, has brought him a temporary following, but his political future remains uncertain.

Neofascism, let alone neo-Nazism, has thus far made no headway in winning significant support in any of the former Communist states. Dictatorship and fascism have been much discredited in eastern Europe as a result of the Communist rule and because of earlier interwar fascism followed by German military occupation. But nationalism is again readily accepted and is being turned into a political force. The nationalist authoritarian dictatorship of the former Communist Slobodan Milošević of Serbia and the conservative nationalist authoritarian regime of Franjo Tudjman of Croatia have brought unexpectedly bloody havoc to their regions, defying international pressure and intervention. But these regimes have not embraced neofascism, even though their ethnocentric nationalism and racism are reminiscent of Nazism.

If the prospects for fascism in Europe, where it made its appearance and reached its highest state, are not promising, has it found a home elsewhere in the world? A number of historians have characterized the Argentinian Perónist regime of 1946–1955, which championed nationalism and social reform, as a form of fascism. Others have dismissed Perónism as a native political movement that was devoid of fascist features. It cannot be denied that Perónism had certain traits of European fascism: the aim (but not the achievement) of a single-party regime, some cultural and philosophical ideas borrowed from European fascism, and expansive foreign policy goals. Yet these characteristics were not sufficient to give the Perónist government the stamp of a full fascist dictatorship. If one takes extreme nationalism, racism, ethnocentrism, one-party political regimes, charismatic leadership, and revolutionary or radical economic and social policies aiming to transform entire societies to be the hallmarks of fascism, then these characteristics can be found in various Middle Eastern and African states, but never all combined in one. Therefore, it is meaningful to point out certain fascist features in the Egyptian regime of Gamal Abdel Nasser in the 1950s and 1960s, the Libyan dictatorship of Muammar al-Qaddafi, the Syrian rule of Hafez al-Assad, and especially the Iraqi dictatorship of Saddam Hussein, but to consider even the most tyrannical and thorough of these regimes a revived total fascist dictatorship would fall short of the full meaning and practice of traditional European fascism in the first half of the twentieth century.

Fascism rose and fell in Europe. It did not develop into a mass movement and a major political force in Italy and Germany just because a new ideology had burst upon the scene, even though its varied ideas inspired many of its followers. Rather, it came about as the product of a combination of factors: distinctive national traditions in states that had only recently achieved their nationhood, a comparatively new state system with early beginnings of liberal democracy but strong organized nationalism, the actions of both fascist and nonfascist leaders, a condition of perceived or actual national defeat or humiliation, distressing socioeconomic and cultural crisis, and a society in which large segments of the people, especially of the lower classes, had lost confidence in the existing political system. It is notable that classical fascism did not become established as a viable political system outside the motherland of Fascism and the fatherland of Nazism except where, propelled by its perceived mission, it was planted by conquest in war and occupation, and then only temporarily. The failure of fascism after 1945 in western Europe can be explained by the absence of most of the factors found in Italy and Germany after the turn of the century and after World War I. In these countries, including Germany and Italy, the immense cultural, social, and economic changes, accompanied by the maturation of democratic political institutions during the last half-century, have made the return of fascism even in a time of severe economic crisis nearly impossible. The same, however, cannot be assumed about the eastern European successor states of the former Soviet Union, Russia itself, and some regions of the former Yugoslavia, all of which have remained relatively untouched by the deep transformations that European societies have experienced in the last fifty years. Even though it is unlikely that traditional fascism can be reenacted as a political system in countries like Russia, Ukraine, Belarus, or Serbia, the emergence of authoritarian nationalist-imperialist regimes could become a new threatening challenge to the West at a future time.

NOTE

1. For a more detailed discussion of neofascism in postwar Europe, see Stanley G. Payne, *A History of Fascism, 1914–1945* (Madison: University of Wisconsin Press, 1995), 496–520; Walter Laqueur, *Fascism: Past, Present, Future* (New York: Oxford University Press, 1996), 93–235; and Roger Eatwell, *Fascism: A History* (New York: Allen Lane Penguin Press, 1996), 245–362.

Biographies: The Personalities Behind Fascism in Europe

Galeazzo Ciano, 1903–1944

Galeazzo Ciano achieved distinction as an Italian statesman and diplomat during the Fascist era. He was born on March 18, 1903, in Livorno, Italy, the son of Constanzo Ciano, who was named Count of Cortellazzo by the king following his war service. Young Ciano completed his law education in Rome in 1925, where his father was serving as a minister in Mussolini's government. After dabbling in journalism and playwriting while pursuing his university education, Ciano entered the foreign service in 1925 and was assigned to diplomatic posts in South America and China. After his recall to Italy, he married Edda Mussolini, Benito Mussolini's eldest child, in 1930 and then returned to China as consul general in Shanghai and later minister plenipotentiary in Peking. In 1933 he was appointed chief of the Duce's press bureau. In the following year he became under secretary of state and in 1935 minister for press and propaganda. An enthusiastic aviator, he served as the commander of a bomber squadron during the Ethiopian war and returned home with several medals for valor. In June 1936, at age thirty-three, he was named foreign minister, much to the surprise, if not shock, of Italian and foreign observers. His rapid rise through the ranks, combined with his arrogance and driving ambition, had made him few friends among the party elders.

In the operation of the Foreign Ministry, Ciano was intent on centralizing ministerial power and conducting diplomacy largely based on his friendships and antipathies among foreign diplomats. His considerable influence during his early years as foreign minister derived from his close relationship with his father-in-law. At the beginning he deviated very little from Mussolini's foreign policy. As minister for press and propaganda, he mobilized the mass media in support of the Ethiopian conquest. As foreign minister, he succeeded in having League of Nations sanctions eased against Italy. In 1936 he prevailed upon a reluctant Mussolini to intervene in Spain rather than to leave it solely to Nazi German intrusion, greatly underestimating the cost to Italy. He welcomed a rapprochement with Germany and, on a visit to Germany, helped establish the Rome-Berlin Axis. In 1937 Ciano was instrumental in aligning Italy with Germany and Japan in the Anti-Comintern Pact. Perhaps his most important diplomatic achievement was his successful effort to thwart France's role in the Balkans. By organizing a coalition of Yugoslavia, Hungary, and Rumania, he neutralized the Little Entente that France had forged in 1921.

Hitler's unilateral annexation of Austria was accepted by the Duce, but Ciano viewed it as a violation of the Axis agreement. The Italian foreign minister was also surprised by the Führer's decision to add the Sudetenland to the German Reich and was angered by Germany's occupation of Bohemia and Moravia and the establishment of Slovakia as a dependent state in March 1939. He reluctantly went along when Mussolini directed him to discuss with Nazi foreign minister Joachim von Ribbentrop Hermann Göring's proposal of the year before to transform the Anti-Comintern Pact into an alliance. In May 1939 Italy and Germany concluded the Pact of Steel. To counteract German influence in the Mediterranean, Ciano energetically pursued intervention in the Balkans, culminating in the invasion of Albania in April 1939 under his direction. The poorly coordinated campaign turned out to be a much more difficult undertaking than Ciano had anticipated. In a way, it was the prelude for the disastrous Italian invasion of Greece that was launched in October 1940.

Ciano's growing fear of German power and his realization of Italy's lack of military preparedness led him to insist on Italian neutrality when Hitler prepared an invasion of Poland in August 1939. Both he and Mussolini were outraged by the Nazi-Soviet Nonaggression Pact. Hitler accepted Italy's nonbelligerence. However, when the German armies invaded the Low Countries and France in May 1940 and France was on the verge of falling, Ciano supported Italy's entry into the war to ensure that Italy did not lose out on war spoils. Ciano even returned to brief service as a bomber pilot.

Various setbacks and especially Italy's military failure in Greece following the October 1940 invasion, which in part was viewed as "Ciano's war," diminished the foreign minister's standing when he returned to the ministry in 1941. Mussolini was losing confidence in him and even became suspicious when rumors spread in early 1943 that he was plotting the overthrow of the Duce. Ciano was forced out of office in February 1943 and appointed Italian ambassador to the Holy See. He was indeed aware of the conspiracies to remove the Fascist dictator and at the July 24–25, 1943, meeting of the Fascist Grand Council voted for Dino Grandi's motion to return to the king the power to conduct the war. Following Mussolini's forced resignation, Ciano was arrested by the Badoglio government and investigated on charges of embezzlement. He fled to Germany and naïvely expected to be allowed to move to South America, but was detained by Nazi authorities. Upon Mussolini's liberation by a German commando in September 1943 and his establishment as the head of the Italian Social Republic, the Germans delivered Ciano into the hands of the rump Mussolini regime. Together with several other Mussolini opponents, he was tried for treason and promptly executed by a shot in the back on January 11, 1944, in Verona. His wife Edda made a vain attempt to save her husband's life through intervention with her father and by threatening the Germans with the publication of the Ciano diaries abroad.

Francisco Franco, 1892–1975

Francisco Franco was a general and leader of the Nationalist forces that overthrew the democratic Republic during the Spanish Civil War, 1936–1939, and established an authoritarian dictatorship. As head of the government of Spain, often called El Caudillo (the Leader), he ruled Spain for nearly forty years. He is often characterized as a fascist ruler and was branded by hostile foreign opinion as the "last surviving Fascist dictator" after the end of World War II. However, even though he used the fascist Falange Party, especially in the early stages of his rule, he never embraced its ideology nor permitted it to dictate his policies. His regime was based on the support of the military, the church, monarchists, and the conservative Spanish elite.

Francisco Franco y Bahamonde was born on December 4, 1892, in El Ferrol, Galicia Province, in Spain, the son of a Spanish administrative naval officer. Although he was originally destined for a career as a naval officer, he had to settle for the army and graduated from the Toledo Infantry Academy at age seventeen. The youthful Franco won rapid promotion in the colonial campaigns in Morocco, becoming the youngest captain in the Spanish army in 1915, and in the 1920s emerged as the head of the Spanish Legion in Morocco, attaining the rank of brigadier general at the age of thirty-three. In 1928 he was appointed commander of Spain's new military academy at Zaragoza and served there during the last years of the monarchy until its end in 1931. In his politics, Franco was conservative to reactionary and disdained leftists and even liberals, but often remained silent on political questions and generally pursued a cautious course.

During the Republican period between 1931 and 1936, Franco's military career was temporarily compromised. The first liberal Republican government exiled him to island command posts outside Spain. When conservative Republican forces gained control, he was fully reinstated, was promoted to major general, and helped suppress a rebellion of Asturian miners in October 1934. This new prominence resulted in his elevation to chief of the Spanish army's general staff in 1935. However, following the leftist Popular Front election victory early in 1936, he was removed to the Canary Islands and in July joined the military conspiracy against the government. On July 18, 1936, he issued a manifesto proclaiming a military rebellion from the Canary Islands and soon landed in Spain. His march on Madrid was thwarted on the outskirts of the city, and it required three more years to subdue all of Spain to his control. As the commanding general of the rebel forces during the Civil War, he made generally cautious moves but managed to advance slowly but steadily with his army, which was regarded as superior in quality to the forces of the Republican government. A significant factor in Franco's military success was continuing heavy German and Italian military support, though his strategy of military attrition was what wore his opponents down. The war was accompanied by widespread atrocities on both sides, and Franco's regime continued with tens of thousands of executions in the first years after the war ended.

Franco's military ability and prestige as well as his proven ability to gain assistance from Nazi Germany and Fascist Italy made him the natural choice for head of the new Nationalist government. He formally assumed this political role on October 1, 1936. He presided over a basically military dictatorship whose civil support was derived largely from the antileftist middle classes. In April 1937 he reorganized the Falange (Spanish fascist party) by creating a union of Falangists, traditional monarchists, and other members of various rightist groups who were willing to join. Franco insisted from the start that it was the government that used the party rather than the other way around. Similarly, the military junta was receiving the support of the Catholic Church. Thus the authoritarian state that came into existence under Franco was never dominated by a monolithic ideological movement but differed from the fascist state models found in Germany and Italy.

When war broke out in September 1939, Franco announced Spain's neutrality. He was keenly aware of his country's exhaustion after three years of costly internecine war, as well as Britain's sea power. His wartime diplomacy was based on realism and good timing and served Spanish interests well. It is likely that if Hitler had been in a position to achieve total victory in the war, Franco would have joined the Axis. He remained fairly sympathetic to Germany's side but denied Hitler the support that he wanted from Spain to take Gibraltar. After a protracted, frustrating interview with Franco on the French-Spanish border in October 1940, Hitler remarked that he would prefer to have three or four teeth pulled rather than face another such session. Yet in 1941 the vehemently anti-Communist Caudillo sent the Spanish Blue Division to fight on the eastern front after Hitler's attack on the Soviet Union. It remained there until March 1944. After World War II, the Spanish government was confronted by the ostracism of the newly formed United Nations. Franco was in part saved economically by a timely commercial treaty offered by the Argentine dictator Juan Perón. As relations worsened between the Soviet Union and the West during the Cold War, Franco was viewed as an anti-Communist statesman, and relations with the West were noticeably regularized starting in 1948. His international standing improved further when the United States entered into an agreement with Spain in 1953 to establish American air and naval bases on Spanish soil.

Franco's domestic policies were somewhat liberalized during the 1950s and 1960s. However, he insisted on keeping the reins of government in his hands to the very end. By referendum, he turned Spain into a monarchy in 1947 while ensuring his own powers as a sort of regent for life. In 1969 he named Juan Carlos, the eldest son of the nominal pretender to the Spanish throne, as his official successor upon his death. Also, starting in 1967, he allowed direct elections for a small minority of deputies to the parliament and significantly moderated censorship in the country. When he died on November 20, 1975, in Madrid, he left a legacy that his successors could begin to transform into a more modern and, after some difficulty, liberal state.

Joseph Goebbels, 1897–1945

Joseph Goebbels became the Nazi movement's master propagandist, chief promoter of the Führer myth, and dictator of media policy and cultural life during the Third Reich. Born in Rheydt in the Rhineland on October 29, 1897, Goebbels grew up in a strict Catholic lower-middle-class family. His father was the head clerk in a small factory. Diminutive in physical stature, Goebbels was also handicapped by a lame right leg and club foot, caused by osteomyelitis in his early boyhood. Rejected for military service during World War I, he pursued university studies in literature and philosophy and obtained a doctorate in literature from the University of Heidelberg in 1921. His efforts to launch a literary career were thwarted, however, for his plays and novels went unpublished, and he failed to obtain a journalism job at the prestigious liberal *Berliner Tageblatt*. After experiencing a political awakening, he joined the Nazi Party in 1924 and became noted as a rabid anti-Semitic speaker, appearing frequently at meetings of extremist nationalist groups. Aware of his oratorical talent, he learned to combine it with a flair for theatrical effects that was to make him, next to Hitler, the most electrifying public speaker of the Nazi movement.

Goebbels's early association with Nazism was with the left wing of the party that was led by Gregor Strasser and emphasized the socialist elements in the party's program. As leading spokesman of the Strasser group in the Rhineland, both in speeches and in articles, Goebbels took issue with the economic and social moderation of various Nazi ideologists and, by implication, Adolf Hitler. However, his political life took a turn after he met Hitler in 1925. One year later, at the Bamberg conference of party delegates and under the sway of the Führer's personality, he switched sides. Hitler rewarded "the little Doctor" by appointing him *Gauleiter* (regional leader) of Berlin and entrusting him with the task of reorganizing the fractured Nazi Party in the national capital. Goebbels's performance lived up to the Führer's expectations. He established his own weekly newspaper called *Der Angriff* (The attack), staged mass rallies, mobilized SA troops to participate in street battles, and fearlessly took his agitation into working-class districts of the city, where socialists and Communists dominated. When Nazi comrades were killed in street or beer-hall brawls, they were solemnly celebrated as martyrs of the cause. One of them, the student Horst Wessel, who was murdered by a rival over a prostitute, was transformed into the supreme Nazi martyr, and his marching SA song became part of the national anthem after 1933.

Basically, Goebbels lacked deep inner convictions and instrumentalized propaganda in an opportunistic, if not cynical, fashion. He considered it his mission to create an image of Hitler for the German public that viewed him as a savior from Jews and Marxists, leading the nation into a heroic future. In the election campaigns of 1932, he excelled in mass persuasion to put Hitler and the Nazis in the center of the political stage. In March 1933 an appreciative Führer appointed his faithful propagandist servant Reich minister of public enlightenment and propaganda. Goebbels quickly exploited this position to gain control of Germany's radio, press, publishing houses, theaters, film industry, and the other arts. One of his first acts as propaganda minister was to call for a boycott of Jewish businesses on April 1. It proved a failure when the majority of the population rejected it. One month later he staged a public burning of books in Berlin, consisting of the works of Jewish, Marxist, and other "undesirable" authors.

At times, Goebbels had to moderate his radical attacks on Jews and other opponents of the Nazi regime due to foreign policy considerations, but on November 9, 1938, he unleashed, while Hitler remained the disguised mover, the *Kristallnacht* (Night of the Broken Glass) pogrom against German Jewry that cost the lives of 91 Jews and resulted in the imprisonment of close to 30,000 Jewish men, the destruction of thousands of Jewish businesses, and the torching of hundreds of synagogues. Goebbels probably expected to regain Hitler's approbation through this infamous anti-Semitic action after he had incurred the Führer's wrath over his passionate love affair with a Czech actress that threatened his marriage. Considering Jews and Gypsies "unconditionally exterminable," he later personally supervised the deportation of Berlin Jews in 1942 with Hitler's full support.

With the outbreak of the war, Goebbels's influence appeared to be slipping. He was not included in the decisions on foreign and military policy. However, after the euphoria of early successes wore off due to the worsening of the war situation for Germany, his star began to rise. When the Allies insisted on unconditional surrender at Casablanca in early 1943, he proclaimed that Germany had no choice except victory or destruction. In February, after the capitulation of Stalingrad, in an emotionally charged speech in Berlin's Sportspalast, he called for mobilization for total war to the thunderous applause of the assembled audience. Months later he prophetically wrote in a Nazi weekly, "We shall go down in history as the greatest statesmen of all time, or as the greatest criminals."[1] To steel the morale of the German populace in the face of mounting military setbacks, he desperately kept alive fantasies of final victory and promises of secret wonder weapons until the very end. When Hitler prepared for his suicide in his Berlin bunker, he appointed Goebbels Reich chancellor, but after only one day in office, the propaganda magician followed his master by taking his own life and that of his wife and six children at the same site on May 1, 1945.

Hermann Göring, 1893–1946

Hermann Wilhelm Göring achieved his prominence as president of the Reichstag, Prussian minister president, commander in chief of the Luftwaffe, and Hitler's deputy and designated successor, "Number Two" in the Third Reich. Born in Rosenheim, Bavaria, on January 12, 1893, Göring grew up in an upper-class family. Impressed by the nationalist and imperialist ideology of his Prussian officer father, young Hermann chose a military career, attended military colleges, and was commissioned in the Imperial German Army. At the outbreak of World War I in 1914, he was an infantry lieutenant, but before long, he joined the Imperial German Air Force as a fighter pilot. He became known as one of the best World War I fighters and was decorated with the highest order, the Pour le Mérite, and the Iron Cross, First Class. In 1918 he was promoted to commander of the Manfred Richthofen Fighter Squadron.

Göring's heroic outlook on life that he had acquired as a Prussian officer and through the comradeship among flyers in the war clashed with the reality of German defeat in 1918 and left him in a state of personal and professional uncertainty. After discharge from the military, he served as a commercial and stunt pilot in Denmark and Sweden for several years. In Sweden, he met his first wife, the aristocratic Karin von Kantzow, with whom he moved to Munich early in 1922. Here he came into contact with the rising Nazi Party, which appeared to offer him the prospect of action and power, loyalty and comradeship. Göring's fame as a fighter pilot and his aristocratic credentials made him a welcome recruit to the fledgling Nazi Party. Hitler, who exerted a considerable spell on the political novice, assigned him the command of the party's paramilitary Storm Troopers or SA Brownshirts in December 1922.

In November 1923 Göring was at Hitler's side in the Munich Beer Hall Putsch and was seriously wounded by a gunshot to his hip. He was arrested, but escaped and fled to Austria. During his convalescence, he lived in Italy and Sweden, where he was forced to attend a clinic for nervous disorders to be cured of the addiction to medical morphine that he had acquired due to the lingering pain of his wound. A political amnesty permitted him to return to Germany in 1927 and to rejoin the Nazi Party. Within a year he was elected to the Reichstag as one of twelve Nazi deputies. During the critical years 1927 to 1934, Göring struggled for power within the Nazi movement and together with Hitler in Germany. More attracted to Hitler's strong personality than to the party, he was instrumental in providing social respectability and contacts with conservative circles and important leaders of big business and industry, all of which helped the Nazi Party to score electoral and political successes. Following the Nazi triumph in the July 1932 election, Göring attained the Reichstag presidency. Upon Hitler's appointment to the chancellorship in January 1933, Göring was rewarded by being named cabinet minister without portfolio, Prussian minister of the interior, thereby taking charge of the largest German police force, and Reich commissioner for aviation. In addition, he was also appointed Prussian minister president. He turned the conservative Prussian police into a state instrument that used ruthless force and terror in crushing political resistance to the Nazi regime. The Reichstag fire of February 1933 gave him a pretext to order the arrest of thousands of Communists, some Social Democrats, and other Nazi opponents and to suspend civil rights.

Göring's own consolidation of power within the Nazi political state was significantly enhanced when he helped mastermind the elimination of his rival Ernst Röhm and other SA leaders during the Blood Purge of June 1934. At the end of the year, he gave up his position as Hitler's minister of police and ceded the leadership of the Gestapo to Heinrich Himmler. However, he was compensated by being appointed Reich forest master and Reich master of the hunt. In March 1935 Hitler named him commander in chief of the newly created Luftwaffe (air force) and entrusted him with the task of the rapid buildup of the aircraft industry and the training of military flyers. In the following year he gained control of economic policy making in Germany as commissioner for the implementation of the Four-Year Plan. Göring's attempt to gain control of the army through intrigue against Field Marshal Werner von Blomberg and General Werner Freiherr von Fritsch was thwarted by Hitler, who assuaged his deputy by giving him a field marshal's baton. One year later, at the outbreak of the war, Hitler officially designated him as his deputy and successor, and in 1940 he named him the first and only Reich marshal.

During the Poland crisis in August 1939, when Hitler was driving events toward war, Göring attempted to limit or prevent it by using Swedish contacts. His doubts about Germany's ability to endure an all-out war were evident when he exclaimed after the British declaration of war had been received on September 3, "If we lose this war, then God help us!"[2] The witty and charming, but also vain, pompous, and egomaniac number two Nazi enjoyed considerable popularity among the German populace, but when, contrary to his assurances, the Luftwaffe failed to wipe out the Allied forces at Dunkirk, fumbled during the Battle of Britain, scored only limited successes against the Soviet Union, and proved unable to protect Germany against massive Allied bombing raids, he lost the confidence of the German people in his leadership and Hitler's as well. The latter in fact became contemptuous of him. Göring's effort to take the reins of power during Hitler's last days in the Berlin bunker led to his expulsion from the party and dismissal from all offices. A temporary arrest by the SS was soon followed by U.S. capture. Tried by the International Military Tribunal at Nuremberg in 1945–1946 and condemned to death, he escaped the hangman's noose by taking cyanide, which he had managed to conceal during his captivity, two hours before his scheduled execution on October 15, 1946.

Dino Grandi, 1895–1988

Dino Grandi was a major figure in Italy's Fascist regime. He was born on June 4, 1895, in Mordano, Italy, the son of a landowner of middle-sized holdings. Educated as a lawyer, he served as a journalist in several nationalist-liberal groups before joining the Italian military in World War I. He received several decorations for valor and attained the rank of captain. After demobilization, he pursued journalism and law and in 1920 joined the Fascist movement. Within a year, he emerged as the leader of a faction within the Fascist movement that disagreed with Mussolini on the issue of pacifying socialist and other groups; he also was opposed to turning the Fascist movement into a party, as Mussolini advocated in late 1921, fearing that this would compromise the future of Fascism. Even though Grandi offered strong opposition to the Fascist leader, he did not break with him, realizing that Fascism could not survive without Mussolini. In October 1922 Grandi participated in the March on Rome that established Mussolini as prime minister.

Grandi's political career received a new boost in 1924 when he was reelected to parliament and chosen vice president of the Chamber of Deputies. He supported Mussolini in the Matteotti affair, believing in the Duce's innocence. In succession he was appointed under secretary of the interior and of foreign affairs. In 1929 he was named minister of foreign affairs. He hoped to use this position to limit the dominance of France on the Continent and to create an expansive Italian colonial empire in Africa. These aims were to be achieved without war and by working through the machinery of the League of Nations. Even though his determination seemed to produce results by 1932, his policies were viewed with suspicion in European diplomatic circles due to his extreme anti-French attitude and indiscreet meddling in the domestic affairs of Austria and Yugoslavia. Mussolini removed him from the foreign ministry and assumed personal control of foreign affairs. Grandi was dispatched as ambassador to London, where he remained until 1939. Here he established contact with members of the British elite and gained a new perspective on world affairs.

Even though Grandi became increasingly critical of Mussolini's policies after the conquest of Ethiopia, which brought closer relations with Nazi Germany and Japan, he remained loyal to the Duce. He fended off severe sanctions against Italy following the invasion of Ethiopia and worked hard to preserve friendly Italo-English relations. Grandi recognized that a careful tactical approach to Germany could strengthen Italy's position in its relations with Britain and France, but he was resolute that if a European war were to break out, Italy must remain in the Anglo-French camp. Mussolini, on the other hand, felt compelled to demonstrate his friendship with

Germany after concluding the Pact of Steel in May 1939 by recalling the anti-German Grandi from London.

Upon his return to Italy, Grandi was appointed minister of justice and president of the Chamber of Fasces and Corporations. He supported Count Ciano in his effort to keep Italy out of the war in the August–September 1939 crisis and continued to pressure Mussolini to refrain from taking precipitous action in the spring of 1940. However, only after Italy's condition worsened due to its defeats in Africa and the Allied invasion of Sicily was Grandi ready to act against Mussolini. At the meeting of the Fascist Grand Council on the night of July 24–25, 1943, he introduced a motion calling for restitution of the king's prerogatives as commander in chief of the armed forces. The motion passed overwhelmingly and enabled Victor Emmanuel to demand Mussolini's resignation. In mid-August Grandi went to Portugal to initiate negotiations for an armistice with the Allies, but his mission was futile since Marshal Pietro Badoglio's government had already established contact with the Allies. American objections denied Grandi a return to Italy, and he remained in Lisbon and then moved on to Brazil. As the chief conspirator against Mussolini, Grandi was sentenced to death in absentia by a Fascist tribunal in 1944. He returned to Bologna in the 1950s and died there on May 21, 1988.

Heinrich Himmler, 1900–1945

Emerging from the middle ranks of the Nazi movement, Heinrich Himmler in the course of a decade and a half came to hold enormous power that was second only to that of Adolf Hitler. As Reichsführer SS (Reich leader of the SS), head of the police, including the Gestapo, and the Waffen SS (fighting arm of the SS), and eventually also minister of the interior, he commanded the Nazi system of institutional control and terror. He presided over a huge concentration-camp empire and was the organizer of the mass program of destruction of millions of Jews and other "undesirables" as the Nazi armies marched through Europe.

Himmler was born in Munich on October 7, 1900, into a respectable, cultured, pious, middle-class Catholic family. His father was a schoolteacher and had once served as tutor of Bavarian royalty. Young Himmler was a star pupil at a secondary school and, after serving as an officer cadet toward the end of World War I, earned a diploma in agriculture from the Technical University in Munich. He never succeeded in civilian life and quite early found his way into various nationalist and paramilitary groups, whose prejudices he appears to have quickly imbibed. In 1923 he joined the National Socialist Party and participated in the ill-fated Beer Hall Putsch of November 1923 as a standard-bearer at the side of Ernst Röhm.

The worldview that he embraced during this formative period combined the image of Germanic racial superiority with extravagant nationalist and anti-Semitic preconceptions.

Himmler remained active in the Nazi movement during the reconstruction period following the failed putsch and Hitler's imprisonment. In 1929 Hitler appointed him Reichsführer SS of the black-shirted organization that served as his personal bodyguard. It was this small elite cadre of several hundred men, which until 1934 remained subordinated to the SA, that the persevering and methodical Himmler built into an overpowering empire in the Nazi state. By 1933 the SS had grown from fewer than 300 men to over 50,000. With Hitler's rise to the chancellorship, Himmler paved his way toward greater power when he became police chief of Munich and shortly afterwards also commander of the political police of Bavaria. Toward the end of 1933, he was put in charge of all political police units outside Prussia, and in 1934 he gained control of the Prussian police and the Gestapo, at first as deputy under Göring. Himmler's career took a major turn as a result of the Röhm purge of June 1934 in which he helped eliminate his former mentor and present superior and other SA leaders by murder. The SS was now separated from the SA and elevated to an independent organization, giving its leader an extraordinary position.

When Himmler was named chief of the German police in June 1936, in addition to continuing as head of the SS, he achieved full command of the political, ordinary, and criminal police throughout the Third Reich, including the concentration-camp system. Together with his deputy Reinhard Heydrich, he was well on his way toward building a power base that rivaled the army and all organizations of the Nazi Party. At the outbreak of the war, the SS was authorized to establish fully armed formations called the Waffen SS, largely elite fighting forces, that reached a strength of 600,000 men at the end of the war. Some of the units under the Waffen SS were entrusted with the guarding of concentration camps and were organized as action groups that carried out the murder of Jews, Gypsies, and other "racially inferior" eastern Europeans. It was in his capacity as Reich commissar for the strengthening of Germandom, added in October 1939 to Himmler's enlarged responsibilities, that he proceeded to translate his extreme racism into fanatical action in eastern Europe. Special SS units terrorized and murdered Jews and others in Poland. Over a million Poles and hundreds of thousands of Jews were driven eastward to create space for the Germanization of western Poland.

Hitler's invasion of the Soviet Union in June 1941 opened the unprecedented program of racial mass extermination, which Himmler in a speech of October 1943 before SS officers extolled as "an unwritten, never to be written, glorious page of our history."[3] Shooting actions of the SS action groups in conquered Soviet territories and permanent extermination camps created in Poland, starting in late 1941 under Himmler's order, claimed the lives of 6 million Jews and millions of others who were deemed to be racially inferior or undesirable. Although no written order by the Führer to Himmler to carry out the "Final Solution" against the Jews has been found, there are good indications that the zealous henchman followed the explicit wishes of his master. In the last years of the war, Himmler had several duties added to his portfolio, making him the most powerful Nazi leader next to Hitler. In 1943 he was appointed minister of the interior, with jurisdiction over the courts and the civil service. Following the failure of the July 1944 attempt on Hitler's life, he became commander in chief of the reserve army, and months later he was given supreme command of Army Group Rhine and Army Group Vistula. In the latter assignment, he failed miserably due to lack of military experience. Seeing the end in sight, Himmler entered into secret negotiations with Western representatives under the supreme delusion that there would be a postwar leadership role for him. An enraged Hitler expelled him from the party and removed him from all offices for treason on April 29, 1945. Following the German surrender, Himmler tried to escape in disguise, but was captured by the British military and committed unheroic suicide by swallowing poison on May 23, 1945, at Lüneburg, Westphalia.

Paul von Hindenburg, 1847–1934

Paul von Hindenburg became a national hero in Germany during World War I. As a revered figure of the German conservatives and the right, he was persuaded against his wishes in 1925 to run for the presidency of the Weimar Republic. Once elected, he dutifully served in office and was reelected in 1932. His advanced age increasingly clouded his independent political judgment and made him subject to the influence of his conservative advisors. In January 1933 he reluctantly consented to the appointment of Adolf Hitler as chancellor, whom he had earlier dismissed as "the Bohemian corporal." By granting Hitler a series of emergency powers, he paved the way for the Nazi dictatorship.

Hindenburg was born in Posen (now Poznan) on October 2, 1847, into a Prussian military family. Drawn into the officer corps, he participated in the Austro-Prussian War of 1866 and the Franco-Prussian War of 1870–1871. Later he joined the general staff and eventually retired as commanding general of an army in 1911. He was recalled to active duty at the outset of the war, and under his command outnumbered German forces defeated the Russian armies advancing into East Prussia. He then was appointed commander in chief of the German armies in the east and as general field marshal was elevated to supreme commander of all German armies in August 1916. Together with his chief of staff, Erich Ludendorff, he became a virtual dictator of Germany by interfering in civilian affairs in order to mobilize all German economic and human resources for the war effort. As the military tide turned against Germany, the two warlords pressured the imperial government to make peace in 1918, thereby escaping much of the blame for the military defeat. Ludendorff resigned even before the war ended, but Hindenburg remained as supreme commander until after the Treaty of Versailles had been signed in June 1919. He thereby ensured an orderly withdrawal and demobilization of German troops from the front lines. After the Treaty of Versailles went into effect, he again retreated into retirement.

At the death of Reich President Friedrich Ebert in 1925, a coalition of conservatives and nationalists prevailed upon the great war hero to run for the presidency of the Weimar Republic. He won by a small margin over the candidate of the center and left parties. Contrary to the expectation of many, Hindenburg observed the provisions of the Weimar constitution despite his monarchist leanings. Under the impact of the Great Depression, parliamentary government began to falter in 1930, and Hindenburg allowed Chancellor Heinrich Brüning, leader of the Catholic Center Party, to govern by emergency decree based on Article 48 of the Weimar constitution. With Brüning's assistance, the aging Hindenburg was reelected president in April 1932, now also with the support of center and left voters, prevailing over Hitler and the Communist leader Ernst Thälmann. However, the reelected Reich president now turned against Brüning and came under the influence of his son Oscar, his chief of the presidential chancellery, Otto Meissner, and the opportunistic Franz von Papen, an archconservative Catholic leader. When Papen and General Kurt von Schleicher, a scheming military politician, failed as short-lived chancellors to contain the Nazis, Hindenburg reluctantly followed the advice of Papen and his close circle to appoint Hitler Reich chancellor, with Papen serving as vice chancellor in a cabinet dominated by non-Nazi ministers. Hitler's advent into governmental power in January 1933 marked the rapid end of whatever authority Hindenburg may have commanded. While the Nazi leader was expanding his base of power, he skillfully exploited Hindenburg's fatherly folk-hero image of the "Wooden Titan" to the advantage of the emerging Nazi regime. Opponents of Hitler repeatedly appealed to Hindenburg to curb the excesses of the Nazis but found him either inaccessible or unable to take resolute action. When Hindenburg succumbed to ill health in Neudeck on August 2, 1934, Hitler, with the consent of the army leadership, succeeded in combining the office of the Reich presidency with the chancellorship.

Adolf Hitler, 1889–1945

The first half of the twentieth century was dominated by several ruthless historical personalities who wielded enormous power as statesmen, and among them Adolf Hitler will be remembered not only as a very powerful dictator but also as a savage destroyer of his own land and much of Europe. Rising from humble social origins, he became the leader of the National Socialist Party at a time when Germany was in deep despair. His oratorical talent and organizational skill enabled him to generate remarkable public support and to build his party into a powerful movement. In his personality traits, he showed courage, perseverance, brutality, vindictiveness, and a total lack of capacity for self-criticism. It is not likely that he would have attained the chancellorship of Germany if, after a promising recovery from the Great War, German society and much of the world had not been plunged into a deep economic depression. A despairing, politically polarized German electorate supported extremist parties in large numbers, thereby further undermining whatever democratic forces remained. With the support of conservative nationalist politicians, Hitler as leader of the largest party was appointed head of the German government. He quickly expanded this position into a totalitarian dictatorship, institutionalized racism as the driving political principle of his policies, and, in the course of half a decade, prepared Germany for war and conquest.

Hitler was born in Braunau am Inn, Austria, on April 20, 1889, the son of a customs official and his third wife, a peasant girl. Young Adolf frequently clashed with his authoritarian father, who was already in his fifties, but found support from his overindulgent young mother. Moody and lazy, Hitler dreamed of becoming an artist or possibly an architect, but lacked both the talent and the perseverance for reaching his goal. In 1903 his father died, but his mother was able to sustain the family with the help of a pension. In secondary school, Hitler excelled in gymnastics, geography, history, and drawing, but his work in mathematics, French, and German was unsatisfactory. In 1905, at age sixteen, he ended his formal learning by leaving school, even though he promised his mother that he would get a higher education. He idled his time away both at home and on trips to Vienna, where he visited museums and occasionally attended operas. In 1907 he applied to the Vienna Fine Arts Academy but failed the entrance examination. The study of architecture was closed to him because he had failed to complete his secondary education. This first blow was followed by a second trauma when his mother succumbed to breast cancer late in 1907. After settling his mother's affairs, he moved permanently to Vienna in 1908, where he lived on his inheritance. A second effort to be admitted to the Fine Arts Academy failed and left him deeply embittered, blaming society and the Jews rather than his own deficiencies. For years, he drifted without permanent employment in Vienna and in 1913 moved to Munich, very likely to avoid the Austrian military service.

In his bohemian years in Vienna, he developed much of his worldview and acquired an early political education by observing the demagogic methods of the popular mayor of Vienna, Karl Lueger. He was also very significantly swayed by the pan-Germanist and anti-Semitic outlook of Georg von Schönerer, another political figure in the Austrian capital. By devouring racist publications of such writers as the defrocked monk Jörg Lanz von Liebenfels and encountering lower-class unassimilated eastern European Jews on Viennese streets, he turned into a rabid anti-Semite. He learned to despise Marxism and democracy, embracing an extreme pan-German nationalism tinged, in addition to anti-Semitism, with anti-Slavic racialism and driven by social Darwinist notions that explained all history in racial terms. As an enthusiastic German nationalist, he joined a Bavarian infantry regiment at the outbreak of the war and served bravely as a dispatch runner throughout the conflict. He was wounded twice and awarded the Iron Cross, Second Class, in 1914 and the Iron Cross, First Class, an exceptional decoration for a commoner, in 1918. However, he never rose above the rank of corporal. In the front lines, he experienced the comradeship and escape from the aimlessness of civilian life that he later always remembered with emotion.

After recovery from temporary blindness suffered in a gas attack toward the end of the war, Hitler was assigned to perform "educational" duties for the army in the summer of 1919, which entailed spying on political parties and agitational work. In September he encountered the small, nationalistic, and anti-Semitic German Workers' Party in Munich, which he was invited to join. Here he discovered his powerful oratorical talent and became the party's main propagandist and, in 1921, its dictatorial leader. The party was renamed the National Socialist German Workers' Party in 1920; Hitler gave it its symbol, the swastika, its greeting, "Heil," and much of its program, which expounded fierce racial nationalism with notions of German *Lebensraum* (living space), anti-Semitism, and opposition to liberal democracy and particularly Marxism.

Because of the havoc caused by the hyperinflation and unrest in parts of Germany, Hitler felt that the Weimar Republic was ready to collapse and staged the Munich Beer Hall Putsch on November 8–9, 1923, in order to seize power in Bavaria and then to march on Berlin. When the putsch failed, Hitler was arrested and put on trial for treason in 1924. He turned the proceedings into a propaganda triumph, declaring that he was not a traitor but the best of Germans who wanted the best for his people. A friendly Bavarian court sentenced him to five years' imprisonment in Landsberg fortress, but he was released after nine months in December. While he was in prison, Hitler wrote *Mein Kampf*, a contorted autobiography and ideological treatise that conveyed his primitive social Darwinism, anti-Semitism, and *Lebensraum* illusion that he attempted to translate into policy once in power. Once freed from prison, he proceeded to rebuild the Nazi Party and resolved to attain power by legal means.

After six years of persevering grassroots work, a new opportunity beckoned as a result of the devastating impact of the Great Depression upon German society, the weakening of the Weimar political system, and the inclination of many voters to turn to political extremists, all of which helped the Nazi Party achieve unexpected victories. In the 1930 elections, the Nazi support swelled from a low of 810,000 popular votes and 12 seats in the Reichstag in 1928 to a dramatic 6,409,000 votes and 107 seats, which made Hitler's party the second largest in Germany. Two years later, the presidential election and two Reichstag elections enabled the Nazis to heighten their agitation among the masses. In July 1932 they became the largest political party of Germany with nearly 14 million votes and 230 Reichstag seats; in November they lost somewhat in popular support (11 million votes, 196 parliamentary seats). However, the Nazi movement with a large paramilitary force of the SA and SS, in addition to the party, maintained the popular momentum to enable Hitler to hold out for the highest governmental post and to proclaim him as a national savior. Intrigue by nationalist politicians and Reich President Hindenburg's failing political acumen facilitated the Nazi leader's appointment as chancellor on January 30, 1933.

Within less than two years, from January 1933 to August 1934, Hitler succeeded in seizing the full reins of power in Germany through a fast-paced series of steps. The Reichstag fire of February 1933 served as a pretext to curtail civil rights. An orchestrated election in March that gave the Nazis a strong plurality but not a majority led him to mastermind the adoption by the Reichstag of a four-year Enabling Act that gave him permanent dictatorial powers. They were used to bring about the control and regimentation (*Gleichschaltung* or coordination) of German institutions in accordance with National Socialist aims and the elimination of trade unions and competing political parties. In June 1934 Hitler engineered the Blood Purge of Ernst Röhm and most of the top SA leaders in order to mollify the army leadership, the only still-independent force that might have challenged him in his quest for autocratic power. When Reich President Hindenburg died in August 1934, army leaders accepted Hitler's merger of the presidency and the chancellorship, which at the same time elevated him to supreme commander of all German armed forces. To ensure their allegiance, officers and soldiers had to swear a personal oath to the Führer.

Hitler demonstrated leadership in pulling Germany out of the economic depression and reducing unemployment between 1933 and 1938, even though it was Hjalmar Schacht who implemented deficit spending, large public works projects, and extensive rearmament programs. When the latter appeared to exceed practical economic bounds, Schacht parted company with the Führer, whose principal goal was to use Germany's economic resources in the pursuit of a vigorous foreign policy. The Nazi leader espoused the notion that the Germanic, or Aryan, race, as the most creative and productive of all races, was destined to rule the world. In Hitler's thinking, Slavs and especially Jews were inferior races and needed to be eliminated as undesirables. Linking the idea of race and space, Hitler insisted that a people's greatness depended on adequate *Lebensraum*, and therefore Germany's future could only be assured through the acquisition of more living space in the east.

During the years of peace after his takeover of power, he exploited the war-weary attitude of the Western democratic powers and managed to abrogate or drastically revise the Versailles Treaty restrictions. In 1933 he withdrew Germany from the Disarmament Conference and the League of Nations. While pretending to be a man of peace, he concluded an unexpected nonaggression pact with Poland in the following year. More ominous was the unilateral introduction of military conscription in 1935 and the remilitarization of the Rhineland in 1936, both of which violated the Treaty of Versailles. Allied protest, only verbal, was ineffective in curbing Hitler's appetite for more foreign policy successes. In March 1938 he annexed Austria, and in September he was prepared to dismember Czechoslovakia by force if necessary, but British and French concessions at the Munich Conference gave him the Sudetenland without firing a shot. In March 1939 the ever-bolder Hitler seized what remained of Czechoslovakia, turning it into a German protectorate and a dependent state. Quite convinced that Britain would not fight, he next demanded the Polish Corridor and the city of Danzig from Poland in preparation for the ultimate conquest of Poland and Russia. To fend off a potential two-front war, he concluded a nonaggression pact with Stalin on August 23, 1939, and then attacked Poland on September 1. When Britain and France honored an earlier promise to come to Poland's defense and declared war on Germany, Hitler was shocked but not deterred from continuing his campaign against the retreating Polish armies.

Hitler's brilliant *Blitzkrieg* (lightning war) strategy—a combination of airplanes, fast mobile armor, and infantry—gave him unprecedented victories in the early years of the war. Poland was defeated in three weeks. After a lull known as *Sitzkrieg* or Phony War, the Nazi armies occupied Denmark and Norway in April 1940 and, on May 10, attacked Holland, Belgium, and France. In one month these powers succumbed to Hitler's onslaught, and the British expeditionary force was driven from the Continent at Dunkirk. However, Britain refused to give in during the Battle of Britain in the summer of 1940, when the Luftwaffe was attempting to bomb the British into submission. Rather than invading the British Isles, Hitler made the most fateful strategic mistake of his career by launching an assault on the Soviet Union in June 1941, after quickly conquering the Balkans. He expected to defeat the Russian armies with a *Blitzkrieg* strike in approximately two months, but when the German forces failed to gain a decisive victory before the onset of the bitter winter, they doomed their chances of winning the war. Hitler burned all his bridges when on December 11, 1941, only days after the Japanese attack on Pearl Harbor, he unilaterally declared war on the United States. The European conflict had become a true world war.

Hitler's war objectives included the achievement of territorial hegemony in Europe from the Atlantic to the steppes of Russia and the enslavement of racially inferior peoples. With the campaign into Russia, a much more sinister plan unfolded: the systematic elimination of racial "undesirables," including close to 6 million Jews and more than 3 million Soviet prisoners of war. In addition, Gypsies and the severely mentally and physically handicapped were also deemed dispensable and slated for elimination. Millions of others perished as victims of political and racial persecution. It is telling that trains that transported millions of Jews to the gas chambers of the killing centers in Poland were often given preference over trains that were supplying the more and more desperate German armies defending the eastern territories against the advancing Red Army.

In the end, Hitler was tragically successful in achieving his second war objective but failed utterly in the first. After the defeat of the German Sixth Army at Stalingrad in January 1943, it was only a matter of time before the once-mighty German armies would be pushed back into their homeland by the relentless pressure of the American, British, Soviet, and other Allied forces. Hitler could not sustain a war of attrition with the limited resources and manpower at his disposal and was thus unable to repeat the kinds of triumphs that marked the early phase of the war. Starting with the campaign into Russia, he demonstrated a fatal underestimation of his enemies. He withdrew from his own people, neither giving public addresses nor visiting bombed cities. After the July 1944 attempt on his life, he lashed out savagely against the conspirators and their families. By early 1945 he retreated to a bunker 55 feet deep under the Reich chancellery garden in Berlin, directing the war increasingly with an air of unreality and giving orders to units that were decimated or no longer existed. Until the very end, he refused to accept any responsibility for his nation's defeat and destruction but blamed it on the Jews and the traitors in the Nazi Party. As far as he was concerned, the German people deserved defeat, for in a great test of wills they had proven inferior to their enemies. He now declared the "racial inferiors" to the east the new masters of Europe. On April 30, 1945, one day after marrying his longtime mistress Eva Braun, he and his new bride committed suicide.

Benito Mussolini, 1883–1945

Benito Mussolini was the founder of Fascism in Italy and became twentieth-century Europe's first fascist dictator. Born into a humble family, he was significantly influenced by his antireligious, anarcho-socialist father. His major achievement as dictator was to restore Italy's confidence in itself after the devastating World War I and its demoralizing aftermath. After restoring stability in domestic affairs, he could have turned the Italian Fascist state into a viable political institution. However, he squandered his moderate domestic successes in the pursuit of aggressive imperialist glory. As a consequence, he became involved in wars and, as his greatest mistake, plunged Italy into World War II, which brought the end of Fascism and its leader.

Mussolini was born on July 29, 1883, in Dovia di Predappio, Forlì, Italy, the eldest son of a blacksmith, who named him after the Mexican revolutionary Benito Juárez. As a child, young Benito was unruly and aggressive but also showed intelligence. He obtained a teaching diploma but had a short-lived career as a schoolmaster. In 1902 he drifted to Switzerland, where he immersed himself in socialism and exposed himself to the writings of Georges Sorel, Louis Blanc, Friedrich Nietzsche, G.W.F Hegel, Vilfredo Pareto, and others without developing a coherent personal philosophy. By 1904 he was back in Italy, served in the military, and ventured more and more into socialist journalism. He established a reputation as a talented, though also dangerous, young socialist. After several years of successful editing of his own socialist newspaper, he was appointed editor of the official Socialist Party's newspaper *Avanti* in 1912. On the eve of World War I, he espoused antimilitarist, antinationalist, and anti-imperialist views, but only two months into the war, he changed his mind and embarked on an interventionist campaign. He resigned from *Avanti* and founded his own newspaper, *Il Popolo d'Italia*, which received assistance from a group of industrialists to fight socialism and from the French to promote Italian intervention.

After being drafted into the army in 1915, he served in the front lines but was wounded by an exploding mortar and was released to resume his antisocialist and ultranationalist journalism. By exploiting the postwar fears of a Bolshevist revolution and the deep discontent with the peace terms, he managed to organize a group of diverse followers into the *Fasci di Combattimento* in March 1919. Although the first program of this "group of fighters," which was nationalist and leftist, scored only electoral defeats, Mussolini's dramatic oratory and his strutting posture caught the imagination of crowds. When strikes threatened the country, the Fascist Blackshirts terrorized Socialists and Catholic leftists, and Mussolini compromised his political message by appealing to both the urban lower middle class and the landowners. By 1921 the Fascist political movement was turned into a party, and with growing numbers and electoral successes, Mussolini was ready to claim governmental power. When a general strike frightened the country in October 1922, he and his Fascist associates threatened to seize the government to restore order by a march on Rome. The king compromised by appointing Mussolini to the prime ministership, hoping thereby to tame the Fascist Party.

Proud to be the youngest prime minister in Italian history, Il Duce (the leader) of the Fascist Party attempted to become the head of a united Italian government. His first cabinet contained a majority of members of other political parties. However, he was granted dictatorial powers for the first year and persuaded the Chamber of Deputies to adopt a law that granted the Fascists a majority in parliament. In 1924 the parliamentary elections gave the Fascists a strong majority without the manipulations of the electoral law and ensured Mussolini's road to full dictatorial power. Even the Matteotti crisis, in which Mussolini appeared to be responsible for the murder of the Socialist deputy, Giacomo Matteotti, did not force his political defeat, since the king did not withdraw support from his prime minister. Starting in early 1925, the Duce was able to consolidate the Fascist regime. By decreasing the role of the cabinet, he had already drawn more legislative and judicial power into his hands. Now he proceeded to outlaw political parties and in 1929 came to terms with the papacy by concluding the Lateran Pacts, which put Vatican City under papal sovereignty and declared Catholicism the official religion of the Italian state.

The Italian people welcomed the restoration of authority following years of strikes and riots. They were attracted to the dramatic techniques and displays of Fascist power reminiscent of Roman times and accepted the dictatorial regime as long as it stabilized the national economy and restored the self-respect of Italy. Late in the 1920s Mussolini launched an extensive program of public works and subsidization of numerous industries. Strikes and non-Fascist labor unions were outlawed, supposedly to banish class struggle and bring about class conciliation. Although workers' conditions improved, industrialists and other property owners gained most in protection. At the same time, a national policy of autarky, or self-sufficiency, brought the tight control of the economy by an ever-expanding bureaucracy. In the 1930s Mussolini sought to realize the full corporate state by restructuring parliament on the basis of "corporations" that represented occupational groups instead of geographical or population units. Even though workers and employers were to have a major voice in this body, the Fascist Party played the decisive role. All these measures brought Mussolini admiration at home and considerable acclaim all over Europe, in Latin America, and in the United States, for they seemed to transform his divided and demoralized country into a vigorous new state.

The Duce might well have remained an admired statesman of the twentieth century if he had not embarked on one of the most fundamental goals of Fascism, the pursuit of war and empire. Relying on bellicose nationalism, he expanded Italy's influence in the Balkans and Austria and in 1935 launched an invasion of Ethiopia as the beginning point of a new Roman Empire. The easy conquest of this unhappy land tempted him to aim for higher stakes, even though he lacked the material resources to sustain an imperialist Italian expansion. After successfully defying the League of Nations over Ethiopia, he intervened in Spain at little gain in prestige and considerable human and material losses. Very significantly, these two adventures alienated Italy's relations with France and Britain and pushed Mussolini into the arms of Hitler. The two fascist dictators admired each other and sustained a personal and, in Hitler's words, brutal friendship to the very end. But Mussolini, although senior in age and time in power, was increasingly forced to subjugate himself to the Führer, whose state commanded superior resources to conduct wars. Dazzled by Hitler on a state visit to Germany in 1937, Mussolini willingly aligned himself with Nazi Germany and imperialist Japan. In 1938 he accepted the German annexation of Austria and supported Hitler against Britain and France at the Munich Conference. He even embraced anti-Semitism and initiated actions against Italian Jews similar to Nazi measures in Germany.

In April 1939 the Duce launched his invasion of Albania and sealed the Axis alliance of 1936 into a military Pact of Steel with Germany in the following month. Expecting to have gained several years of peace until 1942–1943 by entering a military alliance with Germany, Mussolini first attempted mediation and then announced that Italy would be a nonbelligerent when Hitler unexpectedly started war on September 1, 1939. He followed the progress of Hitler's war with growing alarm if not jealousy of German victories. When Nazi armies marched westward and France appeared to be near collapse in June 1940, he convinced himself that it was "necessary" for Italy not to forgo territorial advantages and the glory that came with victory. Expecting to maintain an autonomous role as a belligerent on the side of Germany, he was soon forced into the condition of an inferior partner when the Italians' Greek campaign of 1940–1941 faltered and Mussolini's armies suffered humiliating defeats in Africa in 1941–1942. After the military disasters in the east, he attempted to persuade Hitler to come to a settlement with Stalin and to concentrate all Axis war efforts against the Allies in the west.

With the invasion of Sicily by Allied armies in July 1943, a group of Fascist leaders was ready to remove Mussolini from power in order to prepare Italy's extrication from the war. Under the initiative of Dino Grandi, the Fascist Grand Council, on the night of July 24–25, passed a motion of no confidence in the Duce. When Mussolini reported to the king the next day, he was dismissed from office and put under arrest. Marshal Pietro Badoglio was asked to form a successor government. In September Mussolini was rescued from the mountain stronghold of Gran Sasso by a German commando and taken to Germany. On Hitler's direction, he returned to German-occupied northern Italy in October as puppet head of the Italian Social Republic with headquarters at Gargagno on Lake Garda. He was to fight the Badoglio government and the anti-Fascist Resistance. In April 1945, with the Third Reich collapsing and Allied forces moving closer to Lake Garda, the demoralized Mussolini attempted to flee with his mistress Clara Petacci toward the Austrian border. They were captured by Italian partisans and summarily shot on April 27–28 at Giulino di Mezzegra, Como. The next day their bodies were hung, upside down, from a girder at a filling station in Milan.

Martin Niemöller, 1892–1984

Martin Niemöller was a Lutheran pastor who became a leading opponent of the National Socialist regime. He helped organize the Confessing Church in 1934, a body within the German Evangelical Church that formed the center of Protestant resistance in the Third Reich.

Niemöller was born in Lippstadt, Westphalia, on January 14, 1892, the son of a Lutheran pastor. His early fascination with the sea prompted him to join the imperial navy, and in 1915 he was transferred to submarine service. He served as a submarine commander with distinction, leading several missions against the British and the French. Disillusioned by Germany's defeat and antagonistic to the democracy of the Weimar Republic, he resigned his commission as a naval officer and studied theology with the intention of entering the ministry. After his ordination as a pastor, he was active in church social work and in 1931 was appointed to a pastorate at Berlin-Dahlem. This pulpit served as his platform for his popular sermons after 1933, in which he attacked the Nazi government for blatantly interfering in church affairs.

Niemöller agreed with the National Socialists' antagonism to communism and their aversion to the Weimar Republic, but became alarmed when Hitler attempted to achieve dominance over the Evangelical Church (Lutheran and Reformed) by imposing the neopagan movement of the German Christians under the Nazi-sponsored Reich bishop Ludwig Müller. In September 1933 he and others organized the Pastors' Emergency League to assist non-Aryan pastors or those married to non-Aryans, such as Christian Jews, who were threatened with dismissal, and to serve as an organizational network to resist the Nazi intrusion into church work. In the following year, Niemöller became the leader of a newly created church structure, the Confessing Church, which added lay support to the efforts of the clergy in opposition to the segments of the Lutheran Church dominated by the German Christians. The Confessing Church claimed to be the only duly constituted Protestant church in Germany. Attracting thousands of pastors to its ranks, it managed to maintain itself as the sole coherent opposition among Protestants to the religious policies of the Third Reich. Niemöller's sermons and actions, which brought him considerable popularity throughout Germany and beyond, led to his imprisonment in 1937 and a trial in 1938 on charges of violation of the law and treason. He defended himself by pointing to his patriotic service in war and peacetime and thereby escaped with a moderate sentence, leading to his quick release. Hitler was enraged and had him rearrested and sent as his personal prisoner to the Sachsenhausen concentration camp and, in 1941, to Dachau. Niemöller survived the end of the war and became a prominent but also controversial figure in the postwar life of the church in Germany as an opponent of German rearmament and as an antinuclear spokesperson. He died in Wiesbaden on March 6, 1984.

Franz von Papen, 1879–1969

An archconservative Catholic politician, Franz von Papen briefly served as chancellor in 1932. His conservative "cabinet of barons" was favored by Reich President Hindenburg and mustered the support of the German army and big business, but failed to win a majority in the Reichstag, throwing Papen's political future into doubt. He was forced to resign, but not before he had weakened the already-unstable democratic structure of the Weimar governmental system. Even though General Kurt von Schleicher had proposed Papen to Hindenburg for the chancellorship, Papen turned against him in revenge when Schleicher succeeded him, engaging in intrigues that culminated in the appointment of Adolf Hitler.

Papen was born into a Catholic noble family in Werl, Westphalia, on October 29, 1879. He embarked on a military career and during World War I served as military attaché at the German embassy in Mexico and then in Washington, from which he was expelled for sabotage activities in 1916. During the last years of the war, he was attached to several Turkish armies, largely as chief of staff. As a Catholic Center Party politician in the 1920s, he belonged to the antirepublican right wing that advocated the restoration of the monarchy in Germany. His upper-class connections catapulted him into the limelight of German politics in 1932 when he became chancellor. During his few months in office, he rescinded his predecessor's ban on the SA and SS and permitted them to don their uniforms, replaced republican officials and governors of provinces with authoritarian "nationalists," and appointed himself Reich commissioner of Prussia, the largest state of Germany, after unconstitutionally removing its Social Democratic government.

His most reprehensible act was his conspiratorial effort to depose General Kurt von Schleicher from the chancellorship after he himself had been forced to resign it in December 1932. This was to be accomplished by persuading Hindenburg to dismiss Schleicher and to appoint a Hitler-Papen government. Papen made the scheme plausible by arrogantly insisting that since he commanded the confidence of Hindenburg, he could restrain Hitler in a cabinet made up largely of conservative nationalists. "In two months we shall have Hitler squeezed into a corner so that he squeaks," he boasted.[4] Hindenburg went along with Papen's scheme, and Hitler became chancellor and Papen vice chancellor on January 30, 1933. Too late, Papen discovered that he was no match for the clever and ruthless Nazi leader, who was determined to consolidate his dictatorial position, skillfully exploiting all opportunities to his end. In June 1934 Papen delivered a speech at the University of Marburg in which he called for an end to SA and Nazi Party excesses and greater freedoms. Only a few weeks later Hitler engineered the Röhm purge, and Papen was left to ponder how close he had come to losing his life. After he resigned the vice chancellorship, he continued to accept appointments from Hitler's hands, first as ambassador to Austria and, in 1939, to Turkey, where he remained until the end of the war, deluding himself that he was working for Germany while he was actively serving Hitler. Papen was put on trial before the International Military Tribunal at Nuremberg in 1945 but acquitted in 1946. A denazification court dealt more harshly with him, and he was not formally released until 1949. His memoirs, published in 1952, give no hint that he comprehended how his acts had hastened the demise

of the Weimar Republic and paved the way to Hitler's criminal dictatorship. He died in Oberaspach on May 2, 1969.

Ernst Röhm, 1887–1934

Ernst Röhm joined the Nazi Party at the very start and became a close
associate of Adolf Hitler, who made him chief of staff of the SA. As SA
leader, Röhm wanted to carry the Nazi revolution to a socialist conclusion,
giving the lower-class elements among the Nazi supporters a strong stake
in society and the veterans of the war a dominating place in the German
army. This conception clashed with Hitler's plans to win the traditional
military and industrial elites to his side and climaxed in the bloody purge
of Röhm and his associates in June 1934.

Röhm was born in Munich on November 28, 1887, the son of a well-
established railroad official. After completing secondary education, he attended a military academy and served with distinction as an officer in
World War I, being wounded three times. As a veteran of the war, he
retained the values of the trenches that had been shaped by the camaraderie of the frontline soldiers and were marked by adventurism, if not
restless criminality. He became a perpetual freebooter after 1918 and
found no gainful place in normal civilian life, which he loathed. In 1919
he met Hitler, who introduced him to the fledgling party that he himself
had only recently joined. Röhm's association with Hitler became a close
one personally, even though they differed politically after the abortive
outcome of the Beer Hall Putsch in 1923. Both of them were tried and
received prison sentences, but only Hitler was actually confined to a fortress throughout much of 1924. Hitler learned his lesson from the disastrous putsch and steered the revived party toward a legal takeover of
power. Röhm, who held fast to a revolutionary path to power, treated this
tactic with contempt and drifted away from the Nazi Party. Toward the
end of the 1920s, he left Germany and found employment as a military
instructor in Bolivia for two years.

In 1930 Hitler recalled his comrade and made him chief of staff of the
SA, giving him a relatively free hand in the building of the paramilitary
formation. Spurred by the electoral successes of the party in the 1930
Reichstag elections and benefiting from the worsening conditions of the
Great Depression, the Nazi movement attracted larger and larger masses
of supporters. Röhm capitalized on this groundswell and expanded the
ranks of the SA from 70,000 in 1930 to 170,000 in 1931, enlisting growing
numbers of unemployed and socially displaced Germans. These brown-
shirted SA troopers formed the core of the lower-class street fighters and
toughs who battled Communists and served as instruments of intimidation

and persuasion during Hitler's election campaigns. They became an essential force that ensured his rise to power between 1930 and 1933, and their numbers swelled to 4.5 million men by 1934.

With Hitler in power, Röhm became increasingly angered that while party and SS members were gaining power and privilege in society, the proletarian SA members and their leaders were not sharing the just rewards of the Nazi takeover. He envisaged a Second Revolution in which a people's army would be created by absorbing his SA into the regular German army. His populist rhetoric also attempted to push the Nazi Party into a socialist direction and seemed to work toward a revolutionary conquest of the state, for Röhm refused to rein in the street violence and intimidation of the SA troopers. Röhm's own personal conduct and that of some of his associates, marked by homosexual scandals and wild drinking bouts, as well as reported private outbursts against Hitler, further discredited the SA chief. He managed to alarm the German army generals and alienate the conservative elites that Hitler needed to implement his gradual and seemingly legal takeover of German society. Finally, he also antagonized Hermann Göring and Heinrich Himmler, his two ambitious rivals, who began to urge Hitler to take strong action against their dangerous associate.

A reluctant Hitler, caught between his own party and the conservative leaders in German society, on the one hand, and his closest associate of the years of struggle and the SA, on the other, decided to eliminate Röhm and his senior associates in June 1934. With the help of the SS, the unsuspecting Röhm was rounded up on June 30 while vacationing with other SA leaders south of Munich and was taken to the Stadelheim prison in the city and shot the next day after refusing to commit suicide. The Night of the Long Knives, as the Röhm purge became known, was used by Hitler and his henchmen to liquidate seventy-seven leading Nazis and to settle scores with numerous other political opponents, including General Kurt von Schleicher, by murdering them.

Hjalmar Schacht, 1877–1970

Hjalmar Schacht became noted as a financial wizard during the Third Reich after having gained prominence as an able financial expert in the years before 1933. His early career in banking prepared him for his service as Reich currency commissioner in 1923, in which capacity he was instrumental in stemming the inflation and stabilizing the German mark. Between late 1923 and 1930 he also held the influential position of president of the Reichsbank and participated in the negotiations that revised the German reparations schedule. During this time, he moved closer to the political right. Hitler reappointed him to the presidency of the Reichsbank in 1933 and soon thereafter named him minister of economics. He was very instrumental in the rearmament under Hitler, but developed doubts about the nature of National Socialism and the practicality of some of Hitler's financial policies. In 1937 he resigned from his important positions but remained as minister without portfolio until 1943.

Schacht was born in Tingleff, Schleswig-Holstein, on January 22, 1877, into a family of Danish origin. He grew up in the United States, where his parents had emigrated, but returned to Germany to complete his university education with a doctorate in economics. In 1903 he became head of the archives of the Dresdner Bank and rose to deputy director of the bank by 1908. During the war, he took over the private National Bank for Germany and combined it with the Darmstädter Bank in 1922. Venturing into politics, he was the cofounder of the leftist liberal German Democratic Party in 1918, but left it in 1926 when his political sentiments began to veer to the right. As Reich currency commissioner, he helped eliminate the unprecedented hyperinflation in Germany by carrying out a drastic currency reform in 1924. As president of the Reichsbank, he participated in the negotiations of the Dawes Plan in 1924 that regularized German reparations payments and granted Germany a stabilization loan. Five years later he accepted the Young Plan as head of the German delegation at the reparations conference, but in the following year, 1930, he resigned the Reichsbank presidency in protest over the new regulations incorporated in the new plan. In the very same year he met Hermann Göring and through him, a little later, Adolf Hitler, whose ideas and electoral success of 1930 impressed him. Together with other conservative nationalist politicians, Schacht formed the Harzburg Front in 1931, which was directed against the Weimar Republic, and one year later he called for the appointment of Hitler as Reich chancellor. In the March 1933 election campaign, he prevailed on his banker and industrialist friends to grant the Nazi Party substantial financial support.

Within months after Hitler became chancellor, Schacht was reappointed to the Reichsbank presidency and also took over the Ministry of Economics. In addition, between 1935 and 1937 he functioned as plenipotentiary general of the war economy, which gave him extraordinary powers. His policies and remarkable skills helped to pull the German economy out of the depression, eliminate large-scale unemployment, and set in motion an impressive rearmament program. He negotiated highly profitable bilateral trade agreements with numerous foreign countries. To generate more domestic credit, he created a system of credit notes that financed the rapidly expanding rearmament program. However, with the acceleration of production, the threat of inflation became a concern to Schacht, and he advocated a slowdown in the rearmament program, an option that Hitler rejected. Schacht thereupon resigned as plenipotentiary general of the war economy and economics minister late in 1937. Further disagreements led to his dismissal as president of the Reichsbank in January 1939. Nevertheless, he continued as minister without portfolio until 1943.

During the war years, Schacht established contact with the resistance groups against Hitler, but did not join as a member. He was arrested after the failure of the July 1944 attempt upon the Führer's life and was confined to a concentration camp. To his great disgust, he was charged with organizing Germany for war by the International Military Tribunal at Nuremberg in 1945, but was acquitted at the end of the trial in 1946. He encountered greater difficulties when he was tried by a denazification court and was not able to resume his career until 1950. After that, he embarked on his second career as a financial advisor to developing countries and even managed to accumulate a second fortune. He died in Munich on June 3, 1970.

Claus von Stauffenberg, 1907–1944

Colonel Claus Schenk Graf von Stauffenberg was a major leader of the German opposition against Adolf Hitler during World War II. He helped plan and attempted to carry out the assassination of the Führer in July 1944 in order to topple the Nazi government.

Claus von Stauffenberg was born in Jettingen, Swabia, on November 15, 1907, into an old family of the Württemberg nobility. Despite a somewhat weak constitution, he opted for a military career. A conservative monarchist at heart, he even supported some of the early policies of the Nazi regime, but became greatly disturbed by the anti-Jewish pogrom of *Kristallnacht* in 1938 and Hitler's war strategies in 1939. When the war broke out, he served with distinction as a staff officer in the Polish and French campaigns. In 1940 he was posted to the Army High Command, and during the invasion of the Soviet Union in the following years, he encountered the atrocities against and slaughter of Jews, Russians, and prisoners of war perpetrated by the SS. Early in 1943 he was assigned to Tunisia as an operations officer to a tank division, where he was severely wounded, losing his left eye, his right hand, and part of his left hand. While recovering from his injuries, he decided to become an active member of the Resistance after he concluded that the war was lost and Hitler must be stopped from inflicting utter disaster on the army and Germany.

Stauffenberg's opportunity for action was greatly enhanced when he was posted to Berlin and attached to the command of the Reserve Army in October 1943. This position gave him access to secret information pertaining to the political and military operations of the German army and enabled him to maintain essential contacts with leading members of the Resistance. In June 1944 he was promoted to colonel and appointed chief of staff to General Friedrich Fromm, the commander of the Reserve Army. In this capacity, he gained direct access to Hitler's staff conferences. As a severely disabled war hero, he was also exempt from the searches of persons admitted to Hitler's presence. Stauffenberg was chosen to carry out the assassination and made attempts on three different occasions in July 1944, hoping to kill Hitler together with Göring and Himmler. Twice the attempts were called off because Göring and Himmler were absent. On July 20 Stauffenberg resolved to proceed even if the Führer's two henchmen were not present and deposited a briefcase with a bomb at Hitler's military headquarters in Rastenburg, East Prussia. The device exploded, but Hitler escaped with but a few injuries. Although Stauffenberg was able to fly back to Berlin and initiate the planned coup, the news that Hitler was alive enabled his supporters to rally and thwart any effective action by the conspirators. Stauffenberg and several of his associates were overpowered on the evening of July 20, sentenced by a drumhead courtmartial, and shot in the courtyard of the Berlin War Ministry.

Victor Emmanuel III, 1869–1947

King Victor Emmanuel III of Italy enjoyed a long reign, from 1900 to 1946. It encompassed a period of turmoil and war as well as political change from constitutional monarchy to dictatorship, ending with the establishment of a republic. In his early years on the throne, Victor Emmanuel seemed to be fully committed to maintaining a constitutional monarchy, but in the strife-ridden aftermath of World War I, he decided to appoint Benito Mussolini to the prime ministership in October 1922 when the Fascist leader and his cohorts threatened to march on Rome. He raised no objections when Mussolini assumed more and more dictatorial powers, and he did not intervene when Fascists committed political murder in 1924. The king generally supported Mussolini's aggressive military interventions in Spain, in Ethiopia, and during the first years of World War II. Only when Italy was on the verge of defeat did Victor Emmanuel become a participant in the maneuvers that led to Mussolini's removal from office and arrest in July 1943. Several months later, the royal government made an armistice with the Allies and then declared war on Nazi Germany. These actions did not save Victor Emmanuel's throne. In 1946 he was forced to abdicate, and the monarchy was abolished.

Victor Emmanuel was born in Naples on November 11, 1869, the only son of King Umberto I. After his father's assassination in 1900, he succeeded him on the throne and helped bring to an end years of reactionary rule under his predecessor. In domestic affairs, the new king observed the constitutional practice of appointing prime ministers in accordance with parliamentary majorities. Even though he supported the continuing participation of Italy in the Triple Alliance with Germany and Austria-Hungary, he made overtures to the Triple Entente (France, Russia, and Britain), which allowed Italy to occupy Libya in its war against Turkey in 1911–1912. After the outbreak of World War I, Victor Emmanuel supported Italy's break with the Triple Alliance and intervention in the war on the side of the Triple Entente.

In the postwar years, the king turned his back on political liberalism and constitutional practices. In October 1922, when Mussolini and his Fascist henchmen threatened to seize power by a march on Rome, Victor Emmanuel could have agreed to declare martial law, as his prime minister proposed, but he refused and paved the way for a Fascist authoritarian government by appointing Mussolini to the prime ministership. Two years later, the king again failed to act against the Fascist leader when Mussolini's position had been weakened by his reputed implication in the murder of the Socialist Giacomo Matteotti. The Duce was now able to establish a full dictatorship.

When Mussolini embarked on expansionist adventures and war, Victor Emmanuel lent the ambitious dictator his support. In 1935 he earned another title, emperor of Ethiopia, following the Italian conquest of this African land. He approved Italian intervention in the Spanish Civil War in 1936 and the invasion of Albania in 1939, which made him king of Albania. When the Duce decided to join Hitler in his campaign against France in June 1940, the Italian monarch signed the declaration of war against the Allies without objection. Only when Italy was suffering defeat after defeat under the heavy blows of the Allies and Sicily was being invaded did the timid king join Mussolini's opponents in July 1943. When the Fascist Grand Council voted against the Duce, Victor Emmanuel dismissed him from the prime ministership and had him arrested. The king tried to salvage Italy's and his own fate by establishing a military dictatorship under Marshal Pietro Badoglio and concluding an armistice with the Allies in September 1943. To avoid German arrest, the royal family and Badoglio fled from Rome to the Allies in southern Italy, who in turn compelled the king to declare war on Germany in October. Now fully at the mercy of the Allies, Victor Emmanuel found himself pushed aside by the British and Americans in favor of his son Umberto in 1944 and withdrew from political life. After the war, he formally abdicated in favor of Umberto II in May 1946, but this action failed to save the Italian monarchy, which was formally abolished by popular referendum on June 2,

1946. Victor Emmanuel died in exile in Alexandria, Egypt, on December 28, 1947.

NOTES

1. Joachim C. Fest, *The Face of the Third Reich* (New York: Pantheon Books, 1970), 97.

2. Alan Bullock, *Hitler: A Study in Tyranny*, rev. ed. (New York: Harper and Row, 1962), 550.

3. Karl Dietrich Bracher, *The German Dictatorship: The Origins, Structure and Effects of National Socialism* (New York: Praeger, 1970), 423.

4. Fest, *Face of the Third Reich*, 197.

Primary Documents: Fascism in Europe

Document 1
ADOLF HITLER, *MEIN KAMPF*: SOME KEY IDEAS

Adolf Hitler's principal ideas, which formed much of the content of the Nazi ideology and program, were expounded in his book *Mein Kampf* (My struggle), a curious combination of self-serving autobiography, party history, and vehement political diatribe. He wrote the first volume while he was in prison in 1924; it was published the following year. Subsequently, he dictated a second volume, which appeared in 1926. The two volumes were combined in 1930 and published in bible format; after 1936 the work was regularly presented as a wedding gift to newly married German couples. Although this Hitlerian treatise was translated into sixteen languages and frequently reprinted, it may well have remained the least read book inside and outside of Germany. Hitler's dense prose and especially his extreme ideas made it difficult for any reader to navigate through his tome.

The reprinted excerpts from *Mein Kampf* illustrate some of the major themes that run through Hitler's speeches and ideology. At the basis of his beliefs lay a crude form of social Darwinism: "Man has become great through struggle," he contended. However, humans were engaged in a struggle throughout history that was most of all a racial struggle. Hitler viewed societies as being divided into distinct races whose differing qualities determined everything in the life and culture of societies. Races could be ranked according to their culture-building abilities, with the Aryan or Nordic race, including the Germans, at the top. Throughout the ages, Hitler asserted, the Aryans had demonstrated their superiority in cultural creation and other human qualities. Their greatest foe was the Jews, whom Hitler defined as a demonic antirace incapable of creating a cultural community and threatening the very life and purity of the Aryans. Rather self-righteously he declared: "I believe that I am acting in accordance with the will of the Almighty Creator: *by defending myself against the Jew, I am fighting for the work of the Lord* [italics in the original]. According to the Nazi leader, whatever progressive ideas and institutions had spread throughout modern Western civilization—liberalism, parliamentarism, democracy—were only being used by the Jews to beguile the masses in order to ensure Jewish domination of the world. He especially denounced Marxism as a part of the Jewish conspiracy against the German people. In order to overcome the Jewish drive toward world domination and to save Western civilization from decadence and destruction, the German people must above all safeguard the purity of their race. He decried the mingling of races as defilement of the blood that weakened the stronger and brought physical and intellectual regression of the Aryan race.

HITLER ON MARXISM

I began to make myself familiar with the founders of [Marxism] in order to study the foundations of the movement. If I reached my goal more quickly than at first I had perhaps ventured to believe, it was thanks to my newly acquired, though at that time not very profound, knowledge of the Jewish question. This alone enabled me to draw a practical comparison between the reality and the theoretical flim-flam of the founding fathers of Social Democracy, since it taught me to understand the language of the Jewish people, who speak in order to conceal or at least to veil their thoughts; their real aim is not therefore to be found in the lines themselves, but slumbers well concealed between them.

For me this was the time of the greatest spiritual upheaval I have ever had to go through.

I had ceased to be a weak-kneed cosmopolitan and become an anti-Semite. . . .

The Jewish doctrine of Marxism rejects the aristocratic principle of Nature and replaces the eternal privilege of power and strength by the mass of numbers and their dead weight. Thus it denies the value of personality in man, contests the significance of nationality and race, and thereby withdraws from humanity the premise of its existence and its culture. As a foundation of the universe, this doctrine would bring about the end of any order intellectually conceivable to man. As, in this greatest of all recognizable organisms, the result of an application of such a law could only be chaos, on earth it could only be destruction for the inhabitants of this planet.

If, with the help of his Marxist creed, the Jew is victorious over the other peoples of the world, his crown will be the funeral wreath of humanity and this planet will, as it did thousands of years ago, move through the ether devoid of men.

Eternal Nature inexorably avenges the infringement of her commands.

Hence today I believe that I am acting in accordance with the will of the Almighty Creator: *by defending myself against the Jew, I am fighting for the work of the Lord.*

HITLER ON THE JEWS

... [T]he Jew of all times has lived in the states of other peoples, and there formed his own state, which, to be sure, habitually sailed under the disguise of 'religious community' as long as outward circumstances made a complete revelation of his nature seem inadvisable. But as soon as he felt strong enough to do without the protective cloak, he always dropped the veil and suddenly became what so many of the others previously did not want to believe and see: the Jew....

... [T]he Jew also becomes liberal and begins to rave about the necessary progress of mankind.

Slowly he makes himself the spokesman of a new era.

Also, of course, he destroys more and more thoroughly the foundations of any economy that will really benefit the people. By way of stock shares he pushes his way into the circuit of national production which he turns into a purchasable or rather tradable object, thus robbing the enterprises of the foundations of a personal ownership. Between employer and employee there arises that inner estrangement which later leads to political class division.

Finally, the Jewish influence on economic affairs grows with terrifying speed through the stock exchange. He becomes the owner, or at least the controller, of the national labor force.

To strengthen his political position he tries to tear down the racial and civil barriers which for a time continue to restrain him at every step. To this end he fights with all the tenacity innate in him for religious tolerance....

His ultimate goal ... is the victory of 'democracy,' or, as he understands it: the rule of parliamentarianism. It is most compatible with his requirements; for it excludes the personality—and puts in its place the majority characterized by stupidity, incompetence, and last but not least, cowardice....

... [T]he striving of the Jewish people for world domination ... is just as natural as the urge of the Anglo-Saxon to seize domination of the earth. And just as the Anglo-Saxon pursues this course in his own way and carries on the fight with his own weapons, likewise the Jew. He goes his way, the way of sneaking in among the nations and boring from within, and he fights with his weapons, with lies and slander, poison and corruption, intensifying the struggle to the point of bloodily exterminating his hated foes. *In Russian Bolshevism we must see the attempt undertaken by the Jews in the twentieth century to achieve world domination....*

HITLER ON RACE

For me and all true National Socialists there is but one doctrine: people and fatherland.

What we must fight for is to safeguard the existence and reproduction of our race and our people, the sustenance of our children and the purity of our blood, the freedom and independence of the fatherland, so that our people may mature for the fulfillment of the mission allotted it by the creator of the universe.

Every thought and every idea, every doctrine and all knowledge, must serve this purpose. And everything must be examined from this point of view and used or rejected according to its utility. Then no theory will stiffen into a dead doctrine, since it is life alone that all things must serve....

No more than Nature desires the mating of weaker with stronger individuals, even less does she desire the blending of a higher with a lower race, since, if she did, her whole work of higher breeding, over perhaps hundreds of thousands of years, might be ruined with one blow.

Historical experience offers countless proofs of this. It shows with terrifying clarity that in every mingling of Aryan blood with that of lower peoples the result was the end of the cultured people. North America, whose population consists in by far the largest part of Germanic elements who mixed but little with the lower colored peoples, shows a different humanity and culture from Central and South America, where the predominantly Latin immigrants often mixed with the aborigines on a large scale. By this one example, we can clearly and distinctly recognize the effect of racial mixture. The Germanic inhabitant of the American continent, who has remained racially pure and unmixed, rose to be master of the continent; he will remain the master as long as he does not fall a victim to defilement of the blood.

The result of all racial crossing is therefore in brief always the following:

(a) Lowering of the level of the higher race;

(b) Physical and intellectual regression and hence the beginning of a slowly but surely progressing sickness.

To bring about such a development is, then, nothing else but to sin against the will of the eternal creator....

Everything we admire on this earth today—science and art, technology and inventions—is only the creative product of a few peoples and originally perhaps of *one* race. On them depends the existence of this whole culture. If they perish, the beauty of this earth will sink into the grave with them....

It is idle to argue which race or races were the original representative of human culture and hence the real founders of all that we sum up under the word 'humanity.' It is simpler to raise this question with regard to the present, and here an easy, clear answer results. All the human culture, all the results of art, science, and technology that we see before us today, are almost exclusively the creative product of the Aryan. This very fact admits of the not unfounded inference that he alone was the founder of all higher humanity, therefore representing the prototype of all that we understand by the word "man." He is the Prometheus of mankind from whose bright forehead the divine spark of genius has sprung at all times, forever kindling anew that fire of knowledge which illumined the night of silent mysteries and thus caused man to climb the path to mastery over the other beings of this earth. Exclude him—and perhaps after a few thousand years darkness will again descend on the earth, human culture will pass, and the world turn to a desert.

Source: Adolf Hitler, *Mein Kampf*, trans. Ralph Manheim (Boston: Houghton Mifflin, 1943), 64, 65, 214–215, 286, 288, 290, 305, 314–315, 316, 661. Copyright © 1943, renewed 1971 by Houghton Mifflin Company. Reprinted by permission of Houghton Mifflin Company and Pimlico. All rights reserved.

Document 2
THE POLITICAL IDEAS OF ITALIAN FASCISM

Unlike Nazism, which from the beginning had a clear-cut ideological base, Italian Fascism was slow to develop a doctrinal formulation. Much of this was due to Mussolini's ideological confusion. Having come from a socialist orientation that he never developed into a coherent set of principles, he and his early followers prided themselves on being men of action intent on winning power. Thus the Fascists of the 1920s brought together a mixed coalition of reactionaries, conservatives, and monarchists, as well as republicans, socialists, clericals and anticlericals, and especially nationalists. In 1932, a decade after the march on Rome, Mussolini together with the philosopher and early minister of education Giovanni Gentile, wrote an article on Fascism for the *Enciclopedia Italiana*. It is assumed that the philosophical portion of the article, outlining fundamental ideas, was the work of Gentile, whereas sections that deal with the political and social doctrine, from which the excerpts that follow are taken, are attributable primarily to Mussolini. He stressed that Fascism in the early years was not a doctrine but a faith. It did not accept peace as a lasting condition but promoted heroism and war as creative acts in the life of a people. Fascism rejected Marxian socialism, liberalism, democracy, and government by majority. Mussolini defined the Fascist state as a will to power and empire. Its expression was not so much to be sought in the acquisition of territorial gains or military prowess as in the advancement of morality and the spirit.

BENITO MUSSOLINI: THE POLITICAL AND SOCIAL DOCTRINE OF FASCISM

Above all, Fascism, the more it considers and observes the future and the development of humanity quite apart from political considerations of the moment, believes neither in the possibility nor the utility of perpetual peace. It thus repudiates the doctrine of Pacifism—born of a renunciation of the struggle and an act of cowardice in the face of sacrifice. War alone brings up to its highest tension all human energy and puts the stamp of nobility upon the peoples who have the courage to meet it. All other trials are substitutes, which never really put men into the position where they have to make the great decision—the alternative of life or death. Thus a doctrine which is founded upon this harmful postulate of peace is hostile to Fascism. And thus hostile to the spirit of Fascism . . . are all the international leagues and societies which, as history will show, can be scattered to the winds when once strong national feeling is aroused by any motive— sentimental, ideal, or practical. This anti-pacifist spirit is carried by Fascism even into the life of the individual; the proud motto of the *Squadrista*, "Me ne frego," (I do not fear), written on the bandage of the wound, is an act of philosophy not only stoic, the summary of a doctrine not only political—it is the education to combat, the acceptation of the risks which combat implies, and a new way of life for Italy. Thus the Fascist accepts life and loves it, knowing nothing of and despising suicide; he rather conceives of life as duty and struggle and conquest, life which should be high and full, lived for oneself, but above all for others—those who are at hand and those who are far distant, contemporaries, and those who will come after. . . .

Such a conception of life makes Fascism the complete opposite of that doctrine, the base of the so-called scientific and Marxian Socialism, the materialist conception of history; according to which the history of human civilization can be explained simply through the conflict of interests among the various social groups and by the change and development in the means and instruments of production. That the changes in the economic field . . . have their importance no one can deny; but that these factors are sufficient to explain the history of humanity excluding all others is an absurd delusion. Fascism, now and always, believes in holiness and in heroism; that is to say, in actions influenced by no economic motive, direct or indirect. And if the economic conception of history be denied . . . it follows that the existence of an unchangeable and unchanging class war is also denied. And above all Fascism denies that class war can be the preponderant force in the transformation of society. These two fundamental concepts of Socialism being thus refuted, nothing is left of it but the sentimental aspiration— as old as humanity itself—towards a social convention in which the sorrows and sufferings of the humblest shall be alleviated. But here again Fascism repudiates the conception of "economic happiness." . . .

Fascism denies the materialist conception of happiness as a possibility, and abandons it to its inventors, the economists of the first half of the nineteenth century: that is to say, Fascism denies the validity of the equation, well-being–happiness, which would reduce men to the level of animals, caring for one thing only—to be fat and well-fed—and would thus degrade humanity to a purely physical existence.

After Socialism, Fascism combats the whole complex system of democratic ideology; and repudiates it, whether in its theoretical premises or in its practical application. Fascism denies that the majority, by the simple fact that it is a majority, can direct human society; it denies that numbers alone can govern by means of a periodical consultation, and it affirms the immutable, beneficial, and fruitful inequality of mankind, which can never be permanently leveled through the mere operation of a mechanical process such as universal suffrage. The democratic regime may be defined as from time to time giving the people the illusion of sovereignty, while the real effective sovereignty lies in the hands of other concealed and irresponsible forces. Democracy is a regime nominally without a king, but it is ruled by many kings—more absolute, tyrannical, and ruinous than one sole king, even though a tyrant. This explains why Fascism, having first in 1922 (for reasons of expediency) assumed an attitude tending towards republicanism, renounced this point of view before the March to Rome; being convinced that the question of political form is not today of prime importance. . . .

A party which entirely governs a nation is a fact entirely new to history, there are no possible references or parallels. Fascism uses in its construction whatever elements in the Liberal, Social, or Democratic doctrines still have a living value; it maintains what may be called the certainties which we owe to history, but it rejects all the rest—that is to say, the conception that there can be any doctrine of unquestioned efficacy for all times and all peoples. . . . Political doctrines pass, but humanity remains; and it may rather be expected that this will be a century . . . of Fascism. For if the nineteenth century was the century of individualism (Liberalism always signifying individualism) it may be expected that this will be the century of collectivism, and hence the century of the State. . . .

Every doctrine tends to direct human activity towards a determined objective; but the action of men also reacts upon the doctrine, transforms it, adapts it to new needs, or supersedes it with something else. A doctrine then must be no mere exercise in words, but a living act; and thus the value of Fascism lies in the fact that it is veined with pragmatism, but at the same time has a will to exist and a will to power, a firm front in face of the reality of "violence."

The foundation of Fascism is the conception of the State. . . . Fascism conceives of the State as an absolute, in comparison with which all individuals or groups are relative, only to be conceived of in their relation to the State. . . .

The Fascist State has drawn into itself even the economic activities of the nation, and through the corporative social and educational institutions created by it, its influence reaches every aspect of the national life and includes, framed in their respective organizations, all the political, economic and spiritual forces of the nation. A State which reposes upon the support of millions of individuals who recognize its authority, are continually conscious of its power and are ready at once to serve it, is not the only tyrannical State of the medieval lord nor has it anything in common with the absolute governments either before or after 1789. The individual in the Fascist State is not annulled but rather multiplied, just in the same way that a soldier in a regiment is not diminished but rather increased by the number of his comrades. The Fascist State organizes the nation, but leaves a sufficient margin of liberty to the individual; the latter is deprived of all useless and possibly harmful freedom, but retains what is essential; the deciding power in this question cannot be the individual but the State alone.

The Fascist State is an embodied will to power and government; the Roman tradition is here an ideal of force in action. According to Fascism, government is not so much a thing to be expressed in territorial or military terms as in terms of morality and the spirit. It must be thought of as an empire—that is to say, a nation which directly or indirectly rules other nations, without the need for conquering a single square yard of territory. For Fascism, the growth of empire, that is to say the expansion of the nation, is an essential manifestation of vitality, and its opposite a sign of decadence. Peoples which are rising, or rising again after a period of decadence, are always imperialist: any renunciation is a sign of decay and of death. Fascism is the doctrine best adapted to represent the tendencies and the aspirations of a people, like the people of Italy, who are rising again after many centuries of abasement and foreign servitude. But empire demands discipline, the co-ordination of all forces and a deeply felt sense of duty and sacrifice; this fact explains many aspects of the practical working of the regime, the character of many forces in the State, and the necessarily severe measures which must be taken against those who would oppose this spontaneous and inevitable movement of Italy in the twentieth century, and would oppose it by recalling the outworn ideology of the nineteenth century. . . . for never before has the nation stood more in need of authority, of direction, and of order. If every age has its own characteristic doctrine, there are a thousand signs which point to Fascism as the characteristic doctrine of our time. For if a doctrine must be a living thing, this is proved by the fact that Fascism has created a living faith; and that this faith is very powerful in the minds of men, is demonstrated by those who have suffered and died for it.

Source: Benito Mussolini, "The Political and Social Doctrine of Fascism," *International Conciliation*, no. 306 (January 1935): 7–10, 12–13, 15, 16–17. Reprinted by permission of the Carnegie Endowment for International Peace.

Document 3
HUNGARISM

An interesting variant of German and Italian fascism was Hungarian national socialism, or Hungarism, a doctrine propagated by Ferenc Szálasi, who in 1937 founded Arrow Cross, the Hungarian fascist party. He was of Armenian and German origin and served as a general staff officer before he emerged as the dominant leader of various fascist factions that became united in the Arrow Cross. A man of limited talents, especially when compared to Hitler and Mussolini, he saw himself as the chosen leader of Hungary who was destined to lead the Carpatho-Danubian Great Fatherland, which would encompass much of southeastern and eastern Europe. Along with Nazi Germany and Fascist Italy, this southeastern European fatherland would be one of the dominant forces of the new Europe and the world.

Szálasi's main ideas were developed in *Ut es Cel* (The faith and the goal), a much shorter doctrinal treatise than Hitler's *Mein Kampf*, though perhaps not any less rambling. He saw three leading ideologies in the twentieth century: Christianity, Marxism, and Hungarism. In his view, Christianity was the highest spiritual religion but not a political creed, and Marxism was reduced to materialist tendencies. Hungarism, however, would draw on both Christianity and socialism to form an enlightened national socialism that would be realized in political and social affairs. Szálasi was a devout Catholic and regarded "true Christianity" as an important part of the citizen's life in the Carpatho-Danubian Great Fatherland, while recognizing the Catholic, Protestant, and Orthodox churches. Although he was sometimes regarded as anti-Semitic, he declared himself a-Semitic, maintaining that Jews had no place in a national socialist society. They should not be persecuted but required to emigrate. He believed that the existence of a genuine Turanian-Hungarian race was important for Hungarism but criticized Nazi racial ideas as excessive. Szálasi's party found much of its following among some members of the middle class, the military, and especially workers and peasants. The Arrow Cross was installed in power in Hungary with the help of the German military in the last months of 1944, when Hungary was already being invaded by the Red Army and Hitler and the Nazis found the authoritarian Hungarian regime under Admiral Miklós Horthy defecting from the German alliance.

THE WAY AND AIM OF HUNGARISM

Hungarism is an ideological system. It is the Hungarian practice of the national socialistic view of the world and time spirit.

Not Hitlerism, not fascism, not antisemitism, but Hungarism.

Thus Hungarism means socialism, the tuning together of the moral, spiritual, and material interests of the I and the Us. It has set as its aim not the happiness of the particular privileged individuals or classes, but of the totality of individuals and classes. But Hungarism at the same time also means national socialism, because it fights for the happiness of the most natural community of the people, for the welfare of the nation and through this of every working individual. Hungarism is not designed for the "Mutilated country," neither is it merely designed for the needs of the Hungarian people, but for all the nationalities who live in the Danube basin surrounded by the Carpathian mountains, who are worthy of a country and earth to grow roots in, and who, under the direction and guidance of the Hungarian people, and with them, compose the social, economic, moral, spiritual, material and political unity of the Hungarian nation.

Besides all this, Hungarism is the protector of all the members of its national family who are strewn all over the world and have been forced out [of their country (E. Weber)] by the need to earn a livelihood. Its right and duty is their repatriation into the Great Fatherland.

Hungarism assures peace for the Hungarians and groups of nations living here, the Pax Hungarica, in the Carpathian Danube basin not only by giving a Fatherland and a home to the groups of peoples, furthermore by giving cultural autonomy (language, popular education, self-government and justice, within the framework of self-government and the self-determination of economic interest groups) all these are assured for them within its system of allegiance, but also it will sanction through popular elections based on free assertion of their will, the moral, spiritual, and material well being of the national groups living within the Carpathian Danube basin under the jurisdiction of the Hungarian people. . . .

The basis for this inner peace will be the workpeace of all working classes who live within the nation. This workpeace will hold in inseparable national unity the peasant who supports the nation, the worker who builds the nation, the intelligentsia which leads the nation, the soldier who defends the nation, and the tokens of national immortality: women and youth. Furthermore, it creates: 1) The economic peace which proportionately divides the profits of labor and production between the factors of production, in order to abolish money capitalism and the hopeless misery of the working class. 2) Social peace which ignores privileged classes: feudal, clerical, and liberal capitalist ruling class, upper, middle and lower class, but rather the united socialist community of the workers; and 3) Political peace which does not mislead the political nation with selfish party interests, but in which a single leading political idea directs the community to ensure the welfare of the nation within the community of other European nations. . . .

The Hungarian national socialist economy is inseparable from the Hungarian national socialist moral and spiritual life; its aim being the material welfare of the community of the people. *Thus our national economy and its every part is a means and not an end. . . .*

We cannot bring our fight against the obsolete system of private capital to victory without solving the Jewish question. The realization of the Hungarian national socialist economic system and the solution of the Jewish question are inseparable, one follows from the other, the two tasks are two sides of the same coin.

As a result of our successful work of enlightenment liberal private capitalism has little by little only Jewish followers left. In spite of this the objection is still, though ever more rarely, heard in intellectual circles— especially on the part of the leading intellectuals who have been forced upon the nation, that the solution of the Jewish question by "The German system" would result for this country in upsetting the economic and financial order from one day to the next and that the country's economy and finance could not survive this for a single day. Such a statement is either a fool-hardy lie or criminal stupidity which leads to the misleading, to the ruin, and to the death of the nation. Let there be an end, once and for all to the official superstition that Hungarian life without Jews is unimaginable. Truly, the Hungarian national community can exist without the Jew. Anyhow we shall solve the Jewish question not according to a "foreign system," since the totality of our national socialist practice does not develop according to a foreign system, but according to our peculiar national circumstances and Hungarian national abilities.

Source: Eugen Weber, *Varieties of Fascism* (Princeton, NJ: D. Van Nostrand, 1964), 157–158, 159–160. Reprinted with permission of R. E. Krieger Publishing Company.

Document 4
HITLER'S ENABLING ACT

After Hitler was appointed Reich chancellor on January 30, 1933, he ruled by presidential decree as previous chancellors had done during times when the Reichstag was dissolved. In addition, both before and following the Reichstag fire on February 27, Reich President Paul von Hindenburg granted him emergency powers that enabled the Nazi government to establish a police state by suspending such basic civil liberties as freedom of the press, the right to assemble, and warrants for home searches. However, the Hitler regime still lacked permanent dictatorial power. This was attained when a newly elected Reichstag passed the Enabling Act on March 24, 1933.

In the Reichstag election of March 5, during which the Nazis used strong-arm methods to bolster their parliamentary representation, the Nazi Party still fell short of a majority, attaining only 43.9 percent of the popular vote. With the support of the Nationalists, Hitler could muster a simple Reichstag majority, but he needed a constitutional majority to adopt the Law for the Removal of the Distress of the People and Reich, as the Enabling Act was officially called. Using threats and cajolery, he persuaded the Catholic Center Party to support the extraordinary legislation by promising to respect the rights of the Catholics. In this atmosphere of intimidation, intensified by the arrest of the Communists and the hostile posture of the SA and the SS, only the Social Democrats had the courage to vote against the Enabling Act. It carried 444 to 94 and thus established the legal basis for Hitler's dictatorship, empowering the chancellor and his cabinet to issue laws that deviated from the constitution and to promulgate treaties without the consent of the Reichstag. The duration of the act was initially set for a period of four years. It was renewed by the Nazi-appointed Reichstag in 1937 and in 1939; in 1943 it was extended indefinitely by Führer decree.

ENABLING ACT OF MARCH 1933

The Reichstag has resolved the following law, which is, with the approval of the National Council, herewith promulgated, after it has been established that the requirements have been satisfied for legislation altering the Constitution.

Article 1

National laws can be enacted by the National Cabinet as well as in accordance with the procedure established in the Constitution. This applies also to the laws referred to in article 85, paragraph 2, and in article 87 of the Constitution.

Article 2

The national laws enacted by the National Cabinet may deviate from the Constitution so far as they do not affect the position of the Reichstag and National Council. The powers of the President remain undisturbed.

Article 3

The national laws enacted by the National Cabinet are prepared by the Chancellor and published in the *Reichsgesetzblatt*. They come into effect, unless otherwise specified, upon the day following their publication. Articles 68 to 77 of the Constitution do not apply to the laws enacted by the National Cabinet.

Article 4

Treaties of the Reich with foreign states which concern matters of national legislation do not require the consent of the bodies participating in legislation. The National Cabinet is empowered to issue the necessary provisions for the execution of these treaties.

Article 5

This law becomes effective on the day of publication. It becomes invalid on April 1, 1937; it further becomes invalid when the present National Cabinet is replaced by another.

Berlin, March 24, 1933

Reich's President VON HINDENBURG

Reich's Chancellor ADOLF HITLER

Reich's Minister of the Interior FRICK

Reich's Minister for Foreign Affairs BARON VON NEURATH

Reich's Minister of Finances COUNT SCHWERIN VON KROSIGK

Source: U.S. Department of State, *National Socialism: Basic Principles* (Washington, DC: U.S. Government Printing Office, 1943), 217–218.

Document 5
VICE CHANCELLOR FRANZ VON PAPEN'S MARBURG SPEECH: A CHALLENGE TO HITLER

Franz von Papen was Reich chancellor in 1932 and Hitler's vice chancellor from 1933 to 1934. He was a major figure in the January 1933 political intrigues that enabled Hitler to attain the chancellorship. Determined to gain revenge on his successor in the chancellorship, General Kurt von Schleicher, the wily Papen proposed a right-wing coalition government consisting of the Nazis and the conservative German National People's Party. He persuaded the reluctant Reich President Paul von Hindenburg to accept a joint Hitler-Papen government, assuring him that he and his Nationalist cabinet members would be able to tame and restrain Hitler and the Nazis, since they were to have only three of the twelve cabinet positions. This assumption, however, was a wild delusion, for Hitler skillfully outmaneuvered the opportunist German Nationalists and quickly expanded his dictatorial power.

On June 17, 1934, the increasingly troubled Papen finally ventured an attack on the Nazi policies in a speech to students at the University of Marburg. Expressing the concerns of the Nationalist conservatives, he denounced the Nazification of German institutions and the perpetuation of one-party government. He called for greater political freedom as a means of achieving a more democratic state, the restoration of a just legal system, and the renewal of national life based on Christian conservatism. Hitler was enraged by Papen's speech and called him a "ridiculous dwarf" and a "worm." Joseph Goebbels forbade the dissemination of Papen's speech. In the Röhm purge, which Hitler carried out two weeks after the speech, Papen was put under house arrest and barely escaped with his life. His speech writer, Edgar Jung, a conservative intellectual, was not so lucky. He was arrested by the Gestapo, tortured, and shot.

EXCERPTS FROM FRANZ VON PAPEN'S MARBURG SPEECH

We know that rumors and whispering propaganda must be brought out from the darkness where they have taken refuge. Frank and manly discussion is better for the German people than, for instance, a press without an outlet, described by the Minister for Propaganda "as no longer having a face." This deficiency undoubtedly exists. The function of the press should be to inform the Government where deficiencies have crept in, where corruption has settled down, where grave mistakes have been committed, where incapable men are in the wrong places, where offenses are committed against the spirit of the German revolution. An anonymous or secret information service, however well organized it may be, can never be a substitute for this task of the press. For the newspaper editor is responsible to the law and to his conscience, whereas anonymous news sources are not subject to control and are exposed to the danger of Byzantinism. When, therefore, the proper organs of public opinion do not shed sufficient light into the mysterious darkness, which at present seems to have fallen upon the German public, the statesman himself must intervene and call matters by their right names. . . .

It is a matter of historical truth that the necessity for a fundamental change of course was recognized and urged even by those who shunned the path of revolution through a mass party. A claim for revolutionary or nationalist monopoly by a certain group, therefore, seems to be exaggerated, quite apart from the fact that it disturbs the community. . . .

All of life cannot be organized; otherwise it becomes mechanized. The State is organization; life is growth. . . .

Domination by a single party replacing the majority party system, which rightly has disappeared, appears to me historically as a transitional stage, justified only as long as the safeguarding of the new political change demands it and until the new process of personal selection begins to function. . . .

But one should not confuse the religious State, which is based upon an active belief in God, with a secular State in which earthly values replace such belief and are embellished with religious honors. . . .

Certainly the outward respect for religious belief is an improvement on the disrespectful attitude produced by a degenerate rationalism. But we should not forget that real religion is a link with God, and not substitutes such as have been introduced into the consciousness of nations especially by Karl Marx's materialistic conception of history. If wide circles of people, from this same viewpoint of the totalitarian State and the complete amalgamation of the nation, demand a uniform religious foundation, they should not forget that we should be happy to have such a foundation in the Christian faith. . . .

It is my conviction that the Christian doctrine clearly represents the religious form of all occidental thinking and that with the reawakening of religious forces the German people also will be permeated anew by the Christian spirit, a spirit the profundity of which is almost forgotten by a humanity that has lived through the nineteenth century. A struggle is approaching the decision as to whether the new Reich of the Germans will be Christian or is to be lost in sectarianism and half-religious materialism. . . .

But once a revolution has been completed, the Government only represents the people as a whole and is never the champion of individual groups. . . .

The Government is well informed on all the self-interest, lack of character, want of truth, unchivalrous conduct, and arrogance trying to rear its head under cover of the German revolution. It is also not deceived about the fact that the rich store of confidence bestowed upon it by the German people is threatened. If we want a close connection with and a close association among the people, we must not underestimate the good sense of the people; we must return their confidence and not try to hold them everlastingly in bondage. The German people know that their situation is serious, they feel the economic distress, they are perfectly aware of the shortcoming of many laws born of emergency; they have a keen feeling for violence and injustice; they smile at clumsy attempts to deceive them by false optimism. No organization and no propaganda, however good, will in the long run be able to preserve confidence. I therefore viewed the wave of propaganda against the so-called foolish critics from a different angle than many others did. Confidence and readiness to co-operate cannot be won by provocation, especially of youth, nor by threats against helpless segments of the people, but only by discussion with the people with trust on both sides. The people know what great sacrifices are expected from them. They will bear them and follow the Führer in unflinching loyalty, if they are allowed to have their part in the planning and in the work, if every word of criticism is not taken for ill will, and if despairing patriots are not branded as enemies of the State.

Source: International Military Tribunal, Nuremberg, 1945–1946, *Trial of the Major War Criminals* (Nuremberg: International Military Tribunal, 1948), 16:292–293, 295.

Document 6
DECLARATION OF THE GERMAN EVANGELICAL CHURCH DEFENDING ITS FAITH AND ATTACKING HITLER'S IDEA OF "POSITIVE CHRISTIANITY," AUGUST 1936

In Hitler's drive of *Gleichschaltung*, the policy of coordinating all elements in the Third Reich, political parties and labor unions were quickly dissolved or subordinated to Nazi leadership. However, the established churches remained an obstacle to the Nazi effort to attain total control over German society. Formally the Nazi Party professed to support "Positive Christianity," which was little more than radical ideology expressed in religious terms, but Hitler and many Nazis rejected Christianity. However, in the years before the seizure of power and also in its immediate aftermath, the Nazis refrained from major attacks on the Christian churches. It was clear to many church leaders and theologians that Nazi ideology was incompatible with Christian theology and ethics, but at first they tended to ignore these differences. Pressures began to build, however, when the German Christians, a Protestant pro-Nazi organization within the Evangelical Church, attempted to push for recognition and unification of all Protestant churches in a single Reich church under a Nazi-approved bishop.

In September 1933, to counteract the Nazification move, Martin

Niemöller, pastor at a prominent church in Berlin, called for the establishment of a Pastors' Emergency Union. In a few months 4,000 Protestant pastors had joined it. In the following year many of these pastors helped form the Confessing Church, which soon declared its Provisional Directory to be the legitimate representative of the German Evangelical Church. As actions against Protestant pastors and church groups intensified, leaders of the Confessing Church sent a secret memorandum to Hitler in June 1936, reproving the government's anti-Christian campaign and the lawlessness of the Gestapo. When the text of the memorandum found its way into the foreign press, Nazi attacks against the Confessing Church became more bitter and prompted the Provisional Directory and Brotherhood Council of the Confessing Church to issue the pulpit declaration from which excerpts are printed here. Hitler retaliated by ordering a crackdown on the leaders and pastors of the Confessing Church. By 1937 several hundred pastors were arrested and sent to concentration camps, including Martin Niemöller.

MANIFESTO OF THE GERMAN EVANGELICAL CHURCH, AUGUST 23, 1936

To Evangelical Christians and the Authorities in Germany.

Brethren and Sisters:

The German people are facing a decision of the greatest historical importance.

The question is whether the Christian faith is to retain its right to exist in Germany or not. Today the gospel of Jesus Christ is being attacked here systematically with unequaled violence. This is being done not only by those who reject any belief in God, but also by those who do not wish to deny God, but think they can reject the revelations of Jesus Christ. Powers of the State and of the party are being used against the gospel of Jesus Christ and against those who profess it.

It is hard for us to say this.

The Evangelical Church knows that it is bound to our people and its authorities by the word of God and has its duties toward them. On every Sunday divine aid is asked for the Fuehrer and the Fatherland in the Evangelical Church services. Three years ago millions of Evangelical Germans welcomed the new beginning in the life of our people with warm hearts. They did so with all the more joy because the government of the nation had said in its first proclamation of February 1, 1933, that it would "firmly protect Christianity as the basis of our whole moral system."

It is absolutely fantastic for Evangelical Christians to think that official organs in the German Fatherland turn against the gospel of Jesus Christ. But it is happening, nevertheless.

We have kept silence about this for a long time. We have allowed our-selves to be told that it was only the action of a few individuals who would be called to order. We have waited; we have made representations. . . .

During this year the present acting management and the Council of the German Evangelical Church have sent to the Fuehrer a memorandum making apparent the whole misery and trouble of the Evangelical popu-lation. This memorandum is backed up point for point with detailed evi-dence. With the greatest conscientiousness, this memorandum and its contents were kept secret from the public, indeed even from the members of the Confessional Church, in order to give an opportunity to the Fuehrer of the Reich to give it a thorough examination and at the same time to avoid public misuse of this memorandum. Against our will and without the responsibility of the Confessional Church, this memorandum was pub-lished in the foreign press and thus became known also in Germany.

Now we are forced publicly to stand by our word. Now we must prove to the church what motivates us in connection with our people and our church. It is the duty of the Christian Church freely and publicly to oppose attacks upon the gospel, without fear of man. It is its duty especially to open the eyes of the rising generation to the danger menacing us all. It is in this sense of duty that we speak. . . .

We must have the right publicly and freely to bear witness before the German people of the faith of its fathers. The continual spying upon the work of the church must cease. The ban upon church meetings in public rooms must be lifted; the fetters placed upon the church press and the works of Christian charity must be removed. Above all must a halt be called upon State officials continually interfering in our internal affairs in the interest of those who, by their life and acts, are bringing about the destruction of the Evangelical Church.

A stop must be put to making it impossible for many evangelical Chris-tians to attend divine service through parades, triumphal processions, dem-onstrations, and other affairs just on Sunday forenoon. It must be demanded that the German youth be not so in demand for political and sport service as to prejudice Christian family life and to leave no time for showing loyalty to the church.

Source: International Conciliation, no. 324 (November 1936): 568, 569, 572. Reprinted by per-mission of the Carnegie Endowment for International Peace.

Document 7
PAPAL CONCERNS ON RELATIONS BETWEEN THE CHURCH AND THE GERMAN REICH IN 1937

Unlike the Evangelical Church, the Catholic Church had been a major opponent of Nazism before Hitler's advent to power. Once Hitler became chancellor, the Catholics even tried to wring concessions from the Führer. In March 1933 the Catholic Center Party agreed to support Hitler's Enabling Law, hoping that the Nazi government would guarantee freedom of religion, protection of church institutions, and the preservation of Catholic schools. A concordat negotiated by the Nazi government and the Vatican in July 1933 seemed to assure the church that its relations with the new German state would be based on respect for its special position in society.

In practice, however, the Nazi regime acted quite the contrary. Even though it derived a certain boost to its prestige from the Vatican recognition, the Nazi government soon attacked Catholic organizations, dismissed Catholic teachers, and pressured Catholic youth groups to join the Hitler Youth. Repeated protests by church leaders that the Nazi government was violating the provisions of the concordat and a personal interview of Cardinal Michael von Faulhaber with Hitler in November 1936 failed to persuade Hitler and his government to relax the pressure on the Catholic Church and to moderate its official harassment of Catholics. These circumstances induced Pope Pius XI to issue the general encyclical *Mit brennender Sorge* (With burning anxiety) in March 1937. To be read from Catholic pulpits in Germany, it denounced Nazi attacks on the Catholic Church and expressed deep concern over the oppression of its men and women. The Nazi response to these criticisms was short and harsh. The Nazi authorities intensified their attacks on the Catholic clergy. Hundreds of priests, monks, and nuns were vilified in the press, and many were arraigned on trumped-up charges, ranging from financial improprieties to illicit sexual practices.

EXCERPTS FROM THE ENCYCLICAL *MIT BRENNENDER SORGE* (WITH BURNING ANXIETY), MARCH 14, 1937

To the Venerable Brethren and Archbishops and Bishops of Germany and other Ordinaries in Peace and Communion with the Apostolic See.
Venerable Brethren, Greetings, and Apostolic Blessing.

It is with deep anxiety and growing surprise that We have long been following the painful trials of the Church and the increasing vexations which afflict those who have remained loyal in heart and action in the midst of a people that once received from St. Boniface the bright message and the Gospel of Christ and God's Kingdom. . . .

We turn to you, and through you, the German Catholics, who, like all suffering and afflicted children, are nearer to their Father's heart. At a time when your faith, like gold, is being tested in the fire of tribulation and persecution, when your religious freedom is beset on all sides, when the lack of religious teaching and of normal defense is heavily weighing on you, you have every right to words of truth and spiritual comfort from him whose first predecessor heard these words from the Lord: "I have prayed for thee that thy faith fail not: and thou being once converted, confirm thy brethren" (Luke xxii. 32).

True Faith in God

7. Take Care, Venerable Brethren, that above all, faith in God, the first and irreplaceable foundation of all religion, be preserved in Germany pure and unstained. The believer in God is not he who utters the name in his speech, but he for whom this sacred word stands for a true and worthy concept of the Divinity. Whoever identifies, by pantheistic confusion, God and the universe, by either lowering God to the dimensions of the world, or raising the world to the dimensions of God, is not a believer in God. Whoever follows that so-called pre-Christian Germanic conception of substituting a dark and impersonal destiny for the personal God, denies thereby the Wisdom and Providence of God who "Reacheth from end to end mightily, and ordereth all things sweetly" (Wisdom viii. 1). Neither is he a believer in God. . . .

43. He who searches the hearts and reins (Psalm vii. 10) is Our witness that We have no greater desire than to see in Germany the restoration of a true peace between Church and State. But if, without any fault of Ours, this peace is not to come, then the Church of God will defend her rights and her freedom in the name of the Almighty whose arm has not been shortened. Trusting in Him, "We cease not to pray and to beg" (Col. i. 9) for you, children of the Church, that the days of tribulation may end and that you may be found faithful in the day of judgment; for the persecutors and oppressors, that the Father of light and mercy may enlighten them as He enlightened Saul on the road of Damascus.

Source: The Papal Encyclicals, 1903–1939, trans. Claudia Carlen (Ann Arbor, MI: Pierian Press, 1990), 3:525, 526–527, 534–535. Reprinted by permission of Catholic Mind, America Press, Inc.

Document 8
FROM NUREMBERG LAWS TO KRISTALLNACHT: JEWS IN NAZI GERMANY

Once Hitler became chancellor, Nazi policy toward Jews was implemented in several stages. An organized boycott of Jewish businesses on April 1, 1933, was followed by a series of legal measures, from April to October, designed to eliminate Jews from public life by dismissing them as "non-Aryans." A person who had at least one Jewish parent or grandparent was declared to be of non-Aryan descent. Jews who held civil service positions, which included the state bureaucracy, public schools and universities, and courts, were dismissed. Jews also were excluded from educational and entertainment activities; they could not perform in the theater or in films nor work on newspapers and journals. The admission of Jewish students to institutions of higher learning was limited to 1.5 percent of new admissions.

This rash of measures was followed by a lull until September and November 1935, when the Nuremberg Laws denied full citizenship to Jews and defined Jews more precisely by distinguishing between full Jews and "Reich subjects of mixed, Jewish blood." Full Jews could not vote or hold office; they were forbidden to marry or even engage in extramarital sexual relations with "nationals of German or kindred blood." Employment of Aryan female servants under the age of forty-five was forbidden in Jewish households. Amendments to the original Nuremberg Laws followed and during the course of three years marked the progress of Nazi Jewish policy from discrimination to persecution. Jews were being shut out of German life politically, legally, and socially. During the 1936 Olympic Games in Berlin, the Nazi authorities temporarily suspended some of the most overt anti-Jewish activity visible to outside visitors, but in 1938–1939 the Nazis stepped up actions against Jews, culminating in the November 1938 pogrom known as *Kristallnacht* (Night of the Broken Glass).

In May 1938 major arrests of male Jews were begun, and many were sent "temporarily" to concentration camps. Starting in July, all Jews were required to carry special identification cards and passports and had to add the first name Israel or Sarah to their given names. Harassment and sporadic acts of violence were followed by a dramatic escalation of such acts in the night of November 9–10, 1938, during which a pogrom was initiated by Propaganda Minister Joseph Goebbels. The incident that ostensibly triggered this outburst of massive violence was the assassination of a minor German diplomat in Paris by a seventeen-year-old Polish Jew trying to avenge the expulsion of his parents from Germany. This unprecedented violent action by SA and party groups was dressed up as the "spontaneous reaction of the German people," but was anything but that, as the Heydrich teletype of November 10 shows. Practically all of Germany's 275 synagogues were either destroyed or heavily damaged, over 7,000 Jewish businesses were demolished, many Jewish homes were invaded and vandalized, and over 90 Jews were killed and thousands more tortured. Close to 30,000 Jewish men ended up in concentration camps.

The motive for this new anti-Jewish policy was largely economic, as the follow-up actions of the Nazi leadership substantiate. The Jews of Germany were assessed a so-called indemnity of 1 billion reichsmarks for the death of the German diplomat and had their insurance compensation confiscated. Their businesses and industries were now "Aryanized" and forfeited to the state. Jews in concentration camps were released if their relatives arranged for their emigration or they promised to initiate emigration proceedings. Deprived of their economic existence, Jews were completely excluded from German schools and universities as well as barred from theaters, concerts, museums, and most other public facilities. The ultimate Nazi aim of removing all Jews from Germany seemed in sight.

LAW FOR THE PROTECTION OF GERMAN BLOOD AND GERMAN HONOR OF 15 SEPTEMBER 1935

Thoroughly convinced by the knowledge that the purity of German blood is essential for the further existence of the German people and animated by the inflexible will to safe-guard the German nation for the entire future, the Reichstag has resolved upon the following law unanimously, which is promulgated herewith:

Section 1

1. Marriages between Jews and nationals of German or kindred blood are forbidden. Marriages concluded in defiance of this law are void, even if, for the purpose of evading this law, they are concluded abroad.

2. Proceedings for annulment may be initiated only by the Public Prosecutor.

Section 2

Relation[s] outside marriage between Jews and nationals of German or kindred blood are forbidden.

Section 3

Jews will not be permitted to employ female nationals of German or kindred blood in their household.

Section 4

1. Jews are forbidden to hoist the Reichs and national flag and to present the colors of the Reich.

2. On the other hand they are permitted to present the Jewish colors. The exercise of this authority is protected by the State.

Section 5

1. A person who acts contrary to the prohibition of section 1 will be punished with hard labor.

2. A person who acts contrary to the prohibition of section 2 will be punished with imprisonment or with hard labor.

3. A person who acts contrary to the provisions of sections 3 or 4 will be punished with imprisonment up to a year and with a fine or with one of these penalties.

Section 6

The Reich Minister of the Interior in agreement with the Deputy of the Fuehrer and the Reich Minister of Justice will issue the legal and administrative regulations which are required for the implementation and supplementation of this law.

The law will become effective on the day after the promulgation, section 3 however only on 1 January 1936.

Nurnberg, the 15 September 1935 at the Reich Party Rally of freedom.

The Fuehrer and Reich Chancellor
Adolf Hitler

The Reich Minister of Interior
Frick

The Reich Minister of Justice
Dr. Guertner

The Deputy of the Fuehrer
R. Hess

Reich Minister without portfolio

FIRST REGULATION TO THE REICHS CITIZENSHIP LAW OF 14 NOVEMBER 1935

On the basis of Article 3, Reichs Citizenship Law, of 15 Sept. 1935 . . . the following is ordered:

Article 1

1. Until further issue of regulations regarding citizenship papers, all subjects of German or kindred blood, who possessed the right to vote in the Reichstag elections, at the time the Citizenship Law came into effect, shall, for the time being, possess the rights of Reich citizens. The same shall be true of those whom the Reich Minister of the Interior, in conjunction with the Deputy of the Fuehrer, has given the preliminary citizenship.

2. The Reich Minister of the Interior, in conjunction with the Deputy of the Fuehrer, can withdraw the preliminary citizenship.

Article 2

1. The regulations in Article 1 are also valid for Reich subjects of mixed, Jewish blood.

2. An individual of mixed Jewish blood, is one who descended from one or two grandparents who were racially full Jews, insofar as [he or she] does not count as a Jew according to Article 5, paragraph 2. One grandparent shall be considered as full-blooded if he or she belonged to the Jewish religious community.

Article 3

Only the Reich citizen, as bearer of full political rights, exercises the right to vote in political affairs, and can hold a public office. The Reich Minister of the Interior, or any agency empowered by him, can make exceptions during the transition period, with regard to occupying public offices. The affairs of religious organizations will not be touched upon.

Article 4

1. A Jew cannot be a citizen of the Reich. He has no right to vote in political affairs, he cannot occupy a public office.

2. Jewish officials will retire as of 31 December 1935. If these officials served at the front in the World War, either for Germany or her allies, they will receive in full, until they reach the age limit, the pension to which they were entitled according to last received wages; they will, however, not advance in seniority. After reaching the age limit, their pension will be calculated anew, according to the last received salary, on the basis of which their pension was computed.

3. The affairs of religious organizations will not be touched upon.

4. The conditions of service of teachers in Jewish public schools remain unchanged, until new regulations of the Jewish school systems are issued.

Article 5

1. A Jew is anyone who descended from at least three grandparents who were racially full Jews. Article 2, par. 2, second sentence will apply.

2. A Jew is also one who descended from two full Jewish parents, if: (a) he belonged to the Jewish religious community at the time this law was issued, or who joined the community later; (b) he was married to a Jewish person, at the time the law was issued, or married one subsequently; (c) he is the offspring from a marriage with a Jew, in the sense of Section 1, which was contracted after the Law for the Protection of German Blood and German Honor became effective . . . ; (d) he is the offspring of an extramarital relationship, with a Jew, according to Section 1, and will be born out of wedlock after July 31, 1936. . . .

SECRET COPY OF TELETYPE FROM MUNICH, 10 NOVEMBER 1938, 1:20 A.M.

To all Headquarters and Stations of the State Police.
To all Districts and Sub-districts of the SD.
Urgent! Submit immediately to the Chief or his deputy!
RE: Measures against Jews tonight.

Because of the attempt on the life of the Secretary of the Legation von

Rath in Paris tonight, 9–10 November 1938, demonstrations against Jews are to be expected throughout the Reich. The following instructions are given on how to treat these events:

1. The Chiefs of the State Police, or their deputies, must get in telephonic contact with the political leaders [Gauleitung oder Kreisleitung] who have jurisdiction over their districts and have to arrange a joint meeting with the appropriate inspector or commander of the Order Police [Ordnungspolizei] to discuss the organization of the demonstrations. At these discussions the political leaders have to be informed that the German Police has received from the Reichsfuehrer SS and chief of the German Police the following instructions, in accordance with which the political leaders should adjust their own measures.

a. Only such measures should be taken which do not involve danger to German life or property. (For instance synagogues are to be burned down only when there is no danger of fire to the surroundings) [parenthesis in the original].

b. Business and private apartments of Jews may be destroyed but not looted. The police is instructed to supervise the execution of this order and to arrest looters.

c. On business streets, particular care is to be taken that non-Jewish business should be protected from damage.

d. Foreigners, even Jews, are not to be molested.

2. The demonstrations which are going to take place should not be hindered by the police provided that the instructions quoted above in section 1 are carried out. The police has only to supervise compliance with the instructions.

3. Upon receipt of this telegram, in all synagogues and offices of the Jewish communities the available archives should be seized by the police, to forestall destruction during the demonstrations. This refers only to valuable historical material, not to new lists of taxes, etc. The archives are to be turned over to the competent SD offices.

4. The direction of the measures of the Security Police concerning the demonstrations against Jews is vested with the organs of the State Police, inasmuch as the inspectors of the Security Police are not issuing their own orders. In order to carry out the measures of the Security Police, officials of the Criminal Police as well as members of the SD of the "Verfuegungstruppe" and the allgemeinen [sic] SS may be used.

5. Inasmuch as in the course of the events of this night the employment of officials used for this purpose would be possible in all districts as many Jews, especially rich ones, are to be arrested as can be accommodated in the existing prisons [Haftraeumen]. For the time being only healthy men not too old are to be arrested. Upon their arrest, the appropriate concen-

tration camps should be contacted immediately, in order to confine them in these camps as fast as possible. Special care should be taken that the Jews arrested in accordance with these instructions are not mistreated.

6. The contents of this order are to be forwarded to the appropriate inspectors and commanders of the Ordnungspolizei and to the districts of the SD [SD-Oberabschnitte und SD-Unterabschnitte], adding that the Reichsfuehrer SS and Chief of the German Police ordered this police measure. The Chief of the Ordnungspolizei, has given the necessary instructions to the Ordnungspolizei, including the fire brigade. In carrying out the ordered measures, the closest harmony should be assured between the Sicherheitspolizei and the Ordnungspolizei.

The receipt of this telegram is to be confirmed by the Chiefs of the State Police or their deputies by telegram to the Gestapo, care of SS Standartenfuehrer Mueller.

/s/ Heydrich,
SS Gruppenfuehrer.

Source: U.S. Chief of Counsel for the Prosecution of Axis Criminality, *Nazi Conspiracy and Aggression* (Washington, DC: U.S. Government Printing Office, 1946), 4:8–10, 636–638; 5: 798–800. Here and in the documents that follow, the spellings Fuehrer, instead of Führer, Goering, instead of Göring, and the like of the original document translations have been preserved.

Document 9
HITLER'S FOREIGN POLICY: WAR AND ACQUISITION OF LEBENSRAUM

The roots of World War II lie ultimately in Hitler's ideology. He utterly believed in the ability of the Aryans to create a superior civilization and the leadership role of the Germans in this mission. He also was convinced that nations are militarily successful only if they control a large land mass; he rejected colonies as unsuitable for a large-scale settlement and ineffective in providing national security. In *Mein Kampf*, he asserted that to ensure the dominance of the Aryan race in the Darwinian struggle with inferior races, the Germans must conquer a new empire and become a world power. He proclaimed that "Germany will either be a world power or there will be no Germany." Linking race and space, he believed that Western civilization would decay and that it was the destiny of the German people to replace it with a revitalized new empire that dominated the European continent. To establish this new empire, Germany would need to pursue a vigorous foreign policy that went beyond the restoration of lost territories following World War I and embark on the acquisition of *Lebensraum* (living space) in eastern Europe by wresting land from Russia. Hitler came to believe that a war of conquest of Russian soil would be a relatively easy undertaking, for the Bolshevik revolution had brought the Russian Empire close to collapse. He was convinced that the Slavic masses were incapable of creating a viable state for themselves and that the Jewish Bolshevik leadership could neither organize nor maintain such a state.

HITLER ON FOREIGN POLICY, WAR, AND CONQUEST

The foreign policy of the folkish state must safeguard the existence on this planet of the race embodied in the state, by creating a healthy, viable natural relation between the nation's population and growth on the one hand and the quantity and quality of its soil on the other hand.

As a healthy relation we may regard only that condition which assures the sustenance of a people on its own soil. Every other condition, even if it endures for hundreds, nay, thousands of years, is nevertheless unhealthy and will sooner or later lead to the injury if not annihilation of the people in question.

Only an adequately large space on this earth assures a nation of freedom of existence.

Moreover, the necessary size of the territory to be settled cannot be judged exclusively on the basis of present requirements, not even in fact on the basis of the yield of the soil compared to the population. For ... *in addition to its importance as a direct source of a people's food, another significance, that is, a military and political one, must be attributed to the area of a state.* If a nation's sustenance as such is assured by the amount of its soil, the safeguarding of the existing soil itself must also be borne in mind. This lies in the general power-political strength of the state, which in turn to no small extent is determined by geo-military considerations.

Hence, the German nation can defend its future only as a world power. . . .

If the National Socialist movement really wants to be consecrated by history with a great mission for our nation, it must be permeated by knowledge and filled with pain at our true situation in this world; boldly and conscious of its goal, it must take up the struggle against the aimlessness and incompetence which have hitherto guided our German nation in the line of foreign affairs. Then, without consideration of 'traditions' and prejudices, it must find the courage to gather our people and their strength for an advance along the road that will lead this people from its present restricted living space to new land and soil, and hence also free it from the danger of vanishing from the earth or of serving others as a slave nation.

The National Socialist movement must strive to eliminate the disproportion between our population and our area—viewing this latter as a source

*of food as well as a basis for power politics—between our historical past
and the hopelessness of our present impotence....*

But we National Socialists must go further. *The right to possess soil can
become a duty if without extension of its soil a great nation seems doomed
to destruction.* And most especially when not some little nigger nation or
other is involved, but the Germanic mother of life, which has given the
present-day world its cultural picture. *Germany will either be a world
power or there will be no Germany.* And for world power she needs that
magnitude which will give her the position she needs in the present period,
and life to her citizens.

*And so we National Socialists consciously draw a line beneath the foreign
policy tendency of our pre-War period. We take up where we broke off six
hundred years ago. We stop the endless German movement to the south
and west, and turn our gaze toward the land in the east. At long last we
break off the colonial and commercial policy of the pre-War period and
shift to the soil policy of the future.*

If we speak of soil in Europe today, we can primarily have in mind only
Russia and her vassal border states.

Source: Adolf Hitler, *Mein Kampf*, trans. Ralph Manheim (Boston: Houghton Mifflin, 1943),
   642–643, 645–646, 654. Copyright © 1943, renewed 1971 by Houghton Mifflin Company.
   Reprinted by permission of Houghton Mifflin Company and Pimlico. All rights reserved.

Document 10
THE HOSSBACH MEMORANDUM: HITLER OUTLINES
HIS PLANS FOR EXPANSION IN EUROPE

On November 5, 1937, Hitler called a secret conference in Berlin at
which he expounded his future plans for Germany's expansion.
Among those present were Werner von Blomberg, war minister, Hermann Göring, commander in chief of the Luftwaffe, Werner von
Fritsch, commander in chief of the army, Erich Raeder, commander
in chief of the navy, Konstantin von Neurath, foreign minister, and
Friedrich Hossbach, Hitler's military adjutant. The Führer's aide kept
detailed notes of the conference and days later produced an extensive
transcript, which has become known as the Hossbach Memorandum.

The protocol of the conference was used as a key prosecution document at the Nuremberg trial of 1945–1946 and was cited as clear
evidence of Hitler's premeditated plans for aggression. The majority
of historians of World War II consider the conference minutes one of
the most significant documents relating to the events preceding the
outbreak of the war. In contrast, revisionist historians have questioned
its importance as evidence of Germany's plans for aggression, and a

few have even doubted its authenticity. Revisionists have countered that there were no Nazi plans for conquest, but that Hitler blundered into aggression when faced by events beyond his control.

A plausible explanation of the reason for the conference suggests that Hitler was aware of a quarrel among his staff, especially between Blomberg and Göring, and used the opportunity to expand on his personal plans for the expansion of the armed forces and rearmament in the context of foreign policy. However, the seriousness of his remarks was underscored by his insistence that he wanted his plans to be regarded "as his last will and testament."

The goal sketched by Hitler was basically that earlier expounded in *Mein Kampf*: German acquisition of new living space in the east. He insisted that Germany's needs for raw materials and food could not be satisfied through self-sufficiency but only through conquest of additional living space in the countries surrounding Germany. He conceded that Germany would have to use force and that this could lead to a confrontation with France and Britain. Since Germany's rearmament was nearing completion and, once the height of its military capacity was reached, it only faced decline relative to other European states, it was necessary to take the offensive before other nations finished rearming. Hitler was therefore determined to solve Germany's need for living space no later than 1943–1945. The timing of action was a crucial factor because Hitler saw himself as indispensable to the realization of Germany's goals.

In the short term, under favorable political circumstances, Germany could proceed with the incorporation of Czechoslovakia and Austria as early as 1938. Hitler sketched several scenarios for such a possibility. However, several of those present, notably Blomberg, Fritsch, and Neurath, questioned some of Hitler's pronouncements and expressed doubts about Germany's preparation in the west against France; they opposed any action that might embroil Germany in war against France and Great Britain. Hitler did not take criticism lightly and rejected their arguments. Early in 1938 all three of the old-line conservative objectors were removed from their offices and replaced by compliant appointees.

THE HOSSBACH MEMORANDUM

Berlin, November 10, 1937

MINUTES OF THE CONFERENCE IN THE REICH CHANCEL-LERY, BERLIN,

NOVEMBER 5, 1937, FROM 4:15 TO 8:30 P.M.

Present:The Führer and Chancellor,
        Field Marshal von Blomberg, War Minister,
        Colonel General Baron von Fritsch, Commander in Chief, Army,
        Admiral Dr. h. c. Raeder, Commander in Chief, Navy,

Colonel General Göring, Commander in Chief, *Luftwaffe*,
Baron von Neurath, Foreign Minister,
Colonel Hossbach.

The Führer began by stating that the subject of the present conference was of such importance that its discussion would, in other countries, certainly be a matter for a full Cabinet meeting, but he—the Führer—had rejected the idea of making it a subject of discussion before the wider circle of the Reich Cabinet just because of the importance of the matter. His exposition to follow was the fruit of thorough deliberation and the experiences of his 4½ years of power. He wished to explain to the gentlemen present his basic ideas concerning the opportunities for the development of our position in the field of foreign affairs and its requirements, and he asked, in the interests of a long-term German policy, that his exposition be regarded, in the event of his death, as his last will and testament.

The Führer then continued:

The aim of German policy was to make secure and to preserve the racial community [*Volksmasse*] and to enlarge it. It was therefore a question of space.

The German racial community comprised over 85 million people and, because of their number and the narrow limits of habitable space in Europe, constituted a tightly packed racial core such as was not to be met in any other country and such as implied the right to a greater living space than in the case of other peoples. . . .

Before turning to the question of solving the need for space, it had to be considered whether a solution holding promise for the future was to be reached by means of autarchy or by means of an increased participation in world economy.

Autarchy:

Achievement only possible under strict National Socialist leadership of the State, which is assumed; accepting its achievement as possible, the following could be stated as results:—

A. In the field of raw materials only limited, not total, autarchy.

   1) In regard to coal, so far as it could be considered as a source of raw materials, autarchy was possible.

   2) But even as regards ores, the position was much more difficult. Iron requirements can be met from home resources and similarly with light metals, but with other raw materials—copper, tin—this was not the case.

   3) Synthetic textile requirements can be met from home re-

sources to the limit of timber supplies. A permanent solution impossible.

4) Edible fats—possible.

B. In the field of food the question of autarchy was to be answered by a flat "No." . . .

Participation in world economy:

To this there were limitations which we were unable to remove. The establishment of Germany's position, on a secure and sound foundation was obstructed by market fluctuations, and commercial treaties afforded no guarantee for actual execution. In particular it had to be remembered that since the World War, those very countries which had formerly been food exporters had become industrialized. We were living in an age of economic empires in which the primitive urge to colonization was again manifesting itself; in the cases of Japan and Italy economic motives underlay the urge for expansion, and with Germany, too, economic need would supply the stimulus. For countries outside the great economic empires, opportunities for economic expansion were severely impeded. . . .

Germany's problem could only be solved by means of force and this was never without attendant risk. . . . If one accepts as the basis of the following exposition the resort to force with its attendant risks, then there remain still to be answered the questions "when" and "how." In this matter there were three cases [*Fälle*] to be dealt with:

Case 1: Period 1943–1945

After this date only a change for the worse, from our point of view, could be expected.

The equipment of the army, navy, and *Luftwaffe*, as well as the formation of the officer corps, was nearly completed. Equipment and armament were modern; in further delay there lay the danger of their obsolescence. In particular, the secrecy of "special weapons" could not be preserved forever. The recruiting of reserves was limited to current age groups; further drafts from older untrained age groups were no longer available.

Our relative strength would decrease in relation to the rearmament which would by then have been carried out by the rest of the world. If we did not act by 1943–45, any year could, in consequence of a lack of reserves, produce the food crisis, to cope with which the necessary foreign exchange was not available, and this must be regarded as a "waning point of the regime." Besides, the world was expecting our attack and was increasing its counter-measures from year to year. It was while the rest of the world was still preparing its defenses [*sich abriegele*] that we were obliged to take the offensive.

Nobody knew today what the situation would be in the years 1943–45. One thing only was certain, that we could not wait longer. . . .

If the Führer was still living, it was his unalterable resolve to solve Germany's problem of space at the latest by 1943–45. The necessity for action before 1943–45 would arise in cases 2 and 3.

Case 2:

If internal strife in France should develop into such a domestic crisis as to absorb the French army completely and render it incapable of use for war against Germany, then the time for action against the Czechs had come.

Case 3:

If France is so embroiled by a war with another state that she cannot "proceed" against Germany.

For the improvement of our politico-military position our first objective, in the event of our being embroiled in war, must be to overthrow Czechoslovakia and Austria simultaneously in order to remove the threat to our flank in any possible operation against the West. . . .

On the assumption of a development of the situation leading to action on our part as planned, in the years 1943–45, the attitude of France, Britain, Italy, Poland, and Russia could probably be estimated as follows:

Actually, the Führer believed that almost certainly Britain, and probably France as well, had already tacitly written off the Czechs and were reconciled to the fact that this question would be cleared up in due course by Germany. Difficulties connected with the Empire, and the prospect of being once more entangled in a protracted European war, were decisive considerations for Britain against participation in a war against Germany. Britain's attitude would certainly not be without influence on that of France. An attack by France without British support, and with the prospect of the offensive being brought to a standstill on our western fortifications, was hardly probable. Nor was a French march through Belgium and Holland without British support to be expected; this also was a course not to be contemplated by us in the event of a conflict with France, because it would certainly entail the hostility of Britain. . . .

Italy was not expected to object to the elimination of the Czechs, but it was impossible at the moment to estimate what her attitude on the Austrian question would be; that depended essentially upon whether the Duce were still alive.

The degree of surprise and the swiftness of our action were decisive factors for Poland's attitude. Poland—with Russia at her rear—will have little inclination to engage in war against a victorious Germany.

Military intervention by Russia must be countered by the swiftness of our operations; however, whether such an intervention was a practical contingency at all was, in view of Japan's attitude, more than doubtful.

Should case 2 arise—the crippling of France by civil war—the situation thus created by the elimination of the most dangerous opponent must be seized upon *whenever it occurs* for the blow against the Czechs.

The Führer saw case 3 coming definitely nearer; it might emerge from the present tensions in the Mediterranean, and he was resolved to take advantage of it whenever it happened, even as early as 1938.

Source: Archives of the German Foreign Ministry, *Documents on German Foreign Policy, 1918–1945*, Series D, *1937–1945* (Washington, DC: U.S. Government Printing Office, 1949), 1:29, 30, 31, 34–36.

Document 11
HITLER AND MUSSOLINI DURING THE *ANSCHLUSS*, MARCH 1938

Hitler's first expansionist move after the Hossbach conference led to the annexation of Austria in March 1938. Four years earlier a group of Austrian Nazis hoping to bring about a union with Germany had staged a putsch that resulted in the murder of the Austrian chancellor Engelbert Dollfuss. Mussolini had thwarted that effort by threat of military force. After the debacle of 1934, Hitler resorted to diplomatic means to patch up relations with Austria and to bring it into a closer relationship with the German Reich. Mussolini, on the other hand, though originally opposed to any Austro-German union, for which attitude he had French and British support, moderated his stance once he became involved in war in Ethiopia and in Spain. Still, throughout much of 1937, Hitler was careful not to alienate Mussolini by too forceful a move against Austria.

In February 1938 the Führer was ready to move, having gained assurance that the Duce would not block his action. The occasion arose during a visit for negotiations of the Austrian chancellor Kurt von Schuschnigg to Berchtesgaden, Hitler's mountain resort. Resorting to blatant threats, Hitler demanded that Schuschnigg appoint a Nazi minister of the interior and consent to merging Austria into the German economic system. The Austrian chancellor acceded to Hitler's demands by appointing a Nazi and a Nazi sympathizer to his cabinet, but also called for a plebiscite on the question of Austrian independence. Fearing an unfavorable Austrian vote, Hitler pressured Schuschnigg into postponing any plebiscite. The Austrian leader was, however, soon overwhelmed by Hitler's determination to intervene militarily in Austrian affairs.

But the day before actually invading Austria, Hitler was still concerned about Mussolini's attitude and sent Prince Philip of Hesse to

Rome to hand-deliver his personal message justifying his military intervention. He promised that he would never reopen the issue of the German South Tyroleans, who had been part of Italy since 1919. Hours after Hitler's ambassador had delivered the letter to Mussolini, he telephoned the Führer to report that "the Duce accepted the whole thing in a very friendly manner." Greatly relieved, Hitler responded with expressions of profuse gratitude and pledged to support his fellow Fascist dictator "whatever may happen, even if the whole world were against him."

HITLER'S LETTER SENT TO MUSSOLINI, MARCH 1938

The Führer and Chancellor to Benito Mussolini

March 11, 1938

EXCELLENCY: In a fateful hour I am turning to Your Excellency to inform you of a decision which appears necessary under the circumstances and has already become irrevocable.

((In recent months I have seen, with increasing preoccupation, how a relationship was gradually developing between Austria and Czechoslovakia which, while difficult for us to endure in peacetime, was bound, in case of a war imposed upon Germany, to become a most serious threat to the security of the Reich.

In the course of these understandings [*accordi*], the Austrian State began gradually to arm all its frontiers with barriers and fortifications. Its purpose could be none other than:

1. to effect the restoration at a specified time;
2. to throw the weight of a mass of at least 20 million men against Germany if necessary.

It is precisely the close bonds between Germany and Italy which, as was to be expected, have exposed our Reich to inevitable attacks. Incumbent on me is the responsibility not to permit the rise of a situation in Central Europe which, perhaps, might one day lead to serious complications precisely because of our friendship with Italy. This new orientation of the policy of the Austrian State does not, however, reflect in any way the real desire and will of the Austrian people.))*

For years the Germans in Austria have been oppressed and mistreated by a regime which lacks any legal basis. The sufferings of innumerable tormented people know no bounds. . . .

I am now determined to restore law and order in my homeland and enable the people to decide their own fate according to their judgment in an unmistakable, clear, and open manner.

*The passage in double parentheses was omitted by German insistence when the letter was published.

May the Austrian people itself, therefore, forge its own destiny. Whatever the manner may be in which this plebiscite is to be carried out, I now wish solemnly to assure Your Excellency, as the Duce of Fascist Italy:

1. Consider this step only as one of national self-defense and therefore as an act that any man of character would do in the same way, were he in my position. You too, Excellency, could not act differently if the fate of Italians were at stake, and I as Führer and National Socialist cannot act differently.

2. In a critical hour for Italy I proved to you the steadfastness of my sympathy. Do not doubt that in the future there will be no change in this respect.

3. Whatever the consequences of the coming events may be, I have drawn a definite boundary between Germany and France and now draw one just as definite between Italy and us. It is the Brenner.

This decision will never be questioned or changed. I did not make this decision in 1938, but immediately after the end of the World War, and I never made a secret of it.

I hope that Your Excellency will pardon especially the haste of this letter and the form of this communication. These events occurred unexpectedly for all of us. Nobody had any inkling of the latest step of Herr Schuschnigg, not even his colleagues in the Government, and until now I had always hoped that perhaps at the last moment a different solution might be possible.

I deeply regret not being able to talk to you personally at this time to tell you everything I feel.

Always in friendship,

Yours,

Adolf Hitler

HITLER'S PHONE CONVERSATION WITH PRINCE PHILIP OF HESSE, MARCH 11, 1938

H: I have just come back from Palazzo Venezia. The Duce accepted the whole thing in a very friendly manner. He sends you his regards. He had been informed from Austria, Schuschnigg gave him the news. He had then said it would be a complete impossibility, it would be a bluff, such a thing could not be done. So he was told that it was unfortunately arranged thus and it could not be changed any more. Then Mussolini said that Austria would be immaterial to him.

F: Then, please, tell Mussolini. I will never forget him for this.

H: Yes.

F: Never, never, never, whatever happens. I am still ready to make a quite different agreement with him.

H: Yes, I told him that, too.

F: As soon as the Austrian affair has been settled, I shall be ready to go with him through thick and thin, nothing matters.

H: Yes, my Fuehrer.

F: Listen, I shall make any agreement—I am no longer in fear of the terrible position which would have existed militarily in case we had gotten into a conflict. You may tell him that I do thank him ever so much. Never, never shall I forget that.

H: Yes, my Fuehrer.

F: I will never forget it, whatever will happen. If he should ever need any help or be in any danger, he can be convinced that I shall stick to him whatever might happen, even if the whole world were against him.

H: Yes, my Fuehrer.

Source: Archives of the German Foreign Ministry, *Documents on German Foreign Policy, 1918–1945*, Series D, *1937–1945* (Washington, DC: U.S. Government Printing Office, 1949), 1:573–574, 575–576; U.S. Chief of Counsel for the Prosecution of Axis Criminality, *Nazi Conspiracy and Aggression* (Washington, DC: U.S. Government Printing Office, 1946), 5: 641–642.

Document 12
BENITO MUSSOLINI'S *MARE NOSTRUM* DESIGN

Even before Mussolini embarked on his expansionist moves in the mid-1930s, the Italian dictator had for years championed a scheme of Italian domination of the Mediterranean area. In early February 1939, in a secret session, he outlined to the Fascist Grand Council a concrete strategy for achieving this objective, indicating, however, that Italy would not be ready for war until after 1942. Interestingly, this was also within Adolf Hitler's time frame mentioned in the Hossbach conference when he asserted that Germany's living-space problem would have to be resolved no later than 1943–1945. Mussolini was keenly aware that his aspirations for expansion would sooner or later meet the opposition of Britain and France. He therefore saw the success of his policy ensured only by a close relationship and, in the end, a formal alliance with Nazi Germany.

MUSSOLINI'S FOREIGN POLICY DESIGN, 1939

The fundamental assumption I am making is the following: that states are more or less independent according to their maritime situation. Those states are independent which possess coastlines on the oceans or have free access to the oceans; those states which do not have free access or are trapped inside inland seas are semi-independent. . . . Italy is in an inland sea which is linked to the oceans by the Suez Canal . . . and by the Straits of Gibraltar, dominated by the guns of Great Britain. Italy therefore does not have free access to the oceans; Italy therefore is truly a prisoner in the Mediterranean and the more populated and powerful she becomes the more she will suffer from her imprisonment.

The bars of this prison are Corsica, Tunisia, Malta, Cyprus: the guardians of this prison are Gibraltar and Suez. Corsica is a pistol pointed at the heart of Italy; Tunisia at Sicily, while Malta and Cyprus are a menace to all our positions in the central and eastern Mediterranean. Greece, Turkey and Egypt are states ready to link up with Britain to complete the political and military encirclement of Italy . . . and from this situation . . . we must draw the following conclusions:

1. It is the aim of Italian policy, which cannot have and does not have territorial ambitions in continental Europe, except for Albania, to begin by breaking the bars of the prison.

2. Having broken the bars, Italian policy has just one basic aim: to march towards the ocean. Which ocean? The Indian Ocean through linking up the Sudan, Libya and Ethiopia or the Atlantic Ocean through French North Africa.

In either case we find ourselves confronted by the French and the British. To attempt to solve such a problem without securing our rear in the continent would be stupid. The policy of the Rome-Berlin Axis is therefore the answer to this fundamentally important historical problem.

Source: John Whittam, *Fascist Italy* (Manchester: Manchester University Press, 1995), 164–165. Reprinted by permission of Manchester University Press.

Document 13
THE HITLER-STALIN PACT, 1939

The world was stunned when Nazi Germany and the Soviet Union concluded a nonaggression pact on August 23, 1939. It was the prelude to Hitler's invasion of Poland, which, in turn, triggered World War II when Britain and France declared war on Germany. Since the Nazis and the Communists had been bitter opponents in the past, few people anticipated that Hitler and Stalin would come to an agreement.

After the Western sellout of Czechoslovakia to Hitler at the Munich Conference in 1938, Stalin's concern over security for his country became ever more urgent. In March 1939 he publicly condemned Britain and France for refusing to enter into a collective security arrangement and charged that they were seeking to embroil Germany and the USSR in a war. He pointedly refrained from denouncing Nazism, as he had done in the past. When Hitler occupied rump Czechoslovakia and threatened Poland, Britain and France responded by offering general security guarantees to Poland and Rumania in March and April 1939. The Western powers also wanted the Soviet Union to join them in issuing a declaration promising to protect any neighbor who would resist aggression in order to deter Hitler from the use of force. The Soviets countered with the proposal of a mutual assistance pact that would compel Britain and France to provide military defense to eastern European states. Stalin also wanted maximum territorial concessions in eastern Europe to shore up Soviet defenses.

In the spring of 1939 contacts between the Soviet and German governments increased, even though negotiations with Britain and France also continued. Hitler was reluctant to pursue serious negotiations with the Soviets, fearing that their terms would be excessive and harm German relations with Japan. But once he decided to destroy Poland by force of arms, he had to ensure that the Soviet Union would not join Britain and France in the defense of Poland.

The basic issue that kept the Anglo-French negotiators from reaching an agreement with the Soviets was the flat refusal of the Polish government to allow Soviet troops to be placed on Polish soil. Hitler had no such reservations. He willingly divided Poland with Stalin and conceded Finland, Estonia, and Latvia to the Russian sphere of influence, while Lithuania was to belong to the German sphere. This territorial agreement was added to the official treaty as a secret protocol. After the Nazi defeat of Poland, another treaty was concluded on September 28, 1939, that assigned Lithuania to the Soviet sphere and gave Germany a larger portion of Poland. The terms of the territorial agreements became known after the war, but the Soviet government denied their existence until shortly before the collapse of the Soviet Union.

THE NAZI-SOVIET TREATIES OF AUGUST AND SEPTEMBER 1939

AUGUST 23, 1939.

Treaty of Nonaggression Between Germany and the Union of Soviet Socialist Republics

The Government of the German Reich and the Government of the Union of Soviet Socialist Republics desirous of strengthening the cause of peace between Germany and the U.S.S.R., and proceeding from the fundamental provisions of the Neutrality Agreement concluded in April 1926 between Germany and the U.S.S.R., have reached the following agreement:

Article I

Both High Contracting Parties obligate themselves to desist from any act of violence, any aggressive action, and any attack on each other, either individually or jointly with other powers.

Article II

Should one of the High Contracting Parties become the object of belligerent action by a third power, the other High Contracting Party shall in no manner lend its support to this third power.

Article III

The Governments of the two High Contracting Parties shall in the future maintain continual contact with one another for the purpose of consultation in order to exchange information on problems affecting their common interests.

Article IV

Neither of the two High Contracting Parties shall participate in any grouping of powers whatsoever that is directly or indirectly aimed at the other party.

Article V

Should disputes or conflicts arise between the High Contracting Parties over problems of one kind or another, both parties shall settle these disputes or conflicts exclusively through friendly exchange of opinion or, if necessary, through the establishment of arbitration commissions.

Article VI

The present treaty is concluded for a period of ten years, with the proviso that, in so far as one of the High Contracting Parties does not denounce it one year prior to the expiration of this period, the validity of this treaty shall automatically be extended for another five years.

Article VII

The present treaty shall be ratified within the shortest possible time. The ratifications shall be exchanged in Berlin. The agreement shall enter into force as soon as it is signed.

Done in duplicate, in the German and Russian languages.

Moscow, August 23, 1939.

| For the Government of the German Reich: J. Ribbentrop | With full power of the Government of the U.S.S.R.: V. Molotov |

German-Soviet Boundary and Friendship Treaty

The Government of the German Reich and the Government of the U.S.S.R. consider it as exclusively their task, after the collapse of the former Polish state, to re-establish peace and order in these territories and to assure to the peoples living there a peaceful life in keeping with their national character. To this end, they have agreed upon the following:

Article I

The Government of the German Reich and the Government of the U.S.S.R. determine as the boundary of their respective national interests in the territory of the former Polish state the line marked on the attached map, which shall be described in more detail in a supplementary protocol.

Article II

Both parties recognize the boundary of the respective national interests established in Article I as definitive and shall reject any interference of third powers in this settlement.

Article III

The necessary reorganization of public administration will be effected in the areas west of the line specified in Article I by the Government of the German Reich, in the areas east of this line by the Government of the U.S.S.R.

Article IV

The Government of the German Reich and the Government of the U.S.S.R. regard this settlement as a firm foundation for a progressive development of the friendly relations between their peoples.

Article V

This treaty shall be ratified and the ratifications shall be exchanged in Berlin as soon as possible. The treaty becomes effective upon signature.

Done in duplicate, in the German and Russian languages.
Moscow, September 28, 1939.

For the Government	By authority of the
of the German Reich:	Government of the U.S.S.R.:
J. Ribbentrop	V. Molotov

CONFIDENTIAL PROTOCOL

The Government of the U.S.S.R. shall place no obstacles in the way of Reich nationals and other persons of German descent residing in the territories under its jurisdiction, if they desire to migrate to Germany or to the territories under German jurisdiction. It agrees that such removals shall be carried out by agents of the Government of the Reich in cooperation with the competent local authorities and that the property rights of the emigrants shall be protected.

A corresponding obligation is assumed by the Government of the German Reich in respect to the persons of Ukrainian or White Russian descent residing in the territories under its jurisdiction.

Moscow, September 28, 1939.

For the Government	By authority of the
of the German Reich:	Government of the U.S.S.R.:
J. Ribbentrop	V. Molotov

Secret Supplementary Protocol

The undersigned Plenipotentiaries declare the agreement of the Government of the German Reich and the Government of the U.S.S.R. upon the following:

The Secret Supplementary Protocol signed on August 23, 1939, shall be amended in item 1* to the effect that the territory of the Lithuanian state falls to the sphere of influence of the U.S.S.R., while, on the other hand, the province of Lublin and parts of the province of Warsaw fall to the sphere of influence of Germany (cf. the map attached to the Boundary and Friendship Treaty signed today). As soon as the Government of the U.S.S.R. shall take special measures on Lithuanian territory to protect its interests, the present German-Lithuanian border, for the purpose of a natural and simple boundary delineation, shall be rectified in such a way that the Lithuanian territory situated to the southwest of the line marked on the attached map shall fall to Germany.

Further it is declared that the economic agreements now in force between Germany and Lithuania shall not be affected by the measures of the Soviet Union referred to above.

Moscow, September 28, 1939.

For the Government	By authority of the
of the German Reich:	Government of the U.S.S.R.:
J. Ribbentrop	V. Molotov

Source: U.S. Department of State, *Nazi-Soviet Relations, 1939–1941* Washington, DC: U.S. Government Printing Office, 1948), 76–78, 105–107.

*Item 1 of the Secret Additional Protocol of August 23, 1939, reads: "1. In the event of a territorial and political rearrangement in the areas belonging to the Baltic States (Finland, Estonia, Latvia, Lithuania), the northern boundary of Lithuania shall represent the boundary of the spheres of influence of Germany and the U.S.S.R. In this connection the interest of Lithuania in the Vilna area is recognized by each party."

Document 14
BERLIN-ROME-TOKYO AXIS: TEN-YEAR TRIPARTITE
PACT, SEPTEMBER 1940

Germany, Italy, and Japan signed a ten-year agreement on September 27, 1940, that was to recognize "the leadership of Germany and Italy in the establishment of a new order in Europe" and the leadership of Japan in Greater East Asia in the Far East. The signing parties promised to come to each other's assistance if any of the signatories was attacked by a power not now involved in the European war or in the Sino-Japanese conflict. The purpose of the pact was to keep the United States from intervening in the war. At the same time, the three powers explicitly affirmed the existing German-Soviet relationship, and Hitler even indicated to Stalin that the Soviet Union could join the pact. When Soviet foreign minister Vyacheslav Molotov came to Berlin in November 1940 to discuss outstanding issues concerning German-Soviet relations, the Germans realized that Molotov was neither interested in joining the Tripartite powers nor ready to divide the world, as his German hosts proposed, by giving the Soviet Union a geopolitical sphere in the Near East and the Indian Ocean. All along Hitler was planning an eventual move against the Soviet Union and stepped up military preparations for an attack on Russia after Molotov's visit. Even though Stalin's suspicions were deepened by Molotov's unsuccessful Berlin visit, he did not believe that Hitler was planning an early invasion of the USSR.

Similarly, the United States was not intimidated by the Tripartite pact but intensified its support of China in an effort to counteract Japan's moves in the Far East. In April 1941 Japan concluded a neutrality pact with the Soviet Union and did not side with Hitler in his war against the Soviet Union. However, Hitler, who had repeatedly urged the Japanese to move against Britain, was now joined by Mussolini in immediately declaring war on the United States when the United States declared war on Japan following the Japanese attack on Pearl Harbor in December 1941. Despite the three-power agreement no plans were designed by Germany, Italy, and Japan to coordinate their actions during the course of the war.

TRIPARTITE PACT

September 27, 1940

The Governments of Germany, Italy, and Japan, considering it as a condition precedent of any lasting peace that all nations of the world be given each its proper place, have decided to stand by and co-operate with one another in regard to their efforts in Greater East Asia and regions of Europe respectively wherein it is their prime purpose to establish and maintain a new order of things calculated to promote the mutual prosperity and welfare of the peoples concerned.

Furthermore it is the desire of the three Governments to extend cooperation to such nations in other spheres of the world as may be inclined to put forth endeavors along lines similar to their own, in order that their ultimate aspirations for world peace may thus be realized. Accordingly the Governments of Germany, Italy, and Japan have agreed as follows:

Article 1

Japan recognizes and respects the leadership of Germany and Italy in the establishment of a new order in Europe.

Article 2

Germany and Italy recognize and respect the leadership of Japan in the establishment of a new order in Greater East Asia.

Article 3

Germany, Italy and Japan agree to co-operate in their efforts on the aforesaid lines. They further undertake to assist one another with all political, economic and military means when one of the three Contracting powers is attacked by a power at present not involved in the European War or in the Sino-Japanese Conflict.

Article 4

With a view to implementing the present Pact, Joint Technical Commissions the members of which are to be appointed by the respective Governments of Germany, Italy and Japan will meet without delay.

Article 5

Germany, Italy and Japan affirm that the aforesaid terms do not in any way affect the political status which exists at present as between each of the three Contracting Parties and Soviet Russia.

Article 6

The present Pact shall come into effect immediately upon signature and shall remain in force ten years from the date of its coming into force.

At the proper time before expiration of said term the High Contracting Parties shall, at the request of any of them, enter into negotiations for its renewal.

In faith whereof, the Undersigned, duly authorized by their respective Governments, have signed this Pact and have affixed hereto their Seals.

Done in triplicate at Berlin, the 27th day of September 1940—in the XVIIIth year of the Fascist Era—, corresponding to the 27th day of the 9th month of the 15th year of Syowa.

Joachim v. Ribbentrop

Ciano

Kurusu

Source: Archives of the German Foreign Ministry, *Documents on German Foreign Policy, 1918–1945*, Series D, *1937–1945* (Washington, DC: U.S. Government Printing Office, 1960), 11:204–205.

Document 15
HITLER'S POLITICAL TESTAMENT, APRIL 1945

When Soviet troops were beginning to close in on the Reich chancellery and the Führer's bunker, where Hitler and his entourage were spending their last weeks, the worn-out dictator was coming to terms with his end. In the very early morning of April 29, he married his longtime mistress, Eva Braun. While many of Hitler's circle in the bunker were still celebrating their Führer's wedding, Hitler himself retired with his secretary to dictate his last will and political testament.

As the text of the document indicates, Hitler neither showed regret nor accepted any blame for what his policies had inflicted upon Germany and Europe. He denied that he had wanted war in 1939 and asserted that it had been brought on solely "by those international statesmen who were either of Jewish descent or worked for Jewish interests." It is striking that the Führer's obsession with Jews as the cause of all evil in the world, as he had already claimed in *Mein Kampf*, remained the dominant theme of his very last abject musing. He exhorted his followers who survived to continue building National Socialism while always heeding "the laws of race" and never to relent in their inveterate opposition to "the universal poisoner of all peoples, international Jewry." In the second part of the Political Testament, Hitler also lashed out against several of his closest associates. He expelled Hermann Göring and Heinrich Himmler from the party and dismissed them from all of their offices, charging that they had done immeasurable harm to Germany by engaging in unauthorized negotiations with the enemy and illegally attempting to seize power for themselves. In their places he appointed several successors, among them Grand Admiral Karl Dönitz as president and commander in chief and Joseph Goebbels as Reich chancellor. On the very day that Hitler dictated his testament, he received word that the Duce had died at the hands of partisans and been publicly hanged after his execution. It was this news that impelled Hitler to insist that his remains were to be cremated and all traces of his body were to vanish completely.

ADOLF HITLER: MY POLITICAL TESTAMENT

More than thirty years have now passed since I in 1914 made my modest contribution as a volunteer in the first world-war that was forced upon the Reich.

In these three decades I have been actuated solely by love and loyalty to my people in all my thoughts, acts, and life. They gave me the strength to make the most difficult decisions which have ever confronted to mortal man. I have spent my time, my working strength, and my health in these three decades.

It is untrue that I or anyone else in Germany wanted the war in 1939. It was desired and instigated exclusively by those international statesmen who were either of Jewish descent or worked for Jewish interests. I have made too many offers for the control and limitation of armaments, which posterity will not for all time be able to disregard for the responsibility for the outbreak of this war to be laid on me. I have further never wished that after the first fatal world war a second against England, or even against America, should break out. Centuries will pass away, but out of the ruins of our towns and monuments the hatred against those finally responsible whom we have to thank for everything, International Jewry and its helpers, will grow.

Three days before the outbreak of the German-Polish war I again proposed to the British ambassador in Berlin a solution to the German-Polish problem—similar to that in the case of the Saar district, under international control. This offer also cannot be denied. It was only rejected because the leading circles in English politics wanted the war, partly on account of the business hoped for and partly under influence or propaganda organized by international Jewry.

I also made it quite plain that, if the nations of Europe are again to be regarded as mere shares to be bought and sold by these international conspirators in money and finance, then that race, Jewry, which is the real criminal of this murderous struggle, will be saddled with the responsibility. I further left no one in doubt that this time not only would millions of children of Europe's Aryan peoples die of hunger, not only would millions of grown men suffer death, and not only hundreds of thousands of women and children be burnt and bombed to death in the towns, without the real criminal having to atone for this guilt, even if by more humane means. . . .

I die with a happy heart, aware of the immeasurable deeds and achievements of our soldiers at the front, our women at home, the achievements of our farmers and workers and the work, unique in history, of our youth who bear my name. . . .

Second Part of the Political Testament

Before my death I expel the former Reichsmarschall Hermann Goering from the party and deprive him of all rights which he may enjoy by virtue of the decree of June 29th, 1941, and also by virtue of my statement in the Reichstag on September 1st, 1939, I appoint in his place Grossadmiral Doenitz, President of the Reich and Supreme Commander of the Armed Forces.

Before my death I expel the former Reichsfuehrer-SS and Minister of the Interior, Heinrich Himmler, from the party and from all offices of State. In his stead I appoint Gauleiter Karl Hanke as Reichsfuehrer-SS and Chief of the German Police, and Gauleiter Paul Giesler as Reich Minister of the Interior.

Goering and Himmler, quite apart from their disloyalty to my person, have done immeasurable harm to the country and the whole nation by secret negotiations with the enemy, which they conducted without my knowledge and against my wishes, and by illegally attempting to seize power in the State for themselves. . . .

Finally, let them be conscious of the fact that our task, that of continuing the building of a National Socialist State, represents the work of the coming centuries, which places every single person under an obligation always to serve the common interest and to subordinate his own advantage to this end. I demand of all Germans, all National Socialists, men, women and all the men of the Armed Forces, that they be faithful and obedient unto death to the new government and its President.

Above all I charge the leaders of the nation and those under them to scrupulous observance of the laws of race and to merciless opposition to the universal poisoner of all peoples, international Jewry.

Given in Berlin, this 29th day of April 1945.   4:00 A.M.

Adolf Hitler.

Source: U.S. Chief of Counsel for the Prosecution of Axis Criminality, *Nazi Conspiracy and Aggression* (Washington, DC: U.S. Government Printing Office, 1946), 6:261, 262, 263, 264.

Glossary of Selected Terms

Abwehr (protection). German military espionage and news service agency. It was established in 1920 and given its name to emphasize the defensive function it performed in the German military after World War I. This role changed after 1933 with the Nazi seizure of power when it was attached to the High Command of the armed forces. While Admiral Wilhelm Canaris headed the agency (until his arrest early in 1944), it provided refuge for civilian and military opponents of the Nazi regime.

Anschluss (union). The union of Germany and Austria proclaimed on March 13, 1938. It was forbidden by the Treaties of Versailles and St. Germain of 1919. Hitler pursued the idea of uniting the two countries once in power and carried out the annexation by military threat in 1938. It served as the prelude to further annexations of non-German territory by the Führer, which finally triggered World War II in September 1939.

Anti-Semitism. The term was first used in the second half of the nineteenth century to express animosity toward the Jews. Prejudice against Jews before the nineteenth century was largely based on religious and economic grounds. Modern anti-Semitism, especially starting with the second half of the nineteenth century, has been based on political, economic, and racial considerations. Pseudoscientific theories of so-called Aryan supremacy, which originated in the latter part of the nineteenth and early twentieth centuries, were directed against the Jews and climaxed in Hitler's effort to exterminate the European Jews during the Holocaust.

Arrow Cross. Hungarian Fascist Party, also known as Hungarian National Socialist Party—Hungarist Movement. Named after its emblem, the Arrow Cross was formed by Ferenc Szálasi in 1937 through the merger of three small fascist parties with his own Party of National Will. In October 1944 the German military installed a short-lived Arrow Cross regime, with Szálasi as premier, in the area of Hungary that had not yet been occupied by Soviet forces.

Aryan. Originally the term referred to a group of interrelated Indo-European languages. Aryans reputedly colonized Iran and northern India and gave rise to the Indian subcontinent's Indo-Aryan languages. Nationalists and romanticists in Europe and the United States portrayed them as founders of a flourishing civilization and claimed that Europeans and some Asian peoples were descended from them, but there is no scientific evidence to support such a myth. Nazi Germany embraced the unscientific notions of the myth and regarded the Germanic peoples as the purest descendants of the Aryan race.

Axis Powers. The term describes the cooperation of Nazi Germany and Fascist Italy between 1936 and 1945. Mussolini was the first to refer to the Rome-Berlin Axis in 1936. In May 1939 the two states concluded a formal alliance, the Pact of Steel. In September 1940 Germany, Italy, and Japan signed a Tripartite Pact. As a result, during World War II, the term *Axis Powers* was applied to all three countries and came to include also their eastern European allies, Bulgaria, Hungary, Rumania, and Slovakia.

Beer Hall Putsch. On November 8, 1923, Hitler and his new party tried to seize power in Bavaria during a public meeting in a beer hall in Munich that was being addressed by nationalist political leaders. This attempt was to serve as the prelude for a march on Berlin to overthrow the Weimar Republic. The coup collapsed completely when on the next day a Nazi-led demonstration in the center of the city was met by police fire, killing sixteen Nazi demonstrators. In the aftermath, Hitler was arrested, but his unsuccessful putsch and subsequent trial brought him and his insignificant party headlines in Germany and abroad.

DAF (Deutsche Arbeitsfront, or German Labor Front). Labor organization, established by the National Socialists in May 1933, to replace the labor unions of the Weimar Republic. It was led by Robert Ley and, in the early stages, included, in addition to former members of labor unions, also white-collar groups and management associations. Its function was to represent the interests of every German and to unite workers and employers by providing financial assistance to workers, to set wages, and to use its funds to improve the lives of German workers. It also sponsored the Strength through Joy movement, which offered vacation trips at inexpensive rates. The objective of the party was to integrate labor into the Nazi state. The organization had a membership of 25 million in 1942.

Dopolavoro. The Opera Nazionale Dopolavoro (OND), or Fascist afterwork organization, was established in 1925. This organization for the control of leisure activities was an ambitious attempt to incorporate the adult working population into the emerging Fascist regime. Its activities included almost everything called "mass culture," from bocce games to movies and radio listening. It also offered, especially in the later 1930s, sport, summer camps, and subsidized excursions to the sea and the mountains. The OND enjoyed great popularity, bringing over 3.5 million Italians into its ranks by 1939. Although direct ideological indoctrination was avoided, the organization was viewed as an instrument of propaganda by the regime.

Fasci di Combattimento (Combat Groups). The *Fasci di Combattimento* formed the earliest local organizational cells of Fascism. The first *Fascio* was organized by Benito Mussolini in Milan on March 21, 1919. At first, the structure of the *Fasci* was somewhat informal and flexible as they spread from Milan to other cities of northern and central Italy. They remained a small and fairly insignificant movement until the winter of 1920–1921, when they took the lead in the armed terrorist reaction against the Socialist Party and labor unions, and their membership increased to almost 250,000 by the end of 1921. To rein in the independence of the *Fasci*, Mussolini turned the Fascist movement into a political party in the fall of 1921, with an official program and a tighter organizational structure.

Fascist Grand Council. The Fascist Grand Council was established in December 1922 as a consultative organ of the Fascist Party, or a kind of alternative cabinet, that included all the leading Fascists. It discussed important issues but was completely dominated by Benito Mussolini, who used it to reinforce his authority in the party. In 1928 it acquired legal status and was viewed, in theory, as the most powerful organ of the state and the party. In practice, however, its powers were limited, and Mussolini, as its chairman, called it only at will. Between 1939 and 1943 it was not convened at all. It was ironic that the meeting on the evening of July 24, 1943, which was called on the demand of discontented Fascist leaders, resulted in Mussolini's fall and the collapse of his regime.

Führerprinzip (leadership principle). In *Mein Kampf* Adolf Hitler outlined the antidemocratic concept that decisions in the state must be made by one man, combining "absolute responsibility unconditionally" with "absolute authority." As early as July 1921, Hitler insisted that the *Führerprinzip* (Führer principle) become the law of the Nazi Party. It was applied to all National Socialist organizations, empowering every leader with authority downward and responsibility upward. It formed the basis for the dictatorship of the Third Reich (and other fascist states), with Hitler standing at the top of the party and the state system, having supreme authority and ultimate responsibility for Germany's destiny.

Gauleiter (regional leader[s]). The highest-ranking Nazi Party official below the top Reich leadership. Directly responsible to Hitler, the *Gauleiter* was responsible for all political and economic activities in his region, as well as civil defense and the mobilization of labor. Many *Gauleiter* also served as *Reichstatthalter*, or provincial governors, combining party and state functions. Below the *Gauleiter* was the *Kreisleiter* (district leader).

Gestapo (abbreviation of Geheime Staatspolizei, or Secret State Police). The Gestapo was formed from the Prussian political police by Hermann Göring in April 1933. In the following year, the Gestapo in Prussia came under the partial control of Heinrich Himmler when he was appointed its deputy chief. Himmler, who had headed all political police in Germany since 1933, became the chief of all police forces, political, criminal, and ordinary, in 1936. The Gestapo's primary function was to identify dissidents, complainers, and opponents of the state and to use any method deemed necessary to extract information from them. Enemies of the state could be confined to prison or concentration camp without a trial, making the Gestapo a symbol of the Nazi reign of terror.

Gleichschaltung (Coordination). The term *Gleichschaltung* was first used by the Nazis in March 1933 to describe the effort to synchronize all German political and social organizations with the aims of the National Socialist regime and thereby to subject them to Nazi control. The term had been borrowed from the name of an electrical device that allowed current to flow in only one direction. It referred to the policy of Nazifying state governments and parliaments, political parties, labor unions, youth clubs, and other institutions by either eliminating them or transforming them into National Socialist institutions and associations.

Hitlerjugend (HJ, or Hitler Youth). Hitler firmly believed that a politically trained and athletically steeled youth was essential to the survival of the Third Reich. Originally established in 1926, the Hitler Youth forcibly amalgamated all youth groups in Germany after 1933. Under Baldur von Schirach's leadership, the HJ comprised several formations: the Deutsches Jungvolk, or German Youth Folk (ten- to fourteen-year-old boys), Jungmädel, or Young Girls (ten- to fourteen-year-old girls), the Bund Deutscher Mädel (BDM), or League of German Girls, and the actual HJ for fourteen- to eighteen-year-olds. After 1939 membership in the HJ became compulsory for all healthy German youths. Normally, graduates of the HJ were expected to become members of the Nazi Party. However, war conditions diverted many of them into military service and various auxiliary services.

Iron Guard. Rumanian fascist organization that emerged as a militia arm in 1930 of the Legion of the Archangel Michael, which had been founded by Corneliu Zelea Codreanu several years earlier. Both the Legion and the Guard were suppressed by the Rumanian royal government several times, and Codreanu was shot in 1938. Ion Antonescu, an ultranationalist general, allied with the revived Iron Guard in 1940 when he seized power. Only months later, however, he faced a showdown with the leadership of the Guard due to the violence of its members and their refusal to accept Antonescu as sole commander. The Iron Guard was brutally suppressed, its leaders were driven into exile, and it was never revived.

Kristallnacht (Night of the Broken Glass). Official German name of the pogrom instigated by the Nazi Party against German Jews on November 9–10, 1938. It was justified by an attack of a Jew, Herschel Grynszpan, on a minor German diplomat in Paris and orchestrated as a "spontaneous" action of the masses. In actuality, the pogrom was perpetrated by various Nazi Party formations and resulted in the destruction of over 7,000 Jewish businesses, over 200 synagogues, and the murder of some 100 Jews. It presaged intensified social discrimination against German Jews and the eventual destruction of both German and European Jews during World War II.

Lateran Pacts. Agreements reached between the papacy and the Mussolini government after several years of secret negotiations in February 1929, ending the church-state conflict since the unification of Italy. The pacts recognized the sovereignty of Vatican City, secured the recognition of the Catholic Church as the sole state religion as well as guaranteeing religious education at the secondary level of state schooling and substantive ecclesiastical jurisdiction over marriage and wills, and provided financial compensation to the papacy for the loss of territories as a consequence of the Italian unification. The church, in turn, recognized the Italian state for the first time.

Nazi-Soviet Nonaggression Pact. Sometimes also called the Hitler-Stalin Pact, this agreement between Nazi Germany and Soviet Russia was signed in Moscow by the foreign ministers of the two states on August 23, 1939. It divided eastern Europe into German and Soviet spheres of interest, renounced the use of force against one another, and allowed extensive economic relations to develop. The agreement enabled Hitler to attack Poland without fearing Soviet reaction. Stalin also saw the pact as advantageous, for it prevented a combination of Britain, France, and Germany against his country and gave him territorial acquisitions in eastern Europe. Hitler ended this opportunistic and cynical agreement with his invasion of the Soviet Union in June 1941.

NSDAP (Nationalsozialistische Deutsche Arbeiterpartei, or National Socialist German Workers' Party). The new and permanent name adopted by the Nazi Party in February 1920. Adolf Hitler became the dictatorial leader of the party in July 1921.

Nuremberg Laws. Racial laws promulgated at Nuremberg in September 1935, designed to define the status of Jews in Germany and to restrict them in political and social life. They deprived those Jews of German citizenship who were not of "German or kindred blood" and made marriage or extramarital relations illegal between Germans and Jews.

Röhm Affair or Purge. Sometimes also called the Night of the Long Knives. On June 30, 1934, Adolf Hitler instigated an assassination spree against Ernst Röhm, the leader of the SA, and many of his associates. Röhm called for a second revolution in the direction of socialism in order to reward many of his proletarian SA men and also wanted to merge the SA with the German army. Hitler felt threatened by the aspirations of the SA leader, a close friend of many years, since he needed to keep the goodwill of the army leadership, which vehemently opposed any amalgamation with the SA. The Führer decided to eliminate Röhm when he refused to fall in line.

SA (Sturmabteilung, or Storm Detachment, better known as Storm Troopers). Organized in 1921, the brown-shirted SA served as the paramilitary arm of the Nazi Party. SA men safeguarded Nazi meeting halls, served as bodyguards to party leaders, and fought street battles with the opposition. They also served as propagandists for the party, distributing leaflets and rounding up voters for the Nazi Party in elections. Members were paid out of party funds, and membership increased with unemployment in the late 1920s and early 1930s. Although its ranks increased into the many hundreds of thousands in the Third Reich, the SA played a minor role after Ernst Röhm's purge in 1934.

Squadristi. The *squadristi* were the fighting force of early Fascism and contributed in a decisive way to the emergence of Fascism between 1920 and 1922. The model for this military force was in large part the *arditi*, the demobilized elite shock troops of the Italian army, who served as Mussolini's bodyguard and carried out assaults on socialist publishing houses and offices. When Fascism engaged in an armed terrorist reaction against the Socialist Party and labor unions during the winter of 1920–1921, the *squadristi*, now drawing heavily on youths from the lower middle class as well as students and sons of professional people, pushed for a putsch rather than just a fight against "Bolshevism." After Mussolini attained power over the government, he struggled to control the squads between 1923 and 1925 and finally had them disarmed and disbanded.

SS (Schutzstaffel[n], or protective squad[s]). An elite paramilitary formation, organized first in 1923, that began as Hitler's bodyguard. SS members wore black uniforms until the war. After Hitler appointed Heinrich Himmler Reichsführer SS (leader of the SS) in 1929, the elite organization grew rapidly from fewer than 300 to 52,000 men by the end of 1932. Within the Third Reich, the SS became an independent party organization that controlled the police forces, operated the concentration camps, carried out the Nazi racial policy, and established its own fighting units, the Waffen SS, or armed SS, at the outbreak of the war. The atrocities committed by some SS units and the terror policy of the SS regime gave the organization its notorious reputation.

Totalitarianism. A term that denotes modern dictatorial states that seek to control all aspects of life in a society: political, economic, social, cultural, and educational. Totalitarian governments employ propaganda and censorship, supported by advanced communications technology (press, radio, cinema, television), to impose the aims and policies of the ruling regime on the attitudes, beliefs, and values of all citizens. Under such a regime, the citizen must not only passively accept the ideological goals and values of the dictatorial leader and the party but also internalize them and act on them in everyday activity, as a duty of the individual to the community. More specifically, totalitarian regimes espouse an exclusivist ideology that seeks to explain the main issues and concerns of a society and how the ultimate goal of a society can be realized. A single mass party headed by a dictatorial leader is the carrier of the ideology and, through the government, has full control over the economy, the military, and communications. With the help of regular and secret police, including the use of terror, all dissent and opposition are suppressed. The two notable totalitarian systems that existed in Europe in the twentieth century were Soviet communism under Joseph Stalin and German National Socialism under Adolf Hitler. They had in common all of the characteristics indicated, but one of their chief differences lay in their ultimate aims: Soviet communism pursued the realization of a classless society, whereas Nazism attempted to achieve an empire under the supremacy of the Aryan race. At the same time, both of these systems were ruthless and violent in the pursuit of their goals and totally disregarded ethical and humane values.

Treaty of Versailles. The peace treaty signed on June 28, 1919, by Germany and the victorious Allied powers at Paris. The treaty was forced on Germany by the Big Four and was criticized for its harshness in Germany and the United States, and for its leniency in France and Britain. It assigned to Germany and its allies responsibility for causing the war and imposed heavy reparations on Germany, which were bitterly resented by the German populace. Germany lost all its colonies and considerable territory to Poland in the east. The Rhineland was demilitarized and was to be kept under Allied occupation for fifteen years. German military forces were strictly limited. Most Germans viewed the treaty as a dictated peace, giving the Nazis ample ammunition for their propaganda.

Völkisch. National, ideological ethnic-mindedness. The term conveys a militant Germanic ethnocentrism found in nationalistic movements before and after World War I. The *völkisch* ideology encompassed the idea of an exclusive national community that could not incorporate alien peoples such as Jews because they would be detrimental to the German community. This notion took an extreme expression in the Nazi ideology.

Weimar Republic. The German Republic from 1918 to 1933. Early in 1919, after the defeat of World War I, a National Constituent Assembly met in Weimar, a city known for its liberal cultural heritage. Both the constitution and the German Republic received their name from the city. The new Weimar constitution was considered to be one of the most advanced in the world. However, from the beginning, the Weimar Republic encountered difficulties due to the continued Allied blockade and the reparations. The hyperinflation of 1923 severely weakened the German middle class. When the Great Depression struck in 1930 and brought massive unemployment, the Nazi Party was able to exploit the hardships suffered by much of German society to its political advantage. The economic and social chaos led to political polarization in the electorate and paved the way for Hitler's chancellorship in 1933. This marked the end of the Weimar Republic.

Bibliographical Essay

The bibliography of fascism is quite voluminous, especially on Nazism. In this overview, only works in English have been included that are likely to be useful for further study. The selected titles have been grouped according to broad categories for easier identification. A very comprehensive bibliography of works dealing with fascism in most European languages is Philip Rees, *Fascism and Pre-fascism in Europe, 1890–1945: A Bibliography of the Extreme Right* (Brighton, Sussex, UK: Harvester Press, 1984).

GENERAL HISTORIES OF FASCISM

The standard work on fascism in Europe, with consideration of quasi-fascist groups and movements elsewhere in the world, is Stanley G. Payne, *A History of Fascism, 1914–1945* (Madison: University of Wisconsin Press, 1995). Substantive, judicious, and readable, this impressive work is absolutely essential to any student of fascism. It has a very extensive listing of books and articles on fascism in several languages. A shorter informative account is the very readable book by Walter Laqueur, *Fascism: Past, Present, Future* (New York: Oxford University Press, 1996). It concentrates more on fascist developments after 1945 than on historical fascism. Another recent history is Roger Eatwell's *Fascism: A History* (New York: Allen Lane Penguin Press, 1996), which treats fascism in Italy, Germany, France, and Britain, both before and after 1945. Still useful are several of the older histories of European fascism. Among them, F. L. Carsten, *The Rise of Fascism* (Berkeley: University of California Press, 1967), offers a narrative on Fascism in Italy and National Socialism in Germany as well as fascism in most other European countries, while Eugen Weber, *Varieties of Fascism* (Princeton, NJ: D. Van Nostrand, 1964), in addition to an interpretive narrative, also provides representative documentary selections. An informative anthology of interpretive essays was edited by Walter Laqueur, *Fascism: A Reader's Guide: Analyses, Interpretations, Bibliography* (Berkeley: University of California Press, 1976). An excellent companion piece to the preceding work is Hans Rogger and Eugen Weber, eds., *The European Right: A Historical Profile* (Berkeley: University of California Press, 1965), with essays on the extreme right and fascism in the major European countries by noted historians.

Readers who are interested in analytical concepts that explain fascism will find stimulating suggestions in Stanley G. Payne, *Fascism: Comparison and Definition* (Madison: University of Wisconsin Press, 1980), and in Roger Griffin, *The Nature of Fascism* (London and New York: Routledge, 1991). See also Richard Bessel, ed., *Fascist Italy and Nazi Germany: Comparisons and Contrasts* (Cambridge: Cambridge University Press, 1996), which has essays on society, workers, women, and other topics. Roger Griffin has edited the first comprehensive reader of documentary excerpts drawn from fascist writers and politicians throughout the world and of comments by notable interpreters and critics of fascism, *Fascism* (Oxford: Oxford University Press, 1995).

The interpretation of fascism as a totalitarian phenomenon is reflected in the classic studies by Hannah Arendt, *The Origins of Totalitarianism*, rev. ed. (New York: Harcourt, Brace and World, 1966; first published in 1951), and Carl J. Friedrich and Zbigniew K. Brzezinski, *Totalitarian Dictatorship and Autocracy*, 2nd ed. (Cambridge, MA: Harvard University Press, 1965). The concept went out of vogue among many scholars after the 1960s but has been revived since the 1980s, as Abbott Gleason, *Totalitarianism: The Inner History of the Cold War* (New York: Oxford University Press, 1995), aptly outlines. He reaffirms the fascist origins of the idea of totalitarianism.

BACKGROUND OF FASCISM AND FASCIST REGIMES IN INDIVIDUAL EUROPEAN COUNTRIES

Italy

A good general history of Italy is the balanced and well-researched work of Martin Clark, *Modern Italy, 1871–1995*, 2nd ed. (London: Longman, 1996). Also helpful is Denis Mack Smith, *Italy: A Modern History*, rev. ed. (Ann Arbor: University of Michigan Press, 1969).

A very good brief introduction to the Fascist system is Alexander De Grand, *Italian Fascism: Its Origins and Development*, 2nd ed. (Lincoln:

University of Nebraska Press, 1989). De Grand sees Fascism as a force working within existing social and economic institutions that becomes ideologically and politically fragmented. His bibliographical essay is excellent. Another readable account is Alan Cassels, *Fascist Italy*, 2nd ed. (Arlington Heights, IL: Harlan Davidson, 1985). The narrative is succinct and clear and is followed by a good bibliographical essay. More recent short surveys are John Whittam, *Fascist Italy* (Manchester: Manchester University Press, 1995), which offers a balanced reevaluation of the political, diplomatic, and military developments as well as domestic and cultural aspects; and the fairly analytical work of Philip Morgan, *Italian Fascism, 1919–1945* (New York: St. Martin's Press, 1995). An overview of interpretations can be found in Renzo De Felice, *Interpretations of Fascism* (Cambridge, MA: Harvard University Press, 1977). He tries to draw a line between Mussolini's ideas of Fascism and Hitler's of Nazism.

A remarkable reference book is Philip V. Cannistraro, ed., *Historical Dictionary of Fascist Italy* (Westport, CT: Greenwood Press, 1982). It has informative article-length entries on a great many topics related to Fascism, accompanied by helpful bibliographies. Documents relating to Fascism can be found in Charles Delzell, ed., *Mediterranean Fascism, 1919–1945* (New York: Walker, 1971), and in Adrian Lyttelton, ed., *Italian Fascisms from Pareto to Gentile* (New York: Harper and Row, 1973).

Adrian Lyttelton is also the author of the most important work on the early years of the regime, *The Seizure of Power: Fascism in Italy, 1919–1929* (New York: Charles Scribner's Sons, 1973). Dante L. Germino, *The Italian Fascist Party in Power: A Study in Totalitarian Rule* (Minneapolis: University of Minnesota Press, 1959), is still useful, especially for its good description of the Fascist command structure, but it tends to exaggerate the totalitarian character of the Fascist regime. The Fascist takeover of power at the provincial and local levels reveals some of the interconnectedness between rural and urban political life and social groups, as illustrated by Anthony L. Cardoza, *Agrarian Elites and Italian Fascism: The Province of Bologna, 1901–1926* (Princeton, NJ: Princeton University Press, 1982); Alice A. Kelikian, *Town and Country under Fascism: The Transformation of Brescia, 1915–1926* (Oxford: Clarendon Press, 1986); and Frank M. Snowden, *The Fascist Revolution in Tuscany, 1919–1922* (Cambridge: Cambridge University Press, 1989).

A perceptive study of Mussolini's foreign policy from 1922 through the Ethiopian war, the Spanish Civil War, and Italy's entry into World War II until the Duce's fall in 1943 is Denis Mack Smith, *Mussolini's Roman Empire* (New York: Viking, 1976). Fascist economic policies are extensively examined in A. James Gregor, *Italian Fascism and Developmental Dictatorship* (Princeton, NJ: Princeton University Press, 1979), and Roland

Sarti, *Fascism and the Industrial Leadership in Italy, 1919–1940* (Berkeley: University of California Press, 1971). Relations between the Fascist state and the Catholic Church are discussed in Richard Webster, *The Cross and the Fasces* (Stanford, CA: Stanford University Press, 1960), and John F. Pollard, *The Vatican and Italian Fascism, 1929–32: A Study in Conflict* (Cambridge: Cambridge University Press, 1985).

An important comprehensive treatment of life under Fascism remains Edward R. Tannenbaum, *The Fascist Experience: Italian Society and Culture, 1922–1945* (New York: Basic Books, 1972). Since its publication, several studies have appeared that look at related aspects of Fascist society. Tracy H. Koon, *Believe, Obey, Fight: Political Socialization of Youth in Fascist Italy, 1922–1943* (Chapel Hill: University of North Carolina Press, 1985), helps to understand how Fascists tried to shape the development of the young. An important study of women in Fascist Italy is Victoria De Grazia, *How Fascism Ruled Women: Italy, 1922–1945* (Berkeley: University of California Press, 1992). The same author also wrote *The Culture of Consent: Mass Organization of Leisure in Fascist Italy* (Cambridge: Cambridge University Press, 1981), which examines the regime's efforts to organize consent and create nationwide political culture. However, only superficial ideological consensus was actually achieved. See also Simonetta Falasca-Zamponi, *Fascist Spectacle: The Aesthetics of Power in Mussolini's Italy* (Berkeley: University of California Press, 1997).

Doug Thompson reevaluates the means of Fascism to realize political and cultural control in his *State Control in Fascist Italy: Culture and Conformity, 1925–1943* (Manchester: Manchester University Press, 1991). Racial policies are covered by Meir Michaelis, *Mussolini and the Jews: German-Italian Relations and the Jewish Question in Italy, 1922–1945* (Oxford: Oxford University Press, 1978), Susan Zuccotti, *The Italians and the Holocaust: Persecution, Rescue, and Survival* (New York: Basic Books, 1987), and Jonathan Steinberg, *All or Nothing: The Axis and the Holocaust, 1941–1943* (London: Routledge, 1990). The latter shows that the Italian military leadership refused to carry out Mussolini's directives to deliver Jews into German hands in occupied territories.

Germany

Several general histories provide an excellent background for an understanding of the context of the National Socialist regime. The foremost general treatment is the masterfully written and richly detailed book by Gordon Craig, *Germany, 1866–1945* (New York: Oxford University Press, 1978). A detailed and analytical treatment, with a considerable amount of data, is Volker Berghahn, *Modern Germany: Society, Economy, and Pol-*

itics in the Twentieth Century, 2nd ed. (New York: Cambridge University Press, 1987). An interpretive overview, emphasizing social and cultural aspects, is provided by Mary Fulbrook, *The Divided Nation: A History of Germany, 1918–1990* (New York: Oxford University Press, 1992), and a popular survey, now in its third edition, with a more political bent is Dietrich Orlow, *A History of Modern Germany, 1871 to Present*, 3rd ed. (Englewood Cliffs, NJ: Prentice Hall, 1995).

The literature on Nazi Germany is staggering. A bibliographical guide compiled by Helen Kehr and Janet Langmaid, *The Nazi Era, 1919–1945: A Select Bibliography of Published Works from the Early Roots to 1980* (London: Mansell, 1982), lists over 6,500 titles in English and German. Helpful annotated bibliographies of articles published between 1973 and 1982 are *The Third Reich, 1933–1939: A Historical Bibliography* (Santa Barbara, CA: ABC-Clio, 1984) and *The Third Reich at War: A Historical Bibliography* (Santa Barbara, CA: ABC-Clio, 1984). Several reference tools access information on most conceivable topics and persons related to the Third Reich. They include Christian Zentner and Friedemann Bedürftig, eds., *The Encyclopedia of the Third Reich*, 2 vols. (New York: Macmillan, 1991), Louis L. Snyder, ed., *Encyclopedia of the Third Reich* (New York: McGraw-Hill, 1976), and Robert S. Wistrich, *Who's Who in Nazi Germany*, rev. ed. (London: Routledge, 1995).

The background of the Weimar Republic and the rise of the Nazi movement are covered in A. J. Nicholls, *Weimar and the Rise of Hitler*, 3rd ed. (New York: St. Martin's Press, 1991), and the thought-provoking Detlev J. K. Peukert, *The Weimar Republic: The Crisis of Classical Modernity* (New York: Hill and Wang, 1992). The emergence of paramilitary forces that contributed to Nazism is analyzed by James M. Diehl, *Paramilitary Politics in Weimar Germany* (Bloomington: Indiana University Press, 1977). Richard Bessel and E. J. Feuchtwanger edited *Social Change and Political Development in Weimar Germany* (London: Croom Helm; Totowa, NJ: Barnes and Noble, 1981), which contains essays on significant political and social aspects of the Weimar era. Walter Laqueur, *Weimar: A Cultural History, 1918–1933* (New York: Perigee, 1980), offers an encyclopedic survey of the unusually rich intellectual and cultural ferment of this era, and Peter Gay, *Weimar Culture: The Outsider as Insider* (New York: Harper and Row, 1968), suggests a provocative analysis.

In the past few years, several excellent general treatments of the entire Nazi period have appeared. Alan F. Wilt, *Nazi Germany* (Arlington Heights, IL: Harlan Davidson, 1994), provides an informative short summary that is accompanied by an extensive bibliographical essay. The best text, balanced, thoroughly researched, and well written, with extensive end-of-chapter bibliographical essays, is by Jackson J. Spielvogel, *Hitler and Nazi Germany*, 3rd ed. (Upper Saddle River, NJ: Prentice Hall, 1996). A more elaborate and interestingly written book, rich in substance and analysis and also accompanied by a lengthy bibliography, is Klaus P. Fischer, *Nazi Germany: A New History* (New York: Continuum, 1995). The older standard on the Nazi regime is Karl D. Bracher, *The German Dictatorship: The Origins, Structure, and Effects of National Socialism* (New York: Praeger, 1970). Jeremy Noakes and Geoffrey Pridham, eds., *Nazism, 1919–1945: A History in Documents and Eyewitness Accounts*, 2 vols. (New York: Schocken Books, 1990), offers an excellent compendium of contemporary sources on a vast array of aspects of the Third Reich, with informed and connecting comments. A similarly interesting compilation of lengthier documents, emphasizing social aspects in Nazi Germany, is Benjamin C. Sax and Dieter Kuntz, eds., *Inside Hitler's Germany: A Documentary History of Life in the Third Reich* (Lexington, MA: D.C. Heath, 1992). For historical debates and interpretations of the issues relating to the Hitler regime, Ian Kershaw, *The Nazi Dictatorship: Problems and Perspectives of Interpretation*, 3rd ed. (London: Edward Arnold, 1993), should be consulted. Specific essays or excerpts from books that illustrate the variety of interpretations of Nazi phenomena can be found in Thomas Childers and Jane Caplan, eds., *Reevaluating the Third Reich* (New York: Holmes and Meier, 1993), and Allan Mitchell, ed., *The Nazi Revolution: Hitler's Dictatorship and the German Nation*, 4th ed. (Boston: Houghton Mifflin, 1997).

A helpful summary of the rise of Nazism is provided by Martin Broszat, *Hitler and the Collapse of Weimar Germany* (Leamington Spa: Berg, 1987). Dietrich Orlow, *The History of the Nazi Party*, 2 vols. (Pittsburgh: University of Pittsburgh Press, 1969–1973), is the standard assessment of Hitler's party from its origins to its end. The first volume treats the struggling party from its origins in 1919 to its takeover of the German government in 1933. Harold J. Gordon, *Hitler and the Beer Hall Putsch* (Princeton, NJ: Princeton University Press, 1972), dissects the first Nazi attempt to seize power. Two aspects of the Nazi consolidation of power are examined in Fritz Tobias, *The Reichstag Fire: Legend and Truth* (New York: Putnam, 1964), and in the popular account of the Röhm purge in June 1934 by Max Gallo, *The Night of Long Knives* (New York: Harper and Row, 1972). Historians have given much attention to voting patterns and sociological aspects of the rise and takeover of Nazism. Thomas Childers, *The Nazi Voter: The Social Foundations of Fascism in Germany, 1919–1933* (Chapel Hill: University of North Carolina Press, 1983), and Richard F. Hamilton, *Who Voted for Hitler?* (Princeton, NJ: Princeton University Press, 1982), are fundamental studies of Nazi voters. Michael Kater, *The Nazi Party: A Social Profile of Members and Leaders, 1919–1945* (Cambridge, MA: Harvard University Press, 1983), offers a sociological analysis of the Nazi Party membership.

The role of other segments of society has also been fruitfully examined. Henry A. Turner, *German Big Business and the Rise of Hitler* (New York: Oxford University Press, 1985), shows that support by the industrial and business community of the Nazi Party came largely after Hitler's takeover rather than before. Max Kele, *Nazis and Workers: National Socialist Appeals to German Labor, 1919–1933* (Chapel Hill: University of North Carolina Press, 1972), assesses the Nazi appeal to workers, and Henry A. Winkler, "German Society, Hitler, and the Illusion of Restoration, 1930–1933," *Journal of Contemporary History* 11 (1976): 1–16, reexamines the role of the lower middle class, with emphasis on the small-business community, in the events leading to Hitler's seizure of power.

Regional and local studies of the Nazi rise to power have complemented national histories since the first appearance in 1965 of the perceptive pioneering account by William S. Allen, *The Nazi Seizure of Power: The Experience of a Single German Town, 1922–1945* rev. ed. (New York: Franklin Watts, 1984). One of the most recent treatments of a village is Walter Rinderle and Bernard Norling, *The Nazi Impact on a German Village* (Lexington: University Press of Kentucky, 1993). Other studies have covered the city of Marburg and several German regions: Rudy Koshar, *Social Life, Local Politics, and Nazism: Marburg, 1880–1935* (Chapel Hill: University of North Carolina Press, 1986); Jeremy Noakes, *The Nazi Party in Lower Saxony, 1921–1933* (London: Oxford University Press, 1971); and Geoffrey Pridham, *Hitler's Rise to Power: The Nazi Movement in Bavaria, 1923–1933* (New York: Harper and Row, 1973). Also of considerable interest is David Clay Large, *Where Ghosts Walked: Munich's Road to the Third Reich* (New York: W. W. Norton, 1997).

The workings of the Nazi state have been closely examined in Martin Broszat, *The Hitler State: The Foundation and Development of the Internal Structure of the Third Reich* (London: Longman, 1981). An old classic is Franz L. Neumann, *Behemoth: The Structure and Practice of National Socialism* (New York: Oxford University Press, 1942). Also of interest is Edward N. Peterson, *The Limits of Hitler's Power* (Princeton, NJ: Princeton University Press, 1969), which argues that Hitler's dictatorship was "weak." Jane Caplan, *Government without Administration: State and Civil Service in Weimar and Nazi Germany* (Oxford: Oxford University Press, 1988), examines the Nazis' impact on the bureaucracy. The Nazi legal and judicial system has been analyzed by Ingo Müller, *Hitler's Justice: The Courts of the Third Reich* (Cambridge, MA: Harvard University Press, 1991). On the relationship of the churches to the Hitler regime, the most comprehensive treatment is by Ernst C. Helmreich, *The German Churches under Hitler: Background, Struggle, and Epilogue* (Detroit: Wayne State University Press 1979). Also helpful are John S. Conway, *The Nazi Persecution of the Churches, 1933–45* (New York: Basic Books, 1968), and Guenter Lewy, *The Catholic Church and Nazi Germany* (New York: McGraw-Hill, 1964).

Economic developments and relations between the Nazi government and business and industry can be followed in several studies. R. J. Overy, *The Nazi Economic Recovery, 1932–1938* (London: Macmillan, 1982), gives a brief account of German economic recovery under Hitler. Arthur Schweitzer, *Big Business in the Third Reich* (Bloomington: Indiana University Press, 1964), though dated, is still useful. John Gillingham, *Industry and Politics in the Third Reich: Ruhr Coal, Hitler, and Europe* (New York: Columbia University Press, 1985), is an examination of the relationship between the Nazi state and German industry. Nazi agricultural policies are covered in Gustavo Corni, *Hitler and the Peasants: Agrarian Policy of the Third Reich, 1930–1939* (New York: Berg, 1990).

The place of the medical profession in the Third Reich is assessed by Michael H. Kater, *Doctors under Hitler* (Chapel Hill: University of North Carolina Press, 1989), and its role in racial policies by Robert N. Proctor, *Racial Hygiene: Medicine under the Nazis* (Cambridge, MA: Harvard University Press, 1988), and R. J. Lifton, *The Nazi Doctors: Medical Killing and the Psychology of Genocide* (New York: Basic Books, 1986). Some of the other professions are covered in a longitudinal study by Konrad H. Jarausch, *The Unfree Professions: German Lawyers, Teachers, and Engineers, 1900–1950* (New York: Oxford University Press, 1990). Alan D. Beyerchen, *Scientists under Hitler: Politics and the Physics Community in the Third Reich* (New Haven, CT: Yale University Press, 1977), takes a look at a segment of the scientific community under the Nazis.

German students were heavily represented among the early followers of Hitler. Their role is discussed by Michael Steinberg, *Sabers and Brown Shirts: The German Students' Path to National Socialism, 1918–1935* (Chicago: University of Chicago Press, 1977), and Geoffrey Giles, *Students and National Socialism in Germany* (Princeton, NJ: Princeton University Press, 1985). Youth culture in general is considered by H. W. Koch, *The Hitler Youth: Origins and Development, 1922–1945* (New York: Dorset, 1988), and more specifically by Gerhard Rempel, *Hitler's Children: The Hitler Youth and the SS* (Chapel Hill: University of North Carolina Press, 1989). Life for youth under the Nazis is well related by Willy Schumann in his autobiograpical *Being Present: Growing Up in Hitler's Germany* (Kent, OH: Kent State University Press, 1991).

Several books are noteworthy on the place of women in Nazi society: Claudia Koonz, *Mothers in the Fatherland: Women, the Family, and Nazi*

Politics (New York: St. Martin's Press, 1987), Jill Stephenson, *Women in Nazi Society* (New York: Barnes and Noble, 1975), and the more specialized work by Stephenson, *The Nazi Organisation of Women* (London: Croom Helm, 1981).

The best account to date on how Nazi ideology affected everyday life is Detlev Peukert, *Inside Nazi Germany: Conformity, Opposition, and Racism in Everyday Life* (New Haven, CT: Yale University Press, 1987). Richard Bessel, ed., *Life in the Third Reich* (New York: Oxford University Press, 1987), contains chapters that offer fresh insights into social life. Another very readable book, written as a memoir, is Bernt Engelmann, *In Hitler's Germany: Daily Life in the Third Reich* (New York: Schocken Books, 1986). Still important is David Schoenbaum, *Hitler's Social Revolution: Class and Status in Nazi Germany, 1933–1939* (Garden City, NY: Doubleday, 1966). It argues that Hitler's regime transformed German ideas of class and status.

A good collection of primary sources on Nazi culture is presented in George L. Mosse, *Nazi Culture: Intellectual, Cultural, and Social Life in the Third Reich* (New York: Grosset and Dunlap, 1966). Literature under Nazism is discussed in J. M. Ritchie, *German Literature under National Socialism* (Totowa, NJ: Barnes and Noble, 1983). A well-illustrated survey of the arts is Peter Adam, *Art of the Third Reich* (New York: H. N. Abrams, 1992). Alan E. Steinweis describes how the Nazi government attempted to influence artists and entertainers in *Art, Ideology, and Economics in Nazi Germany: The Reich Chambers of Music, Theater, and the Visual Arts* (Chapel Hill: University of North Carolina Press, 1993). An interesting study that assesses Nazi architecture in a broader context is Barbara Miller Lane, *Architecture and Politics in Germany, 1918–1945* (Cambridge, MA: Harvard University Press, 1968).

There are numerous works on Nazi propaganda. Two helpful introductions are Z.A.B. Zeman, *Nazi Propaganda*, 2nd ed. (London: Oxford University Press, 1973), and Ernest K. Bramsted, *Goebbels and National Socialist Propaganda, 1925–1945* (East Lansing: Michigan State University Press, 1965). See also two books by David Welch, *The Third Reich: Politics and Propaganda* (London: Routledge, 1993), and *Propaganda and the German Cinema, 1933–1945* (New York: Oxford University Press, 1983). The latter analyzes how films were used to mold public opinion. Another basic study is Oron J. Hale, *The Captive Press in the Third Reich* (Princeton, NJ: Princeton University Press, 1964). Ian Kershaw, *The "Hitler Myth": Image and Reality in the Third Reich* (Oxford: Oxford University Press, 1987), explores the Führer's popularity, while Kershaw's *Popular Opinion and Political Dissent in the Third Reich: Bavaria, 1933–1945* (New York: Oxford University Press, 1983) describes the limits of Nazi success in changing attitudes of Germans in Bavaria. The role of heroic Nazi mythology is examined in Jay W. Baird, *To Die for Germany: Heroes in the Nazi Pantheon* (Bloomington: Indiana University Press, 1990).

The role of the SS has been quite carefully studied in several accounts. They include Robert Koehl, *The Black Corps: The Structure and Power Struggles of the Nazi SS* (Madison: University of Wisconsin Press, 1983); Heinz Höhne, *The Order of the Death's Head* (New York: Ballantine, 1971); Helmut Krausnick and Martin Broszat, eds., *Anatomy of the SS State* (New York: Walker, 1968); and Gerald Reitlinger, *The SS: Alibi of a Nation, 1922–1945* (New York: Viking Press, 1968). The leadership of the SS is surveyed in Herbert F. Ziegler, *Nazi Germany's New Aristocracy: The SS Leadership, 1925–1939* (Princeton, NJ: Princeton University Press, 1989). Several studies examine the SS armed forces: Bernd Wegner, *The Waffen SS: Organization, Ideology, and Function* (Oxford: Basil Blackwell, 1990); George H. Stein, *The Waffen SS: Hitler's Elite Guard at War, 1939–1945* (Ithaca, NY: Cornell University Press, 1966); and Charles Sydnor, Jr., *Soldiers of Destruction: The SS Death's Head Division, 1933–1945* (Princeton, NJ: Princeton University Press, 1977), which deals with the SS division that was in charge of concentration and death camps. The machinery of the Nazi police state is investigated by George C. Browder, *Foundations of the Nazi Police State: The Formation of Sipo and SD* (Lexington: University Press of Kentucky, 1990). For a study of the Gestapo, see Robert Gellately, *The Gestapo and German Society* (New York: Oxford University Press, 1990).

For assessments of anti-Semitism in Germany, the Nazi policies toward the Jews, and the Holocaust, only a few works can be mentioned, since the literature on this subject has been practically exploding in the last few decades. Peter G. J. Pulzer, *The Rise of Political Anti-Semitism in Germany and Austria* (New York: Wiley, 1964), looks at anti-Semitism before Weimar and Hitler Germany. Karl A. Schleunes, *The Twisted Road to Auschwitz: Nazi Policy toward German Jews, 1933–1939* (Urbana: University of Illinois Press, 1970), is a classic study of the peacetime years of Jewish persecution in Hitler Germany. Hermann Graml, *Antisemitism in the Third Reich* (Oxford: Basil Blackwell, 1992), also emphasizes the peacetime years. Life for Jewish youth in Nazi Germany is related in Werner T. Angress's memoir, *Between Fear and Hope: Jewish Youth in the Third Reich* (New York: Columbia University Press, 1988). For an assessment of the Holocaust literature, see Michael R. Marrus, *The Holocaust in History* (Hanover, NH: University Press of New England, 1987). Some of the best overall studies of the Holocaust include Yehuda Bauer, *A History of the Holocaust* (New York: Franklin Watts, 1982), a balanced overview; Raul Hilberg, *The Destruction of the European Jews*, 3 vols., rev. ed. (New

York: Holmes and Meier, 1985), from the perspective of the perpetrators; Lucy Dawidowicz, *The War against the Jews, 1933–1945* (New York: Bantam, 1975), from the perspective of the victims; and Martin Gilbert, *The Holocaust: A History of the Jews of Europe during the Second World War* (New York: Holt, Rinehart, and Winston, 1985), who lets many of the victims speak for themselves. On the controversial question of the role of anti-Semitism in bringing on the Holocaust, see Sarah Gordon, *Hitler, Germans, and the "Jewish Question"* (Princeton, NJ: Princeton University Press, 1984); the provocative book of Daniel Jonah Goldhagen, *Hitler's Willing Executioners: Ordinary Germans and the Holocaust* (New York: Alfred A. Knopf, 1996); and the somewhat dissenting book of Henry Friedlander, *The Origins of Nazi Genocide: From Euthanasia to the Final Solution* (Chapel Hill: University of North Carolina Press, 1995).

Spain

Primo de Rivera's dictatorial government in the 1920s, which attempted to carry out major reforms but failed in the end, formed a prelude to Franco's dictatorship. James H. Rial, *Revolution from Above: The Primo de Rivera Dictatorship in Spain, 1923–1930* (Fairfax, VA: George Mason University Press, 1986), provides a good assessment of the elder Primo de Rivera's efforts. The emerging background of Franco's authoritarian rightist regime can be followed in Richard A. H. Robinson, *The Origins of Franco's Spain: The Right, the Republic, and Revolution, 1931–1936* (Pittsburgh: University of Pittsburgh Press, 1970). Primo de Rivera's son José Antonio became the most notable fascist leader and organizer of the Falange in 1933 and 1934. Stanley G. Payne, *Falange: A History of Spanish Fascism* (Stanford, CA: Stanford University Press, 1961), provides the pioneering study of the Spanish fascist party, Falange Española, from its origins to the late 1950s. Payne followed this with a comprehensive political history of the Franco dictatorship, *The Franco Regime, 1936–1975* (Madison: University of Wisconsin Press, 1987), which stresses the eclectic character of Franco's ideas, and, more recently, with a study of *Spain's First Democracy: The Second Republic, 1931–1936* (Madison: University of Wisconsin Press, 1993). Paul Preston, *The Politics of Revenge: Fascism and the Military in Twentieth-Century Spain* (Boston: Unwin Hyman, 1990), contains a collection of essays on the Spanish Right from the 1930s to the 1980s and the army's changing role in politics and society. Italian intervention in the Spanish Civil War is covered in John F. Coverdale, *Italian Intervention in the Spanish Civil War* (Princeton, NJ: Princeton University Press, 1975).

Western Europe

Two books on pre–World War II fascism in France give insights on its development: Robert Soucy, *French Fascism: The First Wave, 1924–1933* (New Haven, CT: Yale University Press, 1986), and Zeev Sternhell, *Neither Right nor Left: Fascist Ideology in France* (Berkeley: University of California Press, 1986). See also the chapter by Eugen Weber on French fascism in Hans Rogger and Eugen Weber, eds., *The European Right* (Berkeley: University of California Press, 1965). The same collection has chapters on England by J. R. Jones and on Belgium by Jean Stengers. For the Netherlands, see Erik Hansen, "Fascism and Nazism in the Netherlands, 1929–1939," *European Studies Review* 11 (1981):355–385.

Central and Eastern Europe

Austrian national socialism from its beginnings to March 1938 (*Anschluss*) is fully discussed by Bruce F. Pauley, *Hitler and the Forgotten Nazis: A History of Austrian National Socialism* (Chapel Hill: University of North Carolina Press, 1981). The Arrow Cross Party in Hungary is examined by István Deák's chapter in Rogger and Webber, eds., *The European Right*, noted earlier, and by Miklós Lackó, a respected Marxist scholar, *Arrow-Cross Men: National Socialists, 1935–1944* (Budapest: Akadémiai Kiadó, 1969), as well as by Nicholas M. Nagy-Talavera, *The Green Shirts and the Others: A History of Fascism in Hungary and Rumania* (Stanford, CA: Hoover Institution Press, 1970). The latter account includes the Rumanian Iron Guard and related movements. For Rumania, see also the lengthy chapter by Eugen Weber in *The European Right*. Some helpful information on fascism in eastern European countries, especially on Poland, Czechoslovakia, and Yugoslavia, since they are not covered by the preceding references, can be gleaned from Peter Sugar, ed., *Native Fascism in the Successor States, 1918–1945* (Santa Barbara, CA: ABC-Clio, 1971). However, the chapters are of uneven quality.

BIOGRAPHIES

Most of the notable fascist personalities have found a biographer. Benito Mussolini has not yet been treated to an exhaustive biography in English. The best political summary of his life is Denis Mack Smith, *Mussolini* (New York: Alfred A. Knopf, 1982). It focuses on the Duce's public life and views him as crucial to the success and failure of Fascism. Ivone Kirkpatrick, a British diplomat who knew Mussolini firsthand, emphasizes foreign policy in his *Mussolini: A Study in Power* (New York: Hawthorn

Books, 1964). Richard Collier, *Duce! A Biography of Mussolini* (New York: Viking Press, 1971), portrays Mussolini as a womanizer and concentrates on his relationship with his family. A revisionist interpretation that views Mussolini not as a demagogue but as a coherent revolutionary thinker is A. James Gregor, *Young Mussolini and the Intellectual Origins of Fascism* (Berkeley: University of California Press, 1979). The Duce's relationship with Hitler, especially after the collapse of the Fascist regime in the summer of 1943, when he was reinstated with the Führer's "help" as head of the neo-Fascist Italian Social Republic, is fully treated by Frederick William Deakin, *The Brutal Friendship: Mussolini, Hitler, and the Fall of Italian Fascism* (New York: Harper and Row, 1962).

Accounts of the lives of Mussolini's immediate associates are scarce. His onetime foreign minister and son-in-law, Galeazzo Ciano, is best remembered for his posthumously published diaries: *The Ciano Diaries, 1939–1943*, edited by Hugh Gibson (Garden City, NY: Doubleday, 1946), and *Ciano's Hidden Diary, 1937–1938*, translated by Andreas Mayor (New York: E. P. Dutton, 1953). No English biography exists of Ciano, but the work of Gordon Craig and Felix Gilbert, eds., *The Diplomats*, 2 vols. (Princeton, NJ: Princeton University Press, 1953), has a chapter that deals with Ciano. Claudio G. Segrè, *Italo Balbo: A Fascist Life* (Berkeley: University of California Press, 1987), offers a political portrait of Balbo as an intelligent and very capable leader and organizer. Harry Fornari, *Mussolini's Gadfly: Roberto Farinacci* (Nashville: Vanderbilt University Press, 1971), presents a somewhat uneven treatment of the radical leader of the Fascist movement.

There is no dearth of reliable biographical literature on the main Nazi leaders. Several decades ago, Joachim C. Fest wrote *The Face of the Third Reich: Portraits of the Nazi Leadership* (New York: Pantheon Books, 1970), containing biographical sketches of all the major Nazi heads. A similar collection of short biographies covering many of the same figures was compiled by Ronald Smelser and Rainer Zitelmann, eds., *The Nazi Elite* (New York: New York University Press, 1993).

Even though many book-length biographies have appeared on Hitler, only a few are good comprehensive scholarly treatments. The two best are by Joachim Fest, *Hitler* (New York: Harcourt Brace Jovanovich, 1974), and Alan Bullock, *Hitler: A Study in Tyranny*, rev. ed. (New York: Harper and Row, 1962). See also Bullock's *Hitler and Stalin: Parallel Lives* (New York: Alfred A. Knopf, 1992), which puts the Nazi leader in the context of his principal antagonist. Also helpful is Werner Maser, *Hitler* (London: Allen Lane, 1973). Robert G. L. Waite, *The Psychopathic God: Adolf Hitler* (New York: Basic Books, 1977), and Rudolph Binion, *Hitler among the Germans* (New York: Elsevier, 1976), are examples of psychobiographies, which have been criticized for relying on much guesswork. Excellent shorter interpretive studies include William Carr, *Hitler: A Study in Personality and Politics* (London: Edward Arnold, 1978); Sebastian Haffner, *The Meaning of Hitler* (Cambridge, MA: Harvard University Press, 1983); Eberhard Jäckel, *Hitler in History* (Hanover, NH: University Press of New England, 1984); and Ian Kershaw, *Hitler* (London: Longman, 1991). For Hitler's youth, see Bradley F. Smith, *Adolf Hitler: His Family, Childhood, and Youth* (Stanford, CA: Hoover Institution Press, 1967), and W. A. Jenks, *Vienna and the Young Hitler* (New York: Columbia University Press, 1960). The best book on the Führer's end is still H. R. Trevor-Roper, *The Last Days of Hitler* (New York: Macmillan, 1947). Hitler should also be read in his own words. His semiautobiograpical *Mein Kampf*, trans. Ralph Manheim (Boston: Houghton Mifflin © 1943, renewed 1971) and his recorded monologues at his headquarters during the war, *Hitler's Secret Conversations, 1941–1944* (New York: Farrar, Straus and Young, 1953), are a good starting point. Most of his speeches were collected by Max Domarus, ed., *Hitler: Speeches and Proclamations, 1932–1945*, 4 vols. (Wauconda, IL: Bolchazy-Carducci, 1990–1997).

Hermann Göring has been the subject of several biographies, but none is definitive. The most reliable account is R. J. Overy, *Goering: The "Iron Man"* (London: Routledge, 1984).

Joseph Goebbels's life is examined in Ernest K. Bramsted, *Goebbels and National Socialist Propaganda, 1925–1945* mentioned earlier, and in Helmut Heiber, *Goebbels* (New York: Da Capo, 1983). Of particular importance as a source for the history of the Third Reich are Goebbels's diaries. Some have appeared in English translation. See, for instance, Fred Taylor, ed., *The Goebbels Diaries, 1939–1941* (New York: Putnam, 1983); Louis P. Lochner, ed., *The Goebbels Diaries, 1942–1943* (1948. Reprint. Westport, CT: Greenwood Press, 1970); and Hugh Trevor-Roper, ed., *Final Entries, 1945: The Diaries of Joseph Goebbels* (New York: Putnam, 1978).

Richard Breitman, *The Architect of Genocide: Himmler and the Final Solution* (New York: Alfred A. Knopf, 1991), concentrates on Himmler's role in the extermination of the Jews. Bradley F. Smith, *Heinrich Himmler: A Nazi in the Making, 1900–1926* (Stanford, CA: Hoover Institution Press, 1971), gives the best scholarly treatment of Himmler's youth and early political career.

Albert Speer, first Hitler's architect and later his armaments minister, has left elaborate writings with insights into the workings of Hitler's inner circle. Speer won some sympathy when he admitted responsibility and guilt at the trial before the International Military Tribunal at Nuremberg in 1945–1946. While serving a twenty-year sentence, he wrote down many of his recollections. Three books appeared in succession: *Inside the Third Reich: Memoirs* (New York: Macmillan, 1970), *Spandau: The Secret Diaries* (New York: Macmillan, 1976), and *Infiltration* (New York: Macmillan, 1981). In the first book, Speer attempts to come to terms with the Nazi regime; in the second, he describes prison life and interactions with fellow inmates; and in the third, he outlines the plans and machinations of Himmler to create an industrial empire under the control of the SS. For critical assessments of Speer's career and his postwar role, see Matthias Schmidt, *Albert Speer: The End of a Myth* (New York: St. Martin's Press, 1984), and Gitta Sereny, *Albert Speer: His Battle with Truth* (New York: Alfred A. Knopf, 1995).

WORLD WAR II IN EUROPE: ORIGINS AND IMPACT

Several works provide a comprehensive view of the coming of the war. They include two books by Gerhard L. Weinberg, *The Foreign Policy of Hitler's Germany: Diplomatic Revolution in Europe, 1933–36* (Chicago: University of Chicago Press, 1970) and *The Foreign Policy of Hitler's Germany: Starting World War II, 1937–1939* (Chicago: University of Chicago Press, 1980); and Donald Cameron Watt, *How War Came: The Immediate Origins of the Second World War, 1938–1939* (New York: Pantheon Books, 1989). Keith Eubank, *The Origins of World War II*, 2nd ed. (Arlington Heights, IL: Harlan Davidson, 1990), offers an excellent synthesis and also an extensive bibliographical essay. Mussolini's part in the making of the war can be followed in Esmonde M. Robertson, *Mussolini as Empire-Builder: Europe and Africa, 1932–36* (New York: St. Martin's Press, 1977), and in MacGregor Knox, *Mussolini Unleashed, 1939–1941: Politics and Strategy in Fascist Italy's Last War* (Cambridge: Cambridge University Press, 1982). Mussolini's alliance with Hitler is discussed in Mario Toscano, *The Origins of the Pact of Steel* (Baltimore: Johns Hopkins Press, 1967). On Hitler's plans for expansion, see Eberhard Jäckel, *Hitler's World View: A Blueprint for Power* (Cambridge, MA: Harvard University Press, 1981); Klaus Hildebrand, *The Foreign Policy of the Third Reich* (Berkeley: University of California Press, 1973); and Norman Rich, *Hitler's War Aims* 2 vols. (New York: W. W. Norton, 1973–1974).

The most important work on the war from a global perspective is the magisterial book of Gerhard L. Weinberg, *A World at Arms: A Global History of World War II* (Cambridge: Cambridge University Press, 1994). Gordon Wright, *The Ordeal of Total War, 1939–1945* (New York: Harper and Row, 1968), is a useful study of the war in Europe, covering political, social, and economic aspects. Peter Calvocoressi, Guy Wint, and John Pritchard, *Total War: The Causes and Courses of the Second World War*, rev. 2nd ed. (New York: Pantheon Books, 1989), also provide a helpful discussion of the major issues relating to the coming of the war and the war itself.

Social and economic developments relating to the war are well covered in Alan S. Milward, *War, Economy, and Society, 1939–1945* (Berkeley: University of California Press, 1977). See also Earl R. Beck, *The European Home Fronts, 1939–1945* (Arlington Heights, IL: Harlan Davidson, 1993), which gives an insightful picture of how the war affected the societies of the Allied and Axis powers. An excellent assessment of the German public's response to the war is found in Marlis Steinert, *Hitler's War and the Germans: Public Mood and Attitude during the Second World War* (Athens: Ohio University Press, 1977). The faltering performance of Italian Fascism on the battlefield is highlighted in Mario Cervi, *The Hollow Legions: Mussolini's Blunder in Greece, 1940–1941* (Garden City, NY: Doubleday, 1971), a discussion of the campaign that paved the way to the Duce's fall in July 1943.

RESISTANCE

A comprehensive treatment of resistance to Italian Fascism, covering twenty years of the regime, and also the partisans' actions against the Italian Social Republic between 1943 and 1945, is Charles F. Delzell, *Mussolini's Enemies: The Italian Anti-Fascist Resistance* (Princeton, NJ: Princeton University Press, 1961; reprinted with new preface (New York: Howard Fertig, 1974). This comprehensive work can be supplemented by Frank Rosengarten, *The Italian Anti-Fascist Press, 1919–1945* (Cleveland, OH: Press of Case Western Reserve University, 1968). See also Maria de Blasio Wilhelm, *The Other Italy: Italian Resistance in World War II* (New York: W. W. Norton, 1988), and David W. Ellwood, *Italy, 1943–1945* (New York: Holmes and Meier, 1985). For a general survey of resistance to fascist occupation throughout Europe, see Henri Michel, *The Shadow War: European Resistance, 1939–1945* (New York: Harper and Row, 1972).

The literature on German resistance to the Hitler regime is quite copious. Only a few accounts can be mentioned here. A very good overall study is Peter Hoffmann, *The History of the German Resistance, 1933–1945* (Cambridge, MA: MIT Press, 1977). Hoffmann also has written a short book, *German Resistance to Hitler* (Cambridge, MA: Harvard University Press, 1988). Joachim C. Fest, noted for his biography of Hitler and sketches of other Nazi leaders, has recently attempted to summarize the current scholarship on the German resistance in *Plotting Hitler's Death: The Story of the German Resistance* (New York: Henry Holt and

Co., 1996). Fest's very readable treatment focuses on the July 1944 plot, whereas the more elaborate study by Theodore S. Hamerow, *On the Road to the Wolf's Lair: German Resistance to Hitler* (Cambridge, MA: Harvard University Press, 1997), treats the ideas and motivations of the resisters. Topical essays dealing with various aspects of the resistance have appeared in David C. Large, ed., *Contending with Hitler: Varieties of German Resistance in the Third Reich* (Cambridge: Cambridge University Press, 1991), and in Michael Geyer and John Boyer, eds., *Resistance against the Third Reich, 1933–1990* (Chicago: University of Chicago Press, 1994). For the Communist resistance, there is the comprehensive work of Allan Merson, *Communist Resistance in Nazi Germany* (London: Lawrence and Wishart, 1985). On the White Rose student group, see Inge Scholl, *Students against Tyranny: The Resistance of the White Rose, Munich, 1942–1943* (Middletown, CT: Wesleyan University Press, 1970), and Annette E. Dumbach and Jud Newborn, *Shattering the German Night: The Story of the White Rose* (Boston: Little, Brown, 1986).

NEOFASCISM

The literature in English on neofascism is remarkably sparse thus far. A very well informed overview can be found in the last chapter "Epilogue: Neofascism: A Fascism in Our Future?" of Stanley Payne, *A History of Fascism, 1914–1945*, noted earlier. Roger Eatwell devotes several good chapters to neofascism in Italy, Germany, France, and Britain in his *Fascism: A History*, noted earlier. Walter Laqueur offers a detailed commentary on neofascism in western European countries, Germany, Italy, and Austria and on postfascism in the Islamic Middle East, North Africa, and eastern Europe and Russia in the longer second half of his *Fascism: Past, Present, Future*, noted earlier. All of these books have good bibliographical references in several languages.

The most detailed work on extremist right-wing groups in West Germany in the immediate postwar period is Kurt Tauber, *Beyond Eagle and Swastika*, 2 vols. (Middletown, CT: Wesleyan University Press, 1967). Another good survey is provided by R. Stöss, *Politics against Democracy: Right-wing Extremism in West Germany* (New York: Berg, 1991). For Italy, see Leonard Weinberg, *After Mussolini: Italian Neo-Fascism and the Nature of Fascism* (Washington, DC: University Press of America, 1979), covering only the first few decades after World War II. Historical Russian right-wing movements have been examined by Walter Laqueur in his *Black Hundred: The Rise of the Extreme Right in Russia* (New York: HarperCollins, 1993).

FASCISM THROUGH FILM

In conclusion, some documentaries and films that have been adapted for educational purposes should be briefly mentioned. Leni Riefenstahl's classic propaganda vehicles *Triumph of the Will* (1935) and *Olympiad* (1938) can be obtained on video from some distribution outlets. A television docudrama, *Mussolini*, starring George C. Scott as Mussolini, was aired on NBC in 1986. It concentrated on the dictator's political career after the march on Rome and his family. Historically more informative is the fast-paced *Mussolini* (1990) documentary narrated by A.J.P. Taylor, a British historian, which can be obtained from the Teachers Video Company. The same outlet also has *The Rise and Fall of Adolf Hitler* (1962), a psychological portrait, narrated by Marlene Dietrich, that has won some acclaim. For similar and additional listings of documentary videos, see the regular catalogs of Films for the Humanities and Sciences. Shorter adaptations for the classroom, usually less than thirty minutes in length, are offered by McGraw-Hill Films, for instance, *Mussolini* (1963) and *The Rise of Adolf Hitler* (1957). For a more general treatment, *Fascist Dictatorships—Second Edition* (1985), turn to Clearvue/eav. It gives an overview of the background, the development, and the legacy of fascism throughout the world. This company also, among others, publishes helpful catalogs featuring CD-ROM material.

Index

About the Author

GEORGE P. BLUM is Professor of History and Chair of the Department at the University of the Pacific. Among his recent publications are articles and chapters in *Research Guide to European Historical Biography* (1992–1993), *Statesmen Who Changed the World* (Greenwood, 1993), *Events That Changed the World in the Twentieth Century* (Greenwood, 1995), and *Encyclopedia of World War II in Europe* (1998).